Homeward

MULTNOMAH WOMEN'S FICTION

Homeward

MELODY CARLSON

This is a work of fiction. The characters, incidents, and dialogues are products of the author's imagination and are not to be construed as real. Any resemblance to actual events or persons, living or dead, is entirely coincidental.

HOMEWARD
published by Multnomah Women's Fiction
a Division of Multnomah Publishers, Inc.

© 1997 by Melody Carlson
International Standard Book Number: 1-57673-029-8

Cover photo by Mike Houska
Cover designed by D² DesignWorks

Printed in the United States of America

Scripture quotations are from: *The Holy Bible,*
New International Version (NIV) © 1973, 1984, by International Bible Society,
used by permission of Zondervan Publishing House

For information:
QUESTAR PUBLISHERS, INC.
POST OFFICE BOX 1720
SISTERS, OREGON 97759

Library of Congress Cataloging--in--Publication Data
Carlson, Melody. Homeward/by Melody Carlson.
p.cm. ISBN 1-57673-029-8 (alk. paper) I. Title.
PS3553.A73257H6   1997   97-11833
  813'.54--dc21   CIP

97 98 99 00 01 02 03 — 10 9 8 7 6 5 4 3 2 1

In loving memory of my grandmother,
Elizabeth Church Haga—
Thank you for your loving and
lifelong devotion to your family.
Your life has taught me much.

A special thanks to the Peart family,
for sharing their cranberry bog with me one crisp fall day.
This is a family who understands both the pain and
the rewards of restoring a neglected cranberry bog.
To Mike, Jim and Janet:
thank you so much for taking the time to teach and
show me the workings of your delightful family business.

Even the sparrow has found a home,
and the swallow a nest for herself,
where she may have her young—
a place near your altar,
O LORD Almighty, my King and my God.

PSALM 84:3

One

FROM THE CORNER OF HER EYE, Meg noticed the flashing blue light in her rearview mirror. She glanced down to check the speedometer and exhaled an impatient breath. Just what she needed—a nice welcome home. She pulled off the freeway, tires skidding in the loose gravel.

The patrolman sauntered up. "Howdy, ma'am," he said with a slight drawl. She greeted him and wondered why some people in southern Oregon sounded like they were from Texas. And why was it that highway patrolmen all seemed to have mustaches?

"License and registration, please," he said. Rain coated his plastic-covered cowboy hat, dribbling down the brim and straight into her car. He obviously had no concern about the damage water could do to leather upholstery. She fumbled with her billfold, then handed him her card and registration with a forced smile.

"Sorry, Officer. You see, I haven't had this car for too long, and I'm still getting used to the cruise control." Not completely true, but worth a shot. Meg smiled again.

"Uh-huh. Nice wheels," he murmured, then moved to the front of her Jaguar to copy the plates. A semi rushed past, spewing a dirty, oily spray onto the sleeve of her silk blouse and into her car. She clenched her teeth, but forced another saccharine smile as the patrolman returned to her window. Maybe there was still a chance he would go easy on her.

"Thing is," he began evenly as he handed her the ticket, "fancy cars like this smash up just the same as any ol' junker. Sometimes worse. I see you're from San Francisco; maybe you didn't know these roads are extra slick up here today. We hadn't had a drop of rain for two weeks. Unusual for March. But I clocked you at eighty-six."

She muttered a cold thanks, with no hint of a smile this time. He tipped his dripping hat and returned to his car. She stared at the name printed neatly across the top of the ticket—*Alexandra Megan Lancaster.* Someone else's name. The *Alexandra* part was from her grandmother, something she'd once been proud of.

Suddenly her chest tightened with the urge to scream. Not over the stupid speeding ticket; no, that would be too simple. This unwelcome rage was vaguely familiar, but it surprised her just the same. She had worked so hard all these years to forget such tiresome things. Was she inviting it all back now, simply by returning?

In another lifetime, she had promised herself she would never return. But this was not the time to dredge up old memories. That would only send her back to San Francisco, and she wasn't ready for that. She needed a break to clear her head, and perhaps it was time to clear up some other things as well. Or at least to try. So she pulled back onto the freeway and decided to blame it on Jerred. Fair or not, it really was his fault that for the first time in nearly twenty years she was going home—at least the closest thing to home she had ever known.

To distract herself, she thought about Jerred. Had it been only two years since he had stepped into her life? It seemed like longer. But then she had just turned thirty-five when they met. How she had celebrated that milestone. Only thirty-five, and at the top of her field. She had carefully played the corporate game and climbed high in the San Francisco advertising firm. And her reward had been a luxurious office with a private bathroom and an assistant who was somewhat efficient. It was all she'd ever hoped for. Wasn't it?

She considered the brief spell in college when she had fantasized about a more creative career: she'd live in a loft in some interesting part of the city and pursue photography or maybe journalism. But she had quickly returned to her senses, reminding herself that such thoughts were probably just carried over from her unconventional upbringing. And by the end of college, money had become important. With bills to juggle and loans to repay, the field of advertising offered the financial security she longed for.

When she first hired on with Montgomery and Tate, she had thought perhaps she'd stay on until her finances were in line, but it didn't take long before she acquired an appetite for the things that money could buy. It was the first time she'd ever worn designer labels and real Italian shoes. And Meg liked being around people who had money. Even more, she liked the power that accompanied that money. It seemed to surround and insulate those who had it. Working twelve-hour days hardly fazed her because she came to believe it was her ticket into their world, a world she had only viewed by pressing her nose to the window.

Then the "golden boy" joined his daddy's firm, and Mr. Montgomery asked her to work with his son—to show him the ropes, so to speak. She'd been somewhat flattered, yet understandably cautious. This upstart wasn't going to pilfer her job. But Jerred Montgomery, with his impeccable manners and boyish charm, quickly won her trust and later—she grimaced at the triteness—her heart. How had she been such a fool? She should have known better. For starters, he was almost ten years younger than she. Why hadn't she recognized that red flag? But Jerred always assured her that "age was a nonfactor." And Meg knew she looked better at thirty-five than ever.

They'd gotten engaged on a picture-perfect New Year's Eve. Jerred's parents had invited them to Lake Tahoe for the holidays, and there was snow on the ground and stars in the sky. She immediately started planning a summer wedding, but then Jerred moved it back. First October, then Christmas—he always had another reason to postpone it. She was patient, turning her energy back to work, making her future father-in-law happier—and richer. Meanwhile, Jerred assured her that being together was what counted. Unfortunately, it didn't count for anything last week. That was when she discovered he was having an affair with his twenty-something secretary, Tiffany.

In her more honest moments, Meg could admit she'd known it even before Tiffany. In some ways, Tiffany provided Meg with the perfect excuse.

Mr. Montgomery had been so kind and fatherly about the whole thing. It only made it harder. The Montgomerys were a fine family, and she once hoped they would become the family she'd always longed for. Meg didn't actually tell Mr. Montgomery about Jerred's part in the breakup, but when he so quickly consented to her month's leave of absence with no loss of position or benefits, she felt certain he knew. Just the same, he made her promise to return as soon as possible. "We don't want to lose you to Crandale permanently," he told her with a kind smile.

Meg frowned as she turned off the freeway toward the coast. Suddenly, it seemed a pretty dismal choice—Crandale or Jerred.

It was Meg's sister, Erin, who had given her the final nudge. The note was actually three months old, something Erin had slipped into a Christmas card, and Meg had only skimmed it at the time. But right after the trouble with Jerred, Meg went on a full-scale cleaning binge in her tiny apartment. She discovered the wrinkled note underneath her sofa. Then suddenly, as she reread the part about her grandmother's deteriorating health, it seemed the perfect excuse. It would allow her to escape San Francisco for a couple of weeks and thus avoid some messy confrontations.

Meg had not warned her sister of this impending visit. She seldom wrote to Erin, and in almost twenty years never phoned her. This sparse communication was Meg's stipulation a long time ago. She originally gave Erin her address with the clear understanding that Erin would never mention it, or their infrequent correspondence, to the rest of her family.

This severing from the family had been important to Meg. And she liked the anonymity—at first. It made her feel free. Jerred had once questioned her lack of family connections, so unlike his close-knit clan. But then his family wouldn't have understood hers, and that had been one more reason to keep them closeted.

The rain stopped, and directly ahead, above the ridge of a fir-covered hill, opened a slit of clear sky so bright it almost hurt her eyes. Meg dug in her purse for sunglasses. The sunlight illuminated the lush fields, creating an almost unreal shade of green. Every leaf and blade of grass seemed to leap out. It was one of her favorite scenes—the rain-washed countryside backdropped by a leaden sky and then spotlighted by the sun. If only she had a camera handy, she would shoot this panorama over and over until she got it just right.

Meg opened the window and let the fresh air blow in. The cool, wet smell reminded her of childhood. How many times had they trekked off to the coast in their rickety old Volkswagen Bug during spring break? Of course, it was only after she and Erin had spent days of strategic pleading and begging to entice Sunny to "please take them to Crandale." Living on a college campus in the radical sixties had seemed less than ideal to Meg, but for some reason Sunny seemed to thrive upon the unrest and would have never considered giving up her professorship in the University of Oregon's art department.

Meg's refuge came in the form of Grandpa's house. They had always called it Grandpa's house. Everyone knew the house belonged to Grandpa and the dress shop belonged to Grandmother. As a child, she never questioned the carefully divided ownership within her grandparents' marriage, or even the nontraditional roles they both lived so naturally. But then nothing in Meg's family had ever been what "should be." Sometimes she imagined she was Alice, living on the other side of the looking glass, where everything was backwards.

At Grandpa's house there seemed to exist some magical element, and Erin and Meg always had high expectations when they went there. Maybe it was because Grandpa truly loved children, or maybe it was just the comforting familiarity of the small coastal town. The two girls spent every vacation moment in Crandale while Sunny took classes and finished graduate school and then started teaching. Grandpa always did the cooking, fixing special dishes they never saw at home. The little cleaning that was done in the big old Victorian house was done by Grandpa's hand as well, but it never bothered Meg that there were cobwebs in corners or that you could write your name on the dusty end tables. Because the best part of staying at Grandpa's was being outside.

Grandpa's grandfather had purchased the several hundred acres right after the turn of the century. He named it Briar Hedge because there was a slight rise between the property and the ocean where a long, thick wall of wild blackberries had grown profusely. Those particular blackberries had been removed long ago, but there were always more than enough blackberry patches to be found close by. The real purpose of Briar Hedge was cranberries. And Meg's favorite thing as a child was to help Grandpa in the cranberry bog. He always made sure a pair of big rubber boots was waiting for her. And when they made the trip into town for supplies, he always let her drive the old truck down the beach road.

Maybe going back wouldn't be so dreadful. Why had she put it off all these years? Sure, some ugly things had been said at Grandpa's funeral, but that was almost twenty years ago. The accusations had been cruel and hateful, spoken in the heat of anger. Some by her, some not. But Grandmother could be dying now. It was time to forgive and forget. Perhaps this would help the old woman go in peace—even if it meant Meg's taking the brunt of the blame. She knew Grandmother would gladly allow that. Besides, it might be worth taking the blame if it would help her avoid that debilitating feeling of guilt, the kind she'd experienced after Grandpa's death.

Meg turned off the main road when she saw the old sign before her. It looked just the same as in the old days, only now it was freshly painted in bright, cheerful colors: *Welcome to Crandale, Home of the Cranberry Carnival.*

She hoped the sign was right. Would she really be welcome?

Two

THE STREET LOOKED CLEANER than she remembered. The old iron lampposts were now painted dark green, and flower boxes swayed in the breeze. Most tourists probably relished the fresh sea air, but to Meg, the familiarity was unsettling. Scents were like that with her; they could penetrate and take her places she had no intention of going.

It was hard to believe she was really here, walking down the same street in the same town she'd once loved. But things looked different now, and of course, she was different, too.

She noticed her reflection in the bakery window. At least the bakery hadn't changed. It even looked like the same old dusty Styrofoam wedding cake sitting in the window with the ever-present dead fly lying feet-up next to the plastic groom.

But she was no longer Meggie, rushing in to buy fresh donuts. Over a decade ago, donuts had been replaced with rice cakes, and she'd put her stair-stepper machine right in front of her TV. Within a year, pudgy Meggie had slowly transformed into a very slender Meg. After losing more than forty pounds, she'd discovered that her legs were actually long, and although she had never considered herself tall at five-foot-six, she suddenly began to hold her shoulders back and to stand up straight. Even her face had changed with the weight loss. Cheekbones had magically appeared, and a nose that had at one time looked too small now fit in rather well.

It had taken time to adjust to her weight loss, and at first she'd found herself thinking from time to time that she was still pudgy Meggie. But over the years she had adapted to her new image, and although she hated to admit it, her confidence level had increased dramatically. Suddenly, the thought of being in Crandale seemed to shatter that confidence, and a deep-rooted fear squeezed her as she imagined herself turning back into pudgy Meggie. Only now she would have wrinkles in place of freckles.

She shoved those ridiculous thoughts aside and crossed the quiet street over to Grandmother's shop, or rather what used to be Grandmother's shop. The faded candy-striped awnings were gone now. What had become of those pasty-faced mannequins and their stiff, shiny hair? Were their rigid bodies heaped together in the back room? Fine gold lettering now swept across the clean plate-glass window, announcing the shop to be Sunny's Gallery.

From the outside, it looked exactly like the sort of place Meg would normally be drawn to, a place where she might browse undisturbed, perhaps pick up an odd piece or two to add to her eclectic collection of objets d'art. Jerred had advised her to select one style and plan around it. But she could never settle on just one; instead she had fallen back into her bohemian way of accumulating what he called junk. Looking back, it seemed the only real part of her life anyway. She was glad she'd ignored his advice.

She hesitated before the beveled glass door. Her hands were actually shaking. It still wasn't too late to change course. Jerred or no Jerred, she could still make it back to San Francisco by tomorrow and be back to work the next day. It wouldn't be comfortable, but it had to be easier than this.

It was funny; after all these years, and all those fights, she couldn't recall one specific thing that she and Sunny had fought about—perhaps because there were so many. Eventually they'd all piled up until she could stand it no longer; the funeral had been the last straw. Meg gave herself a mental shake. Enough remembering!

She squared her shoulders and pushed open the door. A bell tinkled, followed by muted strains of classical music. Sunny had always professed a passion for Mozart, but then she had liked the Beatles almost as much. Behind the counter, a man of about fifty with long, thinning hair pulled into a ponytail stood leafing through a glossy magazine. He nodded in her direction without speaking, and Meg wandered through the gallery just like any other tourist. Yet her heart beat furiously, and her eyes refused to focus on a single piece of art.

The smell in the shop hadn't changed. It was altered somewhat by the scent of a jasmine candle burning on a low, hand-carved coffee table, but that old musty aroma of decaying wood and damp sea air still clung to the seasoned building like a tired old woman hanging on to her last breath of life. With the smell came the unmistakable ring of Grandmother's voice....

"Meggie, for Pete's sake, suck in your stomach and stand up straight! How do you expect this dress to look right when you slump over like a sack of potatoes?" Grandmother scowled up at her with pins puckered in her mouth. She bent her blue-tinted head downward to adjust the hem, giving no apology as a sharp point scratched Meg's bare legs. How was it that a day spent cutting back thorny blackberry bushes around the bog was nothing compared to Grandmother's occasional pinpricks?

Finally Grandmother finished adjusting the hem and turned Meg around to view the results in the mirror. Meg wanted to rip the dress off and dash from the shop. Instead she stood and stared at the hideous garment. It was the most revolting shade of pink, which seemed to make her freckles stand out as if she had some tropical disease. The fabric itself was a stiff polyester that scratched her armpits. The waist was too tight, and the front poufed out over her undeveloped chest. The other shop ladies peered in as if sneaking a preview of a sideshow freak.

"There now," said Grandmother. "That will do nicely for the Cranberry Dance." Meg figured that in that dress she might pass for a gigantic underripe cranberry. She had been twelve that summer, and it was the first time she had ever gotten up the nerve to speak back to Grandmother.

"I don't like it," she said quietly, almost under her breath. "It doesn't fit right, and it's still too long." The pinned-up hem hit her square across the knees, making her protruding legs look like two white stumps. She fought back the tears as she folded her arms across her chest and stood firm. Grandmother's piercing pale blue eyes widened, and Meg felt certain she saw those nostrils flare.

"Well, if it doesn't fit right, it's because you're just too fat. And with those legs, I can't imagine why you'd want it any shorter." Grandmother turned on her heel and huffed off. Meg peeled off the dreadful garment and dumped it into an ugly pink pile. Anger replaced tears as she marched out of the shop, slamming the door behind her.

As she recalled, she'd never entered the shop again—until today.

She walked back to where the dressing rooms once had been. The partition was gone now, and the dressing rooms had vanished. Clean white walls stood in their place, providing a nice backdrop for Sunny's collection of artifacts. The high ceiling was painted flat black and seemed to disappear, except for the bright spotlights that were aimed perfectly at paintings and artifacts. Yes,

Meg had to admit that Sunny still had that special flair. Sunny, who had been completely hopeless at housekeeping—their kitchen could have been a health inspector's nightmare—had always kept their house looking, well, interesting. The decor had consisted of a little bit of everything: dusty peacock feathers in hand-thrown pots, macramé wall hangings, beaded curtains in the doorways.

Meg glanced around the gallery. It was immaculate. Suddenly the old anger churned within Meg—why hadn't Sunny been more of a mother back then? If she had only kept their home half this nice, maybe they would have avoided some of those ridiculous fights. But in those days, Sunny's life had always been on the edge, and often completely out of control.

"Sigfried, I'm back," called a woman's voice. "Tell me again why I offered to chair the Crandale Tourism Committee. Those people are insane! They think that cranberries alone will bring the tourists to town." She laughed.

Meg caught her breath, and her stomach constricted. Sunny's voice sounded the same, yet it was different. It had the same dramatic, well-enunciated tones, but there was some slight change, softer perhaps. Meg froze, pretending to study a woven wall hanging from Nepal, her back to them, as Sunny continued on about the meeting of the Crandale Tourism Committee. At last she paused, and the gallery grew silent except for the small fountain bubbling in the corner and the background music, which had changed from Mozart to Vivaldi.

Heels clicked toward Meg across the polished wooden floor. She felt trapped. *I'm a grown woman,* she told herself, taking a slow, deep, breath. *This is a public place; I have every right to be here.*

"May I help you?" Sunny's tone was warm and friendly, a voice probably reserved for strangers—potential customers. Meg slowly turned and faced her. She watched her mother's expression with some satisfaction; it was like having the upper hand. She waited for that shocked moment of revelation when Sunny recognized her own daughter. Meg had already imagined what the reception would be—very controlled and civilized. Sunny's head cocked to one side in obvious puzzlement, then lit with amazed recognition.

Without warning, Sunny burst into sobs, grabbing Meg and holding her tightly. To Meg's astonishment, she followed suit. Then almost as quickly, they both stopped crying, stepped back, and with embarrassment, dabbed their eyes and noses.

"My dear Sigfried," explained Sunny to the bewildered man at the counter, "this is my own little Meggie, my prodigal daughter come home. I haven't seen her in—well, forever, it seems. Can you mind the shop while we go for a cup of tea?" Sigfried nodded dumbly with wide eyes, and Sunny ushered Meg out the door.

They walked silently down the street until they came to what used to be the Gull's Nest Hotel, now transformed into what looked like a turn-of-the-century tearoom and restaurant. The sign above said *Victoria's*. Meg mulled over the term *prodigal daughter* as they were seated. It wasn't as if she'd run off with the family jewels; actually, she had left with nothing, and everything she had today she had earned herself.

Sunny poured a steaming cup of tea for Meg, then another for herself. She picked up the delicate china cup and slowly sipped, her gaze on Meg, a faint smile playing across her mouth. Her hair was still platinum blonde, and her eyes were the same deep green, which made Meg feel—rather uncomfortably—as if she were staring into her own eyes. Right now those eyes were focused tightly on Meg's.

"Well, Sunny, you haven't changed much," Meg began, forcing herself to push away her childish reaction to her mother's "prodigal daughter" comment. It suddenly seemed strange that she and Erin had never, not even as children, called Sunny

"Mom." It had seemed normal then, but for some reason it now struck her as odd, or dysfunctional, as her therapist would say.

Sunny set down her cup with a clink and shook her head. "Well, I sure can't say the same for you, Meggie." She stared openly, and Meg felt her cheeks grow hot, an irritating habit she hadn't experienced for years. Meg suspected it might be a compliment, but one never knew for sure with Sunny.

"Well, I guess I've lost a few pounds since I last saw you."

"It's more than that, Meggie. Your hair has gotten darker. It used to be so—so red. Now it's more auburn. And it looks softer in that shoulder-length style—much more flattering than those ponytails you used to wear."

"Thanks," said Meg. "I guess."

"And you look, well, older." Sunny laughed.

"After all, it's been nearly twenty years."

Sunny slowly shook her head. "Twenty years since Daddy died? Really? I remember it like yesterday. Just doesn't seem like it.... Where does the time go?" She stared absently across the room, as if looking across time. Her eyes were misty, and Meg noticed how the skin on Sunny's neck sagged a little. She was very thin, maybe too thin, and the wrinkles around her eyes were deeper, but Meg thought Sunny looked pretty good for a woman of sixty.

"Erin wrote me about Grandmother. That's why I'm here, Sunny. How is she? Grandmother, I mean." Meg feared she might be too late; perhaps Grandmother was already dead and buried.

"She's still hanging in there. That woman is amazing. She had a case of pneumonia last December, and the doctor didn't expect her to pull through, what with her heart and all. But here it is March. Not that I want her to kick the bucket, mind you. But you know Grandmother, strong until the end." Sunny laughed.

Meg could think of no response; she just stared woodenly as Sunny pulled out a silver cigarette case.

"Yep, I still smoke, Meggie. It's always been my personal guarantee that I'll never grow to be as old as Mother. Well, that and skydiving." She laughed again, then took a long drag and blew it over her shoulder. The ladies at the next table glared their way, and one of them cleared her throat loudly in an obvious hint.

Meg's face burned in humiliation, just as it had when she was a kid. Sunny had always embarrassed her then. She could always say or do something totally out of the realm of what Meg considered normal. Meg fingered the linen napkin in her lap, reminding herself she was no longer a little girl. Then to her surprise, Sunny glanced at the next table and quickly snuffed out the cigarette in her saucer.

Meg stared in amazement for a moment before speaking. "I thought I might visit Grandmother, if you don't think it'll upset her."

"No, you go ahead. Who knows, she might even want to see you." Sunny laughed again. "It might do her good to see how her little duckling grew into a lovely swan after all."

Meg looked at this strange woman—her mother—and wondered why she couldn't simply give a sincere compliment without disguising it beyond recognition. Well, she would do better than that.

"Your gallery's very nice, Sunny. You've done a fantastic job with it. Erin mentioned once that you've been successful."

Sunny smiled, then frowned. "Sounds like you've been in touch with your sister quite a bit. What is it—some sort of conspiracy against me? Erin never speaks a word of you, even when I ask. For all I knew, you were dead, Meggie."

Meg studied Sunny's expression, trying to discern if she really cared or if it was just theatrics. "I made Erin promise not to mention where I was. We only exchanged cards at Christmas or an occasional birthday, and never anything personal."

"Why, Meggie? Why in the world did you cut out like that? Not a word, nothing. And why have you suddenly come back,

24

unannounced like this, especially after all this time?" Sunny examined Meg closely. "You don't appear to need money.... What's going on, Meggie?"

"I go by Meg now." She stared down at her tea, swirling the golden liquid around in her cup. Suddenly she felt tired. "I don't really know, Sunny. Not exactly. I think it's just time to mend some fences. I never meant to cut the ties so completely—but I was hurt." There, that was honest. That was mature.

"You were hurt? What about me? What about your grandmother?" Sunny's voice rose. Like a little child, Meg suddenly wanted to cover her ears and run from the room. The ladies at the other table simply stared at the spectacle Sunny created. But Sunny had never minded scenes; she always spoke her mind freely. And she'd always enjoyed being the center of attention—any kind of attention.

Suddenly Sunny came to a halt. "I'm—I'm sorry, Meggie." She smiled faintly. "Here you are, back home after all these years, and I'm lecturing you."

Meg could hardly believe her ears. Was this Sunny? Apologizing? She decided to pick up the conversation where she'd left off. "I was just a kid," she explained. "A confused kid. I never wanted to hurt anyone." Part of her wanted to shout, "I just needed someone to love me!" But those words were better left locked inside.

"Oh, let's just forget it, Meg. See there, I called you Meg. It's all just water under the bridge now, anyway. Why don't we move on? And you know, honey, I really am glad you're here." Sunny reached across the table, smiling, and touched Meg's arm.

Part of Meg agreed. She, too, longed to bury the past, just as she'd done for the last twenty years. But another part of her resisted. That little girl inside still cried out with the pain of old wounds. And she knew that being back in Crandale would probably rip open a whole lot more.

25

Three

GRANDPA'S HOUSE WAS A SAD DISAPPOINTMENT. The paint was peeling; the porch sagged, its roof was nearly gone; broken spindles gaped from beneath the warped handrail like missing teeth. The yard, once so full of life and color, was now filled with weeds.

Meg slowly climbed the decrepit steps, mourning the deterioration of Grandpa's house almost as much as she'd grieved over his death. Seeing the old Victorian in such a state was a harsh reminder that he truly was gone, and had been for some time. She'd never really thought of him as gone before. In her childhood memories, he still lived in his house, painted his porch, and flipped cranberry hotcakes high into the air. Today it all seemed dead, with nothing left to remind her of those happier times. She sat down on the top step, and for the second time that day, tears came, hot and wet, streaking down her face. Why hadn't she realized things could never stay the same?

"Hello?" called a small, dark-haired woman from behind the sagging screen door. "Excuse me, can I help you?"

Meg looked up and wiped her nose. "I suppose you must be Rosa. My mother, Sunny, told me about you."

"Oh, yes. And can it be—you are Meggie? All grown up now?

I see your picture upstairs in your grandpa's room. You were a little girl then. But your grandma, she never talks of you." Rosa stepped out on the porch and frowned. "Is something wrong, Meggie? Why do you look so sad?"

"It's okay, Rosa. I'm just feeling a little emotional. It's been so long since I've been back—"

"Rosa," called a voice from inside. "Who's out there?"

Rosa looked at Meg. "You want for me to tell her?"

"No, why don't you let me."

Rosa held the door open, and Meg walked in. To her surprise, it looked almost the same inside as it had when she was a child. Other than some missing pieces of furniture, it was as if she were Meggie again and Grandpa would pop around the corner with a hot loaf of his famous cranberry bread.

"Who's there?" demanded Grandmother shrilly. Meg entered the dimly lit bedroom. It was the same room that Grandmother had slept in when Meg was a girl. Meg stood cautiously in the doorway, wondering what to say. Would Grandmother even want to speak to her? She glanced around the room. Most of the massive cherry bedroom furniture was gone, and in its place was a hospital bed and some other clinical-looking items.

"Hello, Grandmother," she began timidly. "It's me, Meg. I've come to see you."

Grandmother blinked slowly, then stared intently with wide pale eyes. She looked so small and vulnerable in that bed, nothing like the sharp grandmother of Meg's memory.

"Are you trying to give me a heart attack, girl? Is that really you, Meggie? What do you want?" she demanded in a quavering voice.

Meg didn't know what to say, but she drew closer to the bed, leaning over so Grandmother could see her better. This wasn't going to be easy. "I just came to visit you, Grandmother. I saw Sunny today, and I thought I'd come see you, too. I hope you don't mind."

"Humph. Fine thing. You stay away all these years, then come trotting back without a single word of warning. You might have killed me with the shock."

"I'm sorry, Grandmother." Meg stood transfixed, studying her grandmother's wrinkled white hands. The blue veins showed clearly through the translucent skin. In an odd way it was almost beautiful. Finally, Meg pulled a straight chair closer to the bed and sat down.

"I heard you weren't well, Grandmother. I thought I should come while I had the chance. I hoped we could—you know, mend our fences, so to speak."

"Well, what the devil took you so long?"

Meg shook her head, searching for words.

"You should have come back ages ago, Meggie." Grandmother's tone softened.

"You're right, Grandmother. I'm sorry."

Grandmother's blue eyes were much lighter than Meg recalled, and now they stared at Meg as if seeing her for the first time. Then Grandmother smiled faintly.

"My, my, Meggie, you've blossomed into a handsome young woman. How old are you now?"

"Thirty-seven," answered Meg quietly. They were the first words of praise she could remember Grandmother ever speaking to her. "But I'm not exactly a young woman."

Grandmother's laugh sounded like the squawk of an old hen. "Depends on where you're standing, Meggie. I remember when I was thirty-seven. Bennie was in school, and your mother still in diapers. I waited too late to have Sunny—almost killed me, too. Having babies after thirty is no picnic, I can tell you. But I was a businesswoman—probably never should've had a family. It was Stewart's idea to have children, not mine. Do you have any children, Meggie?"

"No, I've been too busy with my career. I'm not even married."

She scooted her chair closer. "I guess I'm a little like you." Meg smiled. It was the first time she'd actually made this connection, but she supposed it was true.

"What, no beaus or anything?"

"Well, I just broke off an engagement." Meg hadn't meant to disclose this little tidbit, but for the first time in her life, she felt an odd sense of kinship with Grandmother. What would it hurt to tell the old woman?

"Tsk, tsk. Well, you know what they say—there's lots of fish in the sea." Grandmother leaned her head back and closed her eyes. Meg wondered if she had worn her out and started to rise.

"Don't go, Meggie." Grandmother's hand reached up. "I've had too much time to lay here and think. I rarely get a chance to visit. Rosa just shuffles in and out with hardly a sentence out of her. Besides, there's a few things I still need to say to you. And I believe there's some things you may need to say to me."

Meg figured that meant a full apology. She had never been good at apologies, but somehow, knowing that Grandmother might not be around for long made it a little easier. Maybe that's what everyone needed—deadlines. Just enough time to get things right. Maybe people would treat each other better.

"Yes, Grandmother, I did come to tell you I'm sorry. I'm sorry for all those wicked things I said after Grandpa's funeral. I was so upset right then. But I know I was way out of line." She looked at Grandmother, whose lips were pressed tightly together as if waiting for Meg to finish. What more was there to say? Did Grandmother want her to beg for forgiveness? "And, Grandmother, you must admit you and Sunny said some pretty mean things to me, too."

"Pish-posh, Meggie. I wasn't fishing for an apology. I'm beyond that sort of pettiness now." Grandmother leaned her head back again, and Meg stared in amazement. She wasn't prepared for this. Grandmother had always owned the role of enemy in

Meg's memory. Now she sounded almost gracious.

"There's so much you couldn't begin to understand, Meggie. You were just too young. And you're right; I wasn't very nice to you that day, or even before then, for that matter. I know you always favored your grandpa, and he spoiled you rotten. He was always catering to you, feeding you sweets and whatnot. And I hounded you to get rid of that baby fat and to act like a lady. Oh, I thought I'd make something of you, Meggie. I was trying to make up for what I never did for Sunny. Looks like you didn't need my help." She sighed. "I never was much good at raising children. Oh, sure, I had fun with Bennie and Sunny when they were young, dressing them up, parading them about, but I never really knew how to be motherly. I'm sure Sunny told you all about that."

Actually, the only thing Meg recalled Sunny saying about her childhood was how she despised the small-town mentality of Crandale. Ironic that she should end up here.

Grandmother was quiet, her eyes closed, and breathing heavily.

"I think I've worn you out, Grandmother. I'd better let you rest," she whispered. Grandmother nodded slightly, then opened her eyes again.

"You've come home, Meggie," she whispered. Meg reached out and touched Grandmother's hand without answering. She didn't want to lie to her grandmother, not on what might be her deathbed. But if Grandmother wanted to believe she'd come to stay, she wouldn't say otherwise. At least not right now.

Out on the beach, Meg walked and walked. For the first time in years, she gave no thought to the time of day, what she was doing, or where she was going. She just walked. Grandpa had loved walking the beaches. She used to walk with him, watching intently as he stooped to examine a shell, a landlocked crab, or whatever else the tide had dragged in. He'd always attached a story to these items of interest, explaining some of the mysteries of the sea and of life. She'd loved being with him and always felt a sense of awe around him. He was so big and strong, so wise. He could do anything, she believed. There wasn't a piece of machinery he couldn't take apart and put back together, better than new.

Yet even as she thought about him with such reverence, she couldn't recall him ever telling her anything personal about himself. He had never spoken of how he'd met Grandmother, his boyhood dreams, or even his grown-up aspirations or disappointments. Maybe he'd had none. To her he remained just Grandpa, frozen in time with his thick white hair and easy pace. He always wore the same hat—a gray tweed tam, yellowed with age. She remembered asking him once if he ever missed his son, Benjamin. Bennie had been ten years older than Sunny. He had died before Meg was born, killed in World War II. But Grandmother had kept a large photo of him on her bedroom dresser. Meg knew this sad event had greatly overshadowed their lives, and it seemed odd that no one ever spoke of him. She knew Bennie had left a widow and a son behind, but the wife lived in California, and the son— she couldn't recall his name, but he would have to be at least fifty by now.

Grandpa's face had grown cloudy the time Meg mentioned Bennie, and she had instantly wished she hadn't. She remembered him saying something like, "Some things just aren't meant to be." She had never known exactly what he'd meant, and she couldn't understand why he didn't regale her with stories about what she imagined to be her war-hero uncle in the same way he told her about the landlocked crab who needed to return to his family in the sea.

The wind picked up, and Meg noticed that a dark bank of clouds had rolled in while she'd been reminiscing. She decided to turn back. She didn't even know where she'd be sleeping tonight. She'd made no arrangements and really didn't want to impose on Rosa, who surely had her hands full with Grandmother.

Finally Meg spotted the old wooden steps set into the edge of the bluff that led up from the beach to Grandpa's house. Just as she reached the top step, it started to pour. She raced to the shelter of the porch.

"Nice car," spoke an unfamiliar voice from the other side of the big wraparound porch. She looked up as a lanky teen stepped into view. He jerked his thumb in the direction of her car parked near what used to be the carriage house. "That your Jaguar?"

"Yes. Who are you?"

He extended his hand. "I'm Jason, and you must be my dad's long-lost cousin Meggie. I guess that makes us like, second cousins, and some sort of once- or twice-removed. I never could figure that part out. Great-grandma tried to explain it once. Anyway, Rosa told me you were here. She was worried you were going to get caught in the rain."

"Really? You're Bennie's grandson? How amazing."

"Well, that's one way of looking at it. My dad says he never even met you. Isn't that totally weird? But Mom and Dad moved here right after Great-grandpa died—I guess that's just after you ran off. I wasn't born yet."

"So you've been living here in Crandale all these years?" Somehow, it didn't seem quite possible that another relative, unknown to her, might inhabit these parts. She felt a sense of betrayal. Of course, that was ridiculous. She hadn't cared enough to come back in all these years, so she could hardly claim any ownership to this house or the town.

"Yep. I was born and raised here. Our house is down a ways on the bluff; you probably saw it from the beach. We used to run the cranberry business, but Dad's been sort of getting out. He says it's a lot of hard work without much payoff. He's thinking about selling off the bog to a developer for a resort. He'll probably tear down this old house, too." He slapped his hand against the wobbly railing.

Meg stared at him in disbelief. "Really? He'd actually tear down Grandpa's house?"

"You mean Great-grandma's house. Yeah, the place is falling down anyway. It'd cost a fortune to fix. But I have to admit I'll miss it some."

Meg nodded sadly. "Guess I'll miss it some, too."

"I wouldn't think you'd care. I mean, you haven't been here in ages."

Meg swallowed the lump in her throat. She could think of nothing more to say to this boy who seemed to think little of tearing down this old house so full of childhood memories.

"You think I could drive it?"

"What?"

"Your car. I never drove a Jag before. You think you'd let me drive it?"

She studied him, noticing that although he had her same coloring, the fair skin with red hair and freckles, he looked nothing like her, or Grandpa, the one who had passed on those Lancaster traits.

"Maybe. But not today. I need to go look up my sister."

"Erin? That's right, she'd be your sister. Man, this is so weird. I just never think about Erin having a sister. I mean, it's like you were just dead or something. Really weird."

"Yeah, I guess it is weird." That seemed to describe it pretty well. "Could you let Rosa know I'm going over to Erin's? I'll be back tomorrow to visit with Grandmother some more."

"Okay. Maybe I can drive your car then."

Meg didn't bother to answer as she dashed through the rain to her car.

Four

MEG WONDERED IF ERIN KNEW she was in town yet. She thought Sunny might have called her; that is, if they were on speaking terms. It seemed that for most of their lives, Sunny and Erin had been in some sort of feud. In fact, Sunny had always seemed to be at odds with someone.

Meg pulled her address book from her purse and looked up her sister's phone number. She turned on her car phone and dialed the number, waiting as the phone rang again and again. Didn't Erin even have an answering machine? Meg studied the address. She thought she recalled where the road was located, but she didn't remember any houses along it.

Erin had mentioned in a Christmas card once that they lived in a small mobile home and it didn't feel very homey at Christmas. Meg tried now to envision Erin, her husband, Tom, and their little kids, but all she could imagine was poor white trash living in a run-down trailer. It wasn't a pleasant thought. She knew that Tom worked in construction and that she had three nieces all under the age of ten. But she hadn't kept very good track of them over the years. She was a pretty poor excuse for an aunt. She did know their names—Jennifer, Hannah, and Ashley—and she thought Jennifer was the oldest, but wasn't sure about the other two.

As she reached the top of a small rise, Meg saw a mailbox with their name: The Edwards Family. She turned down the drive until she came to a large two-story home. It was newly built, but the style was that of the Craftsman era, with a tall, steep-pitched roof, wide eaves, and handsome woodwork that appeared to be hand-done. The wraparound front porch reminded Meg of Grandpa's house.

Was this really where Erin lived? A carved sign on the porch answered her question. She was impressed; Erin and Tom had done well. The driveway made a nice loop that circled in front of the house, and Meg parked on the far side of the loop, then climbed out. She heard what sounded like a large dog barking, but no one answered her knock at the door. She climbed back into her car and studied the place. So this was Erin's house. Nice green lawn, flowers blooming in well-tended beds. Who would have thought? Who would have ever thought.

The last time she'd seen Erin was at the funeral. Erin had been in her early twenties then, and even though it was going out of fashion, Erin still clung tightly to her hippie roots. She'd been living in a commune, supposedly making pottery to sell at arts-and-crafts fairs. Meg remembered that she'd shown up at Grandpa's funeral in a long black dress that looked as if it had been scavenged from someone's attic, along with some clunky lace-up sandals.

Funny how Grandmother had never gotten on Erin's case like she did with Meg. But then Erin had always been the tall, slender, beautiful sister with her flashing dark eyes and straight black hair. She was dramatic and artistic; she could do no wrong. Even when she had joined the commune and taken her vow of poverty, which she obviously must have forsaken somewhere along the way, no one in the family had ever scorned her the way they had Meg.

Erin had taken some art and theater classes in college, but eventually she'd dropped out. A college degree held little interest for a free spirit like her.

It wasn't that Meg had anything against Erin. Nothing more serious than sibling rivalry, anyway. In fact, when they were younger, they had always had great fun together, but then Erin had suddenly grown up while Meg remained a little girl. They had been living just off the university campus then, and Erin started mixing with the college crowd. The same thing had happened to Meg at that age, but when she was the younger child she couldn't understand how it was that Erin had grown up so fast. But Meg had her compensation in the summers. When it was time to go to Crandale, Erin preferred staying with Sunny on campus and joining in the summer fun. Meanwhile, Meg got to stay at Grandpa's house and had Grandpa's attention all to herself. Of course, the drawback was having Grandmother's scrutiny all to herself, as well.

Now Erin had all this, too. It figured. Meg fought down the feeling of envy as she imagined the good life Erin and Tom enjoyed here in this beautiful home with their three darling daughters. This was just the sort of home Meg had imagined she and Jerred would share. Well, Meg had made her choices, or as Grandmother used to say, she'd "made her bed."

Meg noticed the garage door opening, and behind her a dark green Volvo wagon pulled into the driveway. She instantly recognized her sister's face, but the three smaller heads were strangers to her. Her heart started racing. What would Erin think of her? Would she resent the lengthy absence, the lack of communication? The little girls poured out into the garage, each of them carrying grocery bags, the youngest leaving a trail of items behind her. Erin peered curiously at Meg's car, probably wondering who this stranger might be. Meg took a deep breath and climbed out of the car.

"Meggie!" Erin screamed. She threw her purse on the hood of the car and raced over. "Meggie, oh, my gosh, Meggie! Is it really you? Oh, Meggie, you've finally come to your senses and come home!" Erin hugged her tight and then held her at arm's length. "I can't believe it's really you. You look terrific! You're absolutely beautiful. This is so great. Girls, come here and meet your aunt Meggie."

Meg was smiling too. For the first time today, she felt like someone was truly glad to see her—no hoops to jump through, no strings attached. And she didn't even mind being called Meggie. She met the girls. Jennifer, the oldest, was almost ten, with long dark hair and a striking resemblance to Erin as a young girl. Next was Hannah. At six, she had dark curly hair and a pixie face. Last was four-year-old Ashley, with red hair and freckles. The little girls clamored around, asking questions. "When did you get here, Aunt Meggie?" "Did Howard bark at you?" "How long are you staying?" "Do you have any kids, Aunt Meggie?"

Erin laughed. "Why don't we let her come inside and relax before we scare her away." They all grabbed some groceries and carried them inside, where they began unloading them in the big country kitchen.

"Erin, I can't believe it. Your house is beautiful," said Meg as they set the last bag upon the tile-topped counter.

"I suppose you still remember my vow of poverty." Erin laughed. Her big, boisterous laugh was just the same as when they were little. "Well, Tom eventually convinced me there was nothing wrong with living comfortably. Still, we do try to think of others who are less fortunate and help when we can. Tom's very active in Habitat for Humanity—that's a group of volunteers who help build houses for those who can't afford much. But enough of that. Tell me about you. When did you get here? Where are you staying, and for how long?"

"Okay, slow down. I got here this morning around ten. I saw

Sunny and Grandmother. I think I'll find a motel—"

"No way! My sister is not staying in a motel. You will stay here, in our guest room. I insist."

"I don't want to impose—"

"Good grief! I haven't seen you for two decades, and you're worrying about imposing. Meggie, what is wrong with you?" Somehow the way Erin said it sounded like she really wondered. Meg wondered herself. What was wrong with her? How could she have been so stupid, to cut off her own flesh and blood the way she'd done all these years? She felt tears coming again.

"I don't know, Erin."

"Meggie, I'm sorry. I'm just so glad you're here. Don't mind me. You know I always say whatever comes to mind. Not like you. You were always the quiet one. Not that I blame you. I would have done the same if I'd been you."

Meg looked at her sister. "What do you mean?"

"Oh, you know. It seemed like you were always the scapegoat; they were always picking at you—trying to change you and everything. Usually you were pretty quiet about it. At least until the big blowout after Grandpa's funeral. I was pretty strung out that day, but I can still see you in the front room screaming at the two of them. Your face was literally crimson, Meggie." She chuckled, and Meg, for the life of her, tried to see the humor. If only she could laugh too; maybe that would make it all better.

Erin continued. "Grandmother was huffing and puffing like she was just about to explode, and Sunny—" She paused. "Well, we all knew Sunny, as usual, had overimbibed. But you just kept going and going, laying into both of them about how they had killed Grandpa. I wanted to clap—" Erin suddenly stopped. "I'm sorry, Meggie. You probably don't want to talk about all that." She started unpacking groceries. "I'm so glad you're here. I guess I got carried away."

"Well, it may have been amusing for a spectator, but do you

remember what they said to me?"

"Wasn't it their usual diatribe? I think my memory is sort of fuzzy about the rest. Besides, I've heard Sunny's and Grandmother's versions so much, it all gets rather muddled. You know, I don't think I ever heard your version."

Meg had been trying to help by handing Erin things to put away, but she didn't know her way around a kitchen, and kept getting in the way. Finally she pulled up a bar stool and sat down. She watched as Erin quickly shoved things here and there, chattering as she did. She could hear the girls arguing in the den, where Erin had sent them to watch a video.

Erin shoved the last box of cornflakes into the big pantry and turned. "So tell me, Meggie, what is your version?"

Meg tried to think of where to start, how to condense it, and how not to get upset in the telling of it. "Well, when I heard Grandpa had died, I felt like the only person in the world who had ever really cared about me was gone."

Erin frowned. "I cared. I was just too much of a mess to be any help."

"No offense, Erin, but you know we hadn't been close for years. Plus you'd been off in your artsy commune. You seemed pretty checked out. Then Sunny, as usual, was in her own world. Anyway, you know how things were at home, and after I quit high school, Sunny wouldn't even speak to me."

Erin nodded and poured them each a glass of soda. "Well, you must admit, Sunny was pretty miffed when I dropped out of college. Your quitting high school was just a bit too much for the college professor."

"I know, but I was already getting my GED, and high school seemed so juvenile at the time. They treated us like babies. Besides, I'd sorted that all out with Grandpa that summer. He'd offered to pay all my college tuition if I would get in and stick to it."

"Oh, I remember now. But Grandmother had never heard

40

about any of that, and she thought you'd broken Grandpa's heart with your wild and rebellious ways." Erin drew the back of her hand across her forehead in her old dramatic way.

"Yeah, and I was angry with them for allowing him to work himself sick in the cranberry bog. I saw the condition of the house he came home to every night. I was so mad at Grandmother for letting him live like that. It was pitiful."

"Maybe you should have moved down from Eugene to help out." Erin eyed Meg with a look that was more curiosity than accusation.

"Erin, I've struggled with that exact thought for years. I did blame myself. When I got down here, I couldn't believe his house. Piles of filthy dirty dishes, and he'd been eating out of pots and pans. A laundry heap that had been there for weeks—there wasn't a single clean piece of clothing left in his closet, and his sheets were brown. Erin, they were brown with ground-in grime. It was so sad and disgusting. I could have died when I thought of him coming home to that, day after day. But, Erin, I was only seventeen, just a kid. They were the grown-ups; shouldn't they have done something?"

"Think about it, Meggie." Erin took a sip of her soda. "In those days, they rarely thought of anyone other than themselves."

"I'd just been down during the summer, and things hadn't been like that. If only I'd known…" Meg swallowed hard. "The worst part is, during that time I never even wrote or called him. I didn't even come for harvest. Grandmother said I broke his heart. Maybe I did." It was too late; the tears were coming now.

The roar of a pickup truck sounded from the front, and a door slammed.

Erin touched Meg's arm. "You've had a long day, Meg. Why don't you give yourself a little break before dinner? I'll show you the guest room, and you can lie down and relax a bit. You can meet Tom later."

"Thanks, Erin. I'm really sorry I kept away all this time."

She was sorry. Deeply sorry. Here all along had been this wonderful sister, yet she'd deprived herself of the friendship they could have had. She was the one who had sent the cold, brief letters, until Erin had finally kept her notes short and impersonal, too. Why had she been so stupid and stubborn? Where in the world had it gotten her?

Five

LIKE THE REST OF THE HOUSE, the guest room was lovely, with sponge-painted walls in a soft shade of cream and a hand-painted border of ivy around the ceiling. Each ivy leaf was exquisite, with many shades of green blended to perfection. It looked like a real plant. It was obvious that Erin had poured her artistic nature into this home.

Once again, Meg felt an unwanted surge of envy. She had worked so hard putting herself through college, then throwing herself into her career. Now what did she have to show for it? A tiny apartment filled with odds and ends, a designer wardrobe suitable for the office, and, of course, her car. But what was that compared to this? She had no husband or children, and no real home.

She flopped across the bed and stared at the ceiling. Jerred and San Francisco seemed so very far away. Almost unreal. In her memory, Jerred seemed like some nondescript character from a movie that she could barely remember. Had she ever truly known him? What would life have been like if Tiffany hadn't come along and they had gotten married after all? Not like this, surely. And how long would it have been until another "Tiffany" came along? No, it was best that she had escaped Jerred. But what about the rest of her life? Was there anything left in San Francisco worth clinging to? Had she ever really been happy? Her success had been somewhat fulfilling, but what did it mean once she left the office and went home?

She closed her eyes and tried to imagine what kind of a life she would want if she could start all over again. Would money be as important? Where would family fit in? Her life seemed so unsettled, and perhaps now, more than ever, she longed for some stability— something she could cling to, something that would give her roots. But what was it? And where was it? Questions continued to tumble through her mind as she fell asleep. In a half dream, the kind that she always remembered and where she seemed to have some control over the outcome, she found herself chasing several different things all at once and not catching any. In the end she didn't even know what it was that she was chasing.

"Aunt Meggie?" Meg opened her eyes to a round little face peering at her. Chubby fingers touched her arm softly. "Mommy said to tell you it's almost time for dinner."

"Thank you, Ashley." Meg sat up and rubbed her eyes in the semidark room. Ashley, highlighted by a long slat of light pouring in from the hallway, stood looking at her with a puzzled expression, but saying nothing.

"Is something wrong, Ashley?" asked Meg, turning on the small lamp next to the bed.

Ashley nodded. "Mommy says I look like you. But you're all growed up. You're not a girl like me."

Meg laughed. "Your mommy's probably remembering when I was little like you. You see, I was a little girl once, and I probably did look a lot like you." She tousled the carrot red curls. She'd never spent much time with children. In fact, she couldn't remember ever having had a real conversation with a child.

Ashley lowered her chin and said shyly, "I think you're pretty, Aunt Meggie."

Meg smiled. "I think you're pretty too, Ashley." Meg wondered if anyone had ever told her she was pretty as a child. She didn't remember such a thing. Grandpa used to say she was a hard worker, a smart and sturdy girl, but never pretty. She hoped Ashley wouldn't grow up hearing only those things.

Downstairs Meg was introduced to her brother-in-law, and instantly liked him. Tom seemed so down-to-earth, and it was plain to see he adored his wife and daughters. A big man with dark hair and beard and friendly blue eyes, he spoke with obvious enjoyment about his work as a contractor. After a pleasant dinner, Jennifer and Hannah began clearing the table, and Tom started a fire in the big rock fireplace. Erin excused herself to help Ashley get ready for bed.

"I've already told Erin at least ten times what a beautiful home this is," said Meg, "but I haven't told you, Tom. It's really wonderful. Erin says you did most of the work yourself."

"Yeah, it was quite a project. But Erin and I worked together, and, well, it turned out all right." He threw a log on the fire and looked around the spacious living room. "There was a time in life I thought we'd never get ahead. I suppose you heard all about that crazy commune; then we lived in that awful trailer during the recession when I could hardly find work. It hasn't always been like this."

Meg laughed. "Yeah, I remember when Erin went to live in the commune. I thought she'd lost her mind."

He scratched his beard and chuckled. "It does seem strange now, but you know, there's something to be said about some of the values in the commune. Those people did believe in sharing. But unfortunately they started sharing drugs—and even spouses, come to think of it. We were real lucky to get out when we did. Then the girls came along, and we knew we wanted to provide them with something more. Erin never felt like she'd had much of a home. I suppose you know how that goes. She wanted more for

45

our girls. Of course, I did, too." He rubbed his hand over the hand-carved oak mantel. Erin had already explained how all the woodwork had been painstakingly done by Tom.

"Well, this is certainly more than we ever had as girls, Tom. I know Erin appreciates it."

"Do you ever hear from your father, Meg? I know Erin doesn't seem to care much about him. But sometimes I wonder...."

"I tried to track him down once when I was in college. I hoped maybe I could get him to help out financially. I sent a letter to the only address I'd ever had from him; it was off an old birthday card that I'd clung to for years. But my letter came back unopened and stamped 'No Such Address.'"

"I asked Sunny about him once, and she said she thought he was somewhere on the East Coast. But you can never tell with Sunny."

Meg sighed. "I see you know her pretty well."

After Erin rejoined them, they visited on into the night, remembering old times, catching up, and laughing about anything and everything. Before long, Meg felt at home with both of them. They seemed to have the ingredients for what she would consider a pretty good marriage, although she'd never actually seen one up close before. She hadn't even believed such a thing existed. Meg knew that if she had married Jerred, it would have been rocky at best, and probably nowhere near as good as what Erin and Tom had.

"How long have you two been married?" asked Meg.

"You mean legally married, with a license and all?" asked Tom with a twinkle in his eye. "You know me and my old lady had been shacked up quite a few years before she made me tie the knot."

Erin chucked a pillow at him. "I was never your 'old lady,' and you know it! And if I remember right, you're the one who decided it was time to get married."

Tom turned to Meg and grinned. "We met on the commune about sixteen years ago. The first time I saw Erin, she had this long black braid down her back, and she was making a huge pot. I can still see her kicking that wheel with her bare feet, and the mud splattering off the wet clay, just coating her arms and face." He looked at his wife with tenderness. "I always was a softy for girls that liked to play in the dirt. And that's when I fell in love."

Erin smiled at him and continued the story. "It wasn't too long after Tom joined the commune that we both got pretty fed up with all the drugs that were taking over. That's when we decided to leave. Then we lived together for a few years. Grandmother was absolutely livid. Such a scandal. She wouldn't even speak to us. But Sunny was okay with it."

Meg laughed. "Why does that not surprise me?"

"Sure, I was just following in her footsteps, right? Well, fortunately, Tom and I still loved each other by the time I became pregnant with Jenny. About that time we joined a church and started to see life differently. That's when we made it official. Probably not the best way to start a marriage, with a baby on the way, and we've certainly had our tough times. But we both give God the credit for keeping us together and making our marriage great. We celebrated ten official years in December."

"Seems like only yesterday," Tom said sincerely. Then he stood and yawned. "Well, this working boy needs to hit the hay. I'm real glad you've come home, Meg. And you're welcome to stay with us as long as you like."

"That goes double for me, Meg," said Erin. "We still have a lot of catching up to do."

"Thanks, you two. I appreciate the hospitality. I'd really planned to stay in a hotel, but I must admit this is much nicer."

That night, Meg lay in bed replaying Erin's words about giving God the credit. When had Erin gotten acquainted with God? It was Meg who used to be what everyone else called religious. As a teenager, she'd gone to church with Grandpa every chance she got. God had seemed very real then, but somewhere—probably when Grandpa died—she had lost him. And she'd not been able to find him since.

Six

THE NEXT MORNING, MEG WOKE to rain pelting against the window. She looked out to see the two older girls, in bright raincoats and rubber boots, scurrying down the driveway to climb aboard the waiting yellow bus that had already honked its horn twice. In a swoosh of mist and squeaking brakes, they were gone.

Meg looked at her watch. It was half past seven. Normally she'd be in the office by now, probably working on the Lindsey account. Well, that was no longer her problem. She quickly dressed, then sat down. What would she do today? Unaccustomed to leisure, she suddenly felt uneasy. Vacations were foreign to her, and an extended leave of absence was almost frightening. What was she doing to her life?

She took a deep breath and looked out the window again, telling herself it was okay to take it easy for a change. It was the same thing her therapist had been telling her for months, and at fifty bucks an hour. She had to admit, there was something soothing about this place: the yellow school bus, the big fir trees dripping on the black driveway, brightly colored blooms in the flower beds. Erin's house was so provincial, so homey; it begged her to slow down. Yet she'd never managed to slow down in her entire adult life. Would it be possible?

Erin and Meg ate a pleasant breakfast and slowly sipped their second cup of coffee. They talked and talked. Meg mostly talked about Sunny and how frustrating it was to have her for a mother. Sunny, the perennial child, never taking responsibility for relationships, as flighty as a grasshopper, loud and brash, and hopelessly selfish. Suddenly, Meg grew aware of little Ashley sprawled on the floor at their feet, coloring a pair of tigers in a Noah's ark coloring book. Erin did not shoo her away as she had the older girls yesterday when they had discussed sensitive subjects. Maybe Erin thought that younger ears heard less, but Meg knew from experience this wasn't true. Finally, she steered her conversation away from Sunny. She didn't want to be the one to blame for turning a little girl against her grandma. After all, she knew what that was like. Instead, she began to tell Erin about what she'd been doing for the past nineteen and a half years. She even mentioned Jerred and the reasons for her unexpected leave of absence.

"Wouldn't it be hard to go back and work there after all that?" asked Erin as she wiped the countertop.

"I don't know. It's such a different life there. People come and go, and change, and it's all just part of the process. I think I could fit back in if I really wanted to."

"Do you want to?"

"I'm not sure that I do. But on the other hand, I don't know that I'm ready to give it all up, either. Besides, I don't really know what else I'd do. If I got a job in another agency, it probably wouldn't be nearly so high up. Although it might not take too long to work up, if I worked hard..." She sighed. The thought of starting over was almost sickening. Suddenly, she felt as if she were an old woman, over-the-hill and rolling down the other side fast, her best years behind her.

"Enough talk of work," announced Erin. "You're on vacation

right now. You don't need to think about work. I have to take Ashley to a birthday party around eleven; you want to come along? We could look around town, get some lunch."

"Sure. But I promised to go back to see Grandmother today. It was so different yesterday. For the first time, we almost seemed to hit it off. I couldn't believe it. I don't want to miss out on that while I still have the chance. What exactly is wrong with her, anyway? I know she's old, but…"

"I think the only real thing wrong with her is our cousin Abner," said Erin. "Ever since he got it into his head to sell off the bog, he's treated her like an invalid or like she's going senile. Oh sure, she's always had that thing with her heart, even when we were kids. But up until last year she had been as healthy as a horse." Erin glanced down at Ashley and lowered her voice. "Meggie, I actually think Abner wants her to die so he can have the place to do with as he likes. I know it's horrible and suspicious, and not very Christian of me, but I just don't trust him." Erin's eyes flashed the same way they used to when she was a teen getting all worked up over some new cause on the university campus.

"Really? Do you think Abner has something to do with her health?"

"Oh, I don't know. It's not like he's putting arsenic in the well. But I have to admit that I've never really liked our cousin. He's sort of slippery. Look around Grandmother's house and try and remember how many antiques there used to be. Abner has confiscated most of them. I don't know what he does, but my guess is that he sells them to buy his booze. I try and try not to judge him, Meggie. I do want to accept him, but he's always involved in something. Even Sunny says he's just like his dad."

"You mean Bennie? I thought Bennie was supposed to have been such a great guy and all."

"You're still living in childhood memories. Ask some old-timers, and you may hear about a different Bennie. I guess he and

Grandpa never got along too well. I think Bennie was sort of a mama's boy, and maybe that's what came between Grandmother and Grandpa. But then I'm sure that's another story. There's lots we don't know, Meggie. Lots that we can only speculate about. But stick around, and maybe we can figure it all out."

"Aunt Meggie?" asked Ashley, tugging at Meg's arm. "You wanna see my room? I made my bed all by myself."

"What a great idea, Ash," exclaimed Erin. "In fact, why don't you give Aunt Meggie a tour of the whole house while I go take a shower. If she wants to, that is."

"I'd love it," said Meg. "I've been dying to see all the things you've done with this marvelous house, Erin."

They started with Ashley's room. It was yellow and blue, with rabbits and daisies stenciled along the wall right at a child's eye level, obviously the careful handiwork of Erin again. A cozy, padded window seat invited a little girl to curl up with a picture book.

"Oh, Ashley, I love your room. It's perfect."

"This is Molly." Ashley pulled a well-loved rag doll from inside her lumpily made bed and held her up proudly.

"Hello, Molly," said Meg, shaking the little hand of the rag doll. "I certainly hope we didn't wake you."

Ashley giggled and laid Molly back down, this time on top of the pillow. She then took Meg by the hand and showed her the other girls' rooms, much like her own, but each with a different color scheme and each with its own special personality. Hannah's was lavender and green, and a bit messy, but more cluttered than sloppy. Jenny's room was peach and aqua, and very tidy; even her shoes were lined up in the closet. A mural of a little English cottage and flower garden filled one wall. Meg marveled at how pretty the girls' rooms were—they looked like something from a magazine. At the end of the hallway was a nice, roomy bathroom shared by all three girls. Ashley explained that they each had their own special color for towels, washcloths, and toothbrushes.

"One time, I got mixed up and I used Jenny's toothbrush instead of mine," Ashley said sheepishly. "But I never told Jenny."

They walked past the guest room where Meg was staying, with its own private bath. Meg knew she could be comfortable here for a while, but she didn't plan to impose on their hospitality.

"This is Mommy and Daddy's room." Ashley opened the door at the other end of the hall and walked in. Meg heard the shower running but decided a quick look around the bedroom wouldn't hurt—after all, Ashley was the one giving the tour. Situated above the triple-car garage, the room was spacious and beautiful with vaulted ceilings and lots of windows. Almost everything was white and cream, with just a few touches of color carefully placed here and there. Again the eye of the artist at work. Meg wondered how Erin kept everything so clean and white with Tom's work in construction, but she had noticed the roomy bath next to the laundry room downstairs. She also wondered how they had managed to build such a home; it must have cost a fortune.

Ashley then took Meg up a narrow back stairway behind the girls' rooms to show her the playroom that had been created in the attic space. Its sloped low ceiling and little dormer windows made the perfect hideaway. And at last—a messy room! Clutter from toys and craft supplies was everywhere. Childish paintings were taped to the walls, many bearing Hannah's name in big block letters. Hannah had definitely inherited her mother's talent. Meg thought how lucky these girls were and how much she would have loved to have grown up in a beautiful home like this, with a mother and father who cared so dearly.

"This is Jenny's," said Ashley as she knelt before a large Victorian dollhouse. It seemed the decorating was still in process; stacks of wallpaper and fabric were piled neatly on the floor beside it. "Jenny's making it real pretty." The awe showed plainly in Ashley's voice as she peered inside with tiny hands tucked safely behind her back. "I'm not s'posed to touch anything." Meg could feel every fiber of the child longing to handle it, to play with it, to have it for her very own. Meg could relate to Ashley's feelings—she, too, was the outsider looking in.

"What's your favorite thing to play with?" asked Meg, hoping to distract Ashley from the forbidden dollhouse.

"My bunnies." Ashley stood and grinned. "Wanna see?"

"Sure. Where are they?"

Once again Ashley took Meg by the hand, this time leading her down two flights of stairs and then out behind the garden shed where a pair of rabbit hutches stood, with a wide roof overhang protecting them. Ashley carefully opened a wire door, reached in, and pulled out a brindled lop-eared rabbit.

"This is Flopsy. Wanna hold her?"

"How about if I just pet her?" Meg reached out gingerly and touched the rabbit. The fur was incredibly soft. She stroked Flopsy several times, and the rabbit seemed quite calm. For some reason she expected it to leap and run away.

Before she realized what was happening, Ashley had slipped Flopsy into Meg's hands, then turned and extracted the other bunny from its cage. Meg's eyes grew wide as she stared at the rabbit cradled in her arm. Its tiny warm body twitched, and its nose sniffed her fingers curiously. Then it snuggled right into the crook of her elbow, and she was filled with an odd sense of pleasure as she held the little breathing creature.

"And this is Peter." Ashley held out a gray bunny for Meg to see. His eyes were black and bright, and his whiskers wiggled back and forth on his velvety nose.

"I like your bunnies, Ashley. I can see why they're your favorite." After a while, they put the bunnies back, and Ashley carefully gave them fresh food and water. Ashley then showed Meg around the yard. Neat little gravel paths led to various parts of the yard: a vegetable garden, a gazebo, a big wooden swing set, and a little playhouse. Finally, Ashley stopped by what looked like a toolshed.

"This is where Mommy works sometimes." Ashley opened the door to reveal a potter's shed. The pungent smell of clay and dust reminded Meg of childhood days when she used to tag along with Erin to pottery classes. Usually Erin would share a lump of clay, and sometimes, if there was a potter's wheel free, Meg would try her hand at a pot. But she could never make clay do the things that Erin could; instead, she usually wound up with a lopsided, lumpy thing that served as yet another ashtray for Sunny. Even though she knew her sister was five years older and gifted in art, Meg always came away feeling like a failure.

Now as she walked around Erin's workroom, observing the crowded shelves, she was assaulted with the same feeling. There were all kinds of pots and dishes and tiles. All perfectly symmetrical and lovely. Some were glazed in rich shining colors; some plain-looking pieces were still waiting to be fired. A good-sized kiln was in the back of the shed, and judging by the dry warmth of the room, Meg suspected it was running. There were also a large wooden kick wheel and a smaller electric one. Meg could just imagine Erin in here, puttering around. Already, Ashley had climbed onto a stool and was playing with a piece of clay on the workbench.

Meg walked over to another work area and examined a large project. Dozens of square clay tiles were laid in a line, and Meg knew enough about pottery to recognize the intricate design of glazes painted on the dull-looking tiles. They would be beautiful when fired. Behind them, some completed tiles were already stacked. The colors and patterns were stunning, and Meg recognized that they were similar to the ones she had seen in the kitchen and bathrooms.

"Hey, what are you two doing in here?" called Erin.

"I'm getting amazed by my sister's talent," replied Meg, holding up a finished tile in shades of russet, teal, and gold.

"Oh, those aren't anything much. I just make them for Tom's houses." Erin frowned down at Ashley's now clay-smudged denim overalls. "Ashley, is that what you're wearing to Brittany's birthday party?"

Ashley nodded, her chin sticking out.

"Okay, but you'd better change your muddy shoes and wash your hands." She turned to Meg. "Sunny called while you were outside. She asked for you to stop by the shop today. She wants to take you to lunch."

Meg groaned. "It's so hard to be around her."

Erin nodded. "I know."

"But I should probably go anyway."

"If you'd rather go be with Sunny while I take Ashley to the party, I won't mind."

"It's not that I'd rather go. But maybe I should."

"Besides, we'll have lots of time to visit later." Erin checked the temperature on the kiln and turned. "You are going to stay with us for a while, aren't you?"

"Sure. I love it here, Erin. I can't even begin to describe how wonderful it feels to be here. It's like you've created your own little paradise." Meg grinned.

"Thanks. I know what you mean. Sometimes I feel kind of silly. I don't mean to become obsessed with it, and it's not as if I want to create heaven on earth, because I really do believe in heaven. But I just have this strong longing to provide my girls with something special. Something more..." Her voice drifted off.

"I understand completely. And I think it's great, Erin. I'm really proud of you. And as much as I hate to admit it, I'm probably just a little envious—"

"Oh, Meg, you'll probably have all this and more one day," Erin interrupted. "That is, if you want it, I mean. I have a feeling that your coming here is God's way of bringing you something much, much better."

Meg slowly shook her head. "I don't know about that, but I sure hope you're right, Erin. Because right now my life looks pretty bleak."

Seven

ERIN OFFERED TO DROP MEG OFF on her way to delivering Ashley to the party, but Meg declined. As much as she enjoyed Erin's company, she needed her own wheels under her right now.

Instead of heading straight to town, she hopped on the freeway and drove north. She hoped this little drive might help clear her head a bit before her meeting with Sunny. The rain had finally stopped, but the world was still soggy and gray. The hissing of the wet pavement beneath the tires sounded almost musical, and being behind the wheel gave her a feeling of power.

She parked the car on a high viewpoint that looked out over the sea. Even with the gray clouds, the ocean provided a beautiful sight, ever changing with the weather and the season. It was a sight she never tired of. She opened her window and breathed in the fresh, cool air, hoping to absorb some measure of strength from it before she went to see Sunny today. That smell was like nothing else on earth. Part salt, part vegetation—an odd mixture of freshness and decay. Almost like life and death mixed together.

Meg finally pulled into town about half past noon. She stopped by the gallery as Sunny had suggested, and Sigfried told her that Sunny would meet her at the Beach House for lunch at one o'clock, if that was okay. Meg told him that was fine with her, and he turned back to his art magazine behind the counter. She decided to stroll through the gallery again. She had missed so much yesterday; without the distraction of Sunny, she would be able to study the pieces more carefully. Now she noticed the wonderful collection of myrtlewood carvings and several pieces of Erin's pottery, prominently displayed on a center table. Meg wondered if Sunny charged Erin a commission.

"So, are you going to be in town for long?" Meg turned to see Sigfried standing just a few feet away, his arms folded tightly across his chest. He looked as if he were mentally measuring her up, as if he didn't quite approve of Sunny's "prodigal daughter."

"I don't really know." She set down the pottery vase and returned his gaze. What did he want from her?

"Well, you certainly took Sunny by surprise."

Meg nodded absently. He puckered his mouth and rubbed his chin, still examining her in that calculating way.

"You know," he began slowly, "Sunny doesn't need a lot of stress right now." His eyes met hers evenly, almost like a challenge.

"Who does?" she answered coolly, resenting his interference. Just who was this guy to Sunny anyway? And what did he think she planned to do to her own mother?

The corners of his mouth turned up ever so slightly. Not quite a smile, but not really a smirk either. "Looks like there's a lot of your mom in you."

Suddenly she felt angry. She wanted to lash out at this strange man who knew nothing about her. She wanted to scream, "What do you know about me or my mother? And what right do you have to judge me?" But instead she gritted her teeth and politely told him that she had better be on her way, then stepped out the door feeling frustrated and unreasonably furious. The worst part was not knowing exactly why she was so angry.

The sun was still shining between the rolled-back clouds, and she decided to walk up the hill to the Beach House. Maybe it would cool her head. She didn't normally think of herself as an overly emotional person; in fact, Jerred had occasionally accused her of being without feelings altogether. Then again, she did recall that her therapist had told her that she had a tendency to repress negative feelings and that someday she would have to face them. Well, hopefully today was not the day. She took a deep breath, hoping to settle her nerves, then realized she was just downwind from the wharf. The pungent smell of rotting fish guts was just about enough to make her lose any appetite she might have hoped to have for lunch with Sunny.

She slowly climbed the hill, remembering how many times she had come this way as a child. She could remember hot summer days when she had huffed and puffed up this very hill on some crazy errand for Grandmother—taking a spool of pink thread to crabby Mrs. Henderson or picking up some fresh produce from old Mr. Lee's garden. It wasn't until Meg was a teen that she figured out that this was Grandmother's way of ensuring that she got some extra exercise. Thinking of Grandmother made Meg resent the fact that she was not spending more time with her. After all, that had been the primary purpose of this trip. Now, here she was tromping off to lunch with Sunny. Well, she wouldn't linger over the meal. And afterward she would go straight to see Grandmother.

She opened the door of the restaurant, and despite herself, she smiled. Nothing had changed in here at all. Same old glass-topped counter filled with shells and driftwood. Same old fish tank sunk into the wall. Perhaps the fish had changed—or did fish live long lives?

"Hello," called Sunny, waving from the dark interior of the restaurant. Meg frowned momentarily. Why in the world would Sunny choose a booth without a view? Meg slid into the vinyl seat across from her mother and forced her lips to smile.

"Is this okay?" asked Sunny, gesturing to the booth.

Meg's eyes darted to the more open area in the back where a large bank of windows looked out over the sea. "This is fine," she lied, her voice flat and dull.

"We can move," offered Sunny. "It's just where the hostess seated me, and I was—"

"It's okay," said Meg in what she knew was an irritated voice. *Oh boy, here we go.*

Sunny pushed back a strand of platinum hair and leaned forward with bright eyes. "I still can't believe you're here, Meg. It's just so great after all these years."

Meg folded her hands in her lap. "Yes, it seems rather unbelievable to me, too."

Sunny smiled, and Meg felt a small flicker of hope, but she knew better than to set any expectations. She had grown wiser in her old age.

"Tell me, Meg—what have you been doing all these years? I chatted with Erin for a few minutes this morning, so I know a little, but I'd like to hear it from you."

"Well, after I put myself through college, I went to work at a large advertising agency in San Francisco. It wasn't exactly what I thought I wanted to do, but I had to take a good job in order to pay off my college loans and—"

"And what did you really want to do?" asked Sunny, apparently oblivious to the part about loans and bills and how hard Meg had had to work just to survive, let alone put herself through school.

"I don't know...." Meg's voice faltered, and she felt a frown crease her forehead. Had she ever really known? Sure, she'd had some longings, but they had never seemed realistic or practical. And now everything seemed so foggy.

"Well, if you knew that it wasn't what you really wanted to do, didn't you have any idea what it was that you *did* want to do?

What were your real dreams, your highest aspirations?"

"I don't know," snapped Meg. This wasn't a conversation she wanted to have with Sunny. It was a private thing. Something she would share only with a close friend. She had never even discussed this subject with Jerred.

"Okay, then. Tell me about your work," Sunny said as if conceding a pawn in a chess game. "Do you like it?"

"Yes, it's interesting, and it was a great opportunity for me. When I started, it was still a young company—family-owned and small enough for me to work my way up the ladder. And it was challenging, at first. I worked hard and put in long hours, and I was rewarded—"

"Then why did you leave?"

Meg frowned and looked at the table. Had she told Sunny about her leave of absence? Perhaps Erin had mentioned something about Jerred. Oh well, what did it really matter anyway? Sunny was, after all, her mother.

"I'm sorry, hon," said Sunny, waving her hand. "I shouldn't be so intrusive. But you know how I am about these things."

Meg sighed and rolled her eyes. No, she didn't really know how Sunny was. In fact, she wondered if she really knew this woman at all. "It's no big secret," continued Meg. "I took a leave of absence because the boss's son and I were engaged; then I broke it off, and it was just difficult to be in the same workplace right after that. But my job is still there, and my boss wants me back, and I still have my apartment. It's not as if I left for good."

"You broke it off?"

"Broke off what?" Meg tried to remember the context. "Oh, you mean the engagement. Yes, I broke it off. Well, I suppose it was mutual, in a way."

"Did you love him?"

Meg looked at Sunny in amazement. "Love him? We were engaged! Of course I loved him."

63

"Really." It was more statement than question, and Sunny had a knowing look in her eye as if she didn't completely believe Meg's story.

"Excuse me," said a plump, sweet-voiced waitress. "Can I take your order now?" Sunny began to order while Meg quickly scanned the menu, settling on a Caesar salad with grilled chicken. The waitress thanked them and left.

"Did you know that Caesar salad has three times as much fat as a cheeseburger?" asked Sunny in a voice loud enough for the surrounding tables to hear.

Meg felt her cheeks heating up. "Really? Well, we have to splurge now and then, don't we?"

"Sure. Eat, drink, and be merry," Sunny said, holding up her water glass in a mock toast, "for tomorrow we may die."

"Cheers," said Meg flatly. She sipped her water and studied Sunny, wondering vaguely why her mother wasn't drinking anything stronger than water.

"What was his name?" asked Sunny.

"Who?"

"The man you jilted."

"I didn't jilt him. And his name was, rather is, Jerred."

"Did he love you?"

Meg pressed her lips together and inhaled through her nose, holding the breath inside her chest for a long moment as if she might explode like a balloon. It was an old habit from childhood, a habit she thought she had broken long ago.

Sunny smiled and waved her hand in dismissal. "No, you don't have to answer that one. I'm sure he loved you, Meg. Why wouldn't he?"

Meg felt as if she were on a wild carousel ride, being jerked up and down, and around and around. How did Sunny manage to do it with so little effort? Or was she completely unaware of the effect she had on others?

"Do you still do photography?" asked Sunny as the waitress set down their food.

"No. I never really did photography. I just dabbled."

"Nonsense. You were an excellent photographer."

Meg almost dropped her fork. "Since when? And says who?"

"Says I." Sunny pointed her steak knife at Meg. "And anyone who ever looked at your photos."

"Really?" Meg stared at her mother. Was this the truth, or was Sunny just playing with her again? It could be a setup.

Sunny nodded and continued to cut her filet without looking up. "You showed a lot of promise, Meg. I really thought that you would follow through with it. And it seemed as though you liked it a lot."

"I might have liked it. But I got so busy at work, and there just never seemed to be time—"

"And that's exactly the problem with most people. They think there's never enough time. And then before you know it," she said as she laid down her knife and snapped her fingers, "it's gone!"

Meg considered this. "I suppose you're right. In fact, I was just thinking about digging out my camera. I hope that I brought it with me, or maybe I left it in storage.... I can't really remember. I did leave pretty quickly."

"Aha," said Sunny.

"Aha, what?"

"So there was a broken heart."

"No. Not a broken heart. But, if you must know, Jerred and I did not part on particularly happy terms."

"Another woman then?"

"What makes you think it wasn't me? Couldn't there have been another man?"

"Then why would you come up here?" Sunny studied Meg, her brows slightly lifted. "Why wouldn't you go off with the other man?"

"I see what you mean. Okay." She spoke as if to a small child. "Yes, you're right, Sunny. There was another woman. And, of course, Jerred said he didn't love her."

"Sure." Sunny rolled her eyes. "That's what they all say."

Meg looked at Sunny in surprise. Of course, how could she have forgotten? Sunny had survived a number of failed romances herself.

"Well, never mind that." Sunny waved her hand again. "Men. Who needs them anyway?" She winked.

Meg shook her head. "Sure, who needs—"

"And," Sunny interrupted as she rumbled through an over-sized purse, "I happen to have something for you." She pulled out an old 35 mm camera that Grandpa had gotten Meg for her six-teenth birthday. She handed it to her with a sly smile. Meg fondled the camera in disbelief. She knew every part of it.

"I thought I lost this at that photography workshop!"

"You did. Remember Professor Clampton? Well, he found it a few years later when he was cleaning out the back of his van so he could sell it. Lucky for you that Grandpa had put your name on it."

Meg popped open the back. "It looks fine. Do you think it still works?"

"Sure. I've used it a few times. I didn't think you'd mind. If you'd ever written, I would have gladly sent it to you." The last sentence had a barb in it, and Meg felt it dig in deep. She set down the camera and looked at Sunny, whose face had suddenly grown dark.

"Sunny, I already said that I was sorry. How many times do you want me to apologize? I can't turn back the clock. What do you want me to do?"

Suddenly, Sunny's face crumpled, and she began to sob into her hands. When she looked up, there were huge black streaks of mascara lining her cheeks. *Please don't do this, Sunny,* thought Meg

66

as her fists clenched tightly. She longed to slip out unnoticed, but of course, her conscience would not allow that. Instead, she glanced around to see curious eyes staring as Sunny dabbed at her eyes with a napkin and sniffed loudly. Meg's face burned. This had always been Sunny's answer when things got tough. Turn on the tears and talk about the difficulty of being a single parent. That would settle everything. And it had always worked. Both Meg and Erin had easily succumbed to their mother's tears. They would feel so guilty that they would quickly brush aside whatever conflict was at hand—under the rug and out of sight.

"Are you okay now?" asked Meg in a voice that sounded hard and cold.

Sunny looked up with a blotchy face. "I'm sorry. I didn't mean for that to happen. I didn't want to be like this. There's so much I want to tell you, but I just don't know how...."

Sure, thought Meg. But instead she asked, "Do you want to go now?" The waitress had already quietly slipped the bill on the table, discreetly keeping her eyes away from their little spectacle, as if she too wanted them to slip away and take their problems elsewhere.

"No, not yet. I'd like a cup of coffee." Sunny pulled out a compact and quickly repaired her face, then flagged down the waitress and ordered a cup of coffee. "And I'd like to see your dessert tray," said Sunny to the bewildered waitress.

Meg decided to have coffee, too. She felt beaten. She didn't know what to say or do. Being with Sunny was like having the life sucked out of her. She watched as Sunny calmly ate a piece of lemon pie. Meg had no more appetite and nothing to say. At last, it was time to go.

"Where's your car, Meg?" asked Sunny as Meg lingered uncomfortably in the parking lot.

"I walked."

"Well, let me give you a ride then—"

"No, I'd like to walk," Meg answered quickly. "After all, I need to work off all those fat grams from the salad, right?"

"I guess so," said Sunny. "Will I see you later?"

"Sure." Sunny looked as if she was about to say something, but Meg beat her. "I'm going to see Grandmother now. Thanks for lunch. Good-bye." She waved and started down the hill.

The clouds were back now and the breeze had picked up. Meg's jacket was in the car, but she didn't care. She would rather face the worst elements than spend another moment with Sunny.

Eight

GRANDMOTHER WAS SITTING UP IN BED when Meg walked into the room. The shades were up, and the afternoon sunlight filtered weakly through the sheer curtains. Grandmother wore a soft pink embroidered bed jacket, and there seemed to be a bit of color in her alabaster cheeks today.

"You're looking better, Grandmother," said Meg as she sat down. "How are you feeling?"

"Oh, I never feel very well. My back pains me something awful. It's horrible to grow old, Meggie, just horrible."

Meg nodded. She had hoped to have another good conversation with Grandmother, but this wasn't starting out well. "I had lunch with Sunny today. We ate at the Beach House."

"The Beach House. I used to love going for lunch there. Back in the days when I could get out. Life's no use when you're stuck in bed all day."

"Can't you ever get up?"

"It would kill me to get up. My heart's giving out on me, Meggie. I should be dead by summer."

Meg nodded solemnly. "I'm staying at Erin's place. Have you been out there before?"

"Oh, sure. I used to go out there every once in a while when I wasn't so ill. Never could take too much of those girls, though. They're nice, I suppose, but they make too much noise for me. I never did have much tolerance for children. But the two older girls, Hannah and Jennifer, they are pretty little things. They look just like Erin when she was a girl. Pretty, pretty." She smacked her lips as if she were talking about candy.

"And Ashley is very sweet," said Meg defensively. "She's pretty in her own way."

"Well, I don't know that I'd go calling that one pretty," Grandmother grumbled. She leaned over and peered at Meg with open curiosity. "But then again, you can never tell what she might grow up to be. Never can tell."

Meg smiled. "Lucky for Ashley, right?"

Grandmother grinned. "So, how long are you here, Meggie?"

"You mean here at Briar Hedge?"

"No, I mean here in town, to visit. When do you have to leave?"

"I don't know."

Grandmother's brow furrowed. "Don't you have to get back to your job?"

"I have a month's leave, but you never know—I might quit my job." Meg wasn't sure why she said that, but it was too late to take it back.

Grandmother's jaw dropped. "Quit your job? Whatever for? Do you have something better lined up?"

Meg shook her head.

"Well, for heaven's sake, Meggie. What would you do then? You know, you can't just live on thin air."

Meg wondered why it seemed to matter so much. Why should Grandmother care? But she answered anyway. "Don't worry, I'm sure I'll go back. But I thought this might be a good time to figure things out."

Grandmother nodded wisely. "Oh, I see. It's that young man, isn't it? Are you waiting for him to come up here and take you back with him?"

"Take me back?" Meg winced at the shrillness in her voice. "No. Nothing like that."

"Well, I just can't figure you, girl. Guess I never could." Grandmother leaned her head back and closed her eyes.

"I hope I haven't worn you out. Maybe I should let you rest." Meg reached out and touched Grandmother's frail hand, suddenly fearful for the old woman's health. She had almost forgotten her fragile state, especially when Grandmother had been so animated moments before.

"I'm fine. Just a little tired, Meggie. Think I'll take a little nap. Don't go just yet. Go have yourself a cup of tea or something. I think Jason dropped by some cookies that his mother made. Phoebe's not the best-looking gal, but she sure can cook, and it's nice of her to think of me. Have you met your cousin Abner and his family yet?"

"I met Jason. He seems like a good kid."

Grandmother nodded, eyes still closed.

"You rest, Grandmother. I'll be back in an hour or two." Meg tucked in the comforter a little more snugly. The house felt drafty and damp, and Meg had noticed space heaters here and there. She wondered if the old oil furnace still worked.

Grandmother was already asleep by the time she tiptoed out of the room and found Rosa in the kitchen. "It feels a little cool in Grandmother's room, Rosa. Is the furnace working okay?"

Rosa rolled her eyes. "Nothing in this old house works okay. It's falling down around our ears, and Mrs. Lancaster doesn't want anything fixed. They say it's not because she is poor but because she is tighter than a dime-store girdle."

Meg laughed. "Is that so?"

Rosa's hand flew to her mouth. "I'm sorry, Meggie. I forget she

71

is your grandmother. Please forgive me."

"It's okay, Rosa. I used to say the same thing myself. We'll have to see what we can do to fix this place up a bit. It's one thing to die of old age, but hypothermia is something else."

"Would you like some tea, Meggie?"

"I'd love some. Do you mind if I take it outside with me? I want to snoop around and see what else needs fixing."

"No problem." Rosa grinned and poured her a steaming mug. Meg could tell by the smell that it was Earl Grey. Grandmother had always loved Earl Grey tea; she said it reminded her of lavender.

Outside, Meg sat down on the porch steps and pulled a small notepad from her purse. She began jotting down the things she had noticed were in need of attention, starting with the sad-looking porch. By the time she'd worked her way around to the back of the house, she was forced to flip over to a fresh sheet of paper.

"Who are you?" said a gruff voice. Meg looked up to see a dark-haired middle-aged man. He looked vaguely familiar, but she wasn't sure why. She studied him for a moment, trying to place his face.

"Bennie!" she finally exclaimed. He looked bewildered. "No, of course you're not Bennie. But you look like his photo. You must be Bennie's son. Abner, isn't it?"

"Well, I know who I am. But the question is, who are you?"

His rudeness was somewhat jarring, but she decided to stay congenial. "I'm sorry. I'm your cousin, Meg Lancaster. I'm here visiting Grandmother."

He looked at her with undisguised curiosity, his dark eyes cold. What was it Erin had said? Slippery. Yes, that seemed to describe him.

"So, what are you doing back here?" He gave her a sideways glance and jerked his thumb toward the back of the house.

"Grandmother is taking a nap, and I wanted to have a look around." She wanted to tell him that she used to spend every summer and holiday here, that she had always roamed wherever she pleased, and that she knew every inch of Briar Hedge—from the two-and-a-half-story house to the barn to the twenty bogs—like the back of her hand. But instead she evenly returned his stare.

"What are you writing?" He leaned over as if to read from her notepad.

She flipped the pad over in her hand and looked back at his fleshy face. He might have been good-looking when he was younger, but he had the kind of looks that went soft and nondescript with age. "I was making a list." She spoke slowly, as if he were not very smart. "It looks like things have gotten a little rundown and neglected around here, and I thought I'd help Grandmother see that some things get fixed—"

"No need for that," he interrupted. "Grandmother should be going into a nursing home before long, anyway. I've got my wife checking out some possibilities for her."

"Does Grandmother know about this?"

"It's not really your business, Meggie—Meg—whatever your name is. And I suggest you keep out of things that don't concern you."

"How would you know what does or does not concern me?"

"Well, you never came back all these years. Then you come waltzin' in here just when it looks like Grandmother may be buying the farm. Pretty convenient timing, if you ask me." His eyes narrowed, and he curled up his lip, snorting loudly.

Meg stared in disbelief. She couldn't think of a single polite response to his nasty accusations. What burned even more was that it was partly true. She certainly couldn't deny that she had stayed away all these years, but his insinuation that she'd come back for anything beyond reconciliation was loathsome. And he was equally loathsome. She turned and walked away without saying a word. She was glad she wasn't a man, because every bit of her wanted to punch his big red nose.

It had only been a short while since she'd left Grandmother, so she decided to go down to the beach to blow off some steam. Maybe she could walk it off. The wind had picked up, and the stinging breeze felt cool on her hot cheeks. How was it that a perfect stranger could infuriate her like that? And to think he was her own cousin! No wonder Erin had complained, and Erin was not one to easily find fault with people. Meg thought about what he'd said about the nursing home, and wondered what Sunny would think about that. Maybe Sunny wouldn't care. Maybe she had allowed Abner to call the shots when it came to Grandmother. Sunny and Grandmother never had gotten along very well, anyway.

Well, with or without Sunny, Meg was willing to stand up to that goon of a cousin. And she knew Erin would help, too. Maybe Tom could come over and make some of the repairs and check out the furnace situation. She wondered why he hadn't thought of it already. By the time she'd walked a good mile down the beach, she had a plan all worked out in her head. She was ready to turn back and, if necessary, face Cousin Abner all over again.

Fortunately, Abner was nowhere in sight, and Meg spent the rest of the afternoon visiting with Grandmother. She didn't mention Abner's rude accusations or complete lack of manners. She didn't want to offend Grandmother. After all, Abner was her grandson.

"How has the bog been doing, Grandmother?" Meg asked. After suffering through a long speech about the effects of aging and Grandmother's temperamental bowels, Meg was looking for anything to change the subject.

"Not well. Abner says that putting money into the bog is like pouring water down a rat hole. I guess it's just no use. People aren't buying cranberry products these days."

"Says who?"

"Oh, Abner, of course. He knows all about these things. He reads about it a lot. He says there's no reason to keep the bog. The price of cranberries is so low, it's pointless."

"That's too bad. I always liked the bog. I was planning to go out and have a look tomorrow, if you and Abner don't mind."

"There's not much to see, Meggie. Last time I saw it, it was getting overgrown with weeds. I expect it's probably even worse now." Grandmother shook her head.

"Well, I don't understand how the price of berries could be so low that it wouldn't be profitable to keep the bog up and harvest what little you could. I wouldn't think there'd be much expense to it. After all, you still have the equipment, don't you?"

"I suppose, but I've let Abner take care of things ever since he moved up here after your grandfather died."

Meg looked at her hands, wondering what right she had to make such a fuss about the bog. It really was none of her business.

"I know how much you loved the bog, Meggie. You got that from Grandpa, that's for sure."

"I just think it would break his heart to see the bog going to weed and returning to the land. He worked so hard on it. And those cranberries were like his babies."

Grandmother chuckled slightly. "You got that right. Stewart was plumb crazy about cranberries. I never saw anything like it. You know, Meggie, I never thought I'd say it, but I sure do miss some of his cranberry concoctions."

Meg smacked her lips. "Like his cranberry bread."

"Or his cranberry jam."

"How about his cranberry candy?"

"Stop, Meggie. You're making me hungry."

"It's probably getting close to your dinnertime, anyway. I suppose I should go. Erin is expecting me back."

"Will you come back tomorrow, Meggie?" Grandmother's eyes lit up like those of a small child anticipating Christmas morning.

It seemed like only yesterday that Grandmother had been scolding her and Meg had been the one looking up with pleading eyes.

"Yes, I'll come again tomorrow. I'll probably be around so much that you'll get sick of me before long."

"I don't think so, dear. My days are dull and dreary, and you are like a breath of fresh air and sunshine." Grandmother smiled.

"Thanks, Grandmother."

"And Meggie?"

"Yes?"

"If you want to look into the bog, you have my permission. I still own it, you know. If you think it can be saved or made profitable again, you're welcome to look into it. I know it would make your grandfather happy."

"Really? Are you serious?"

"Of course. You know me, Meggie, businesswoman to the bone. If there's profit to be made off of those old bogs, then let's go after it. I don't like to see anything go to waste."

"Thanks, Grandmother. I'd like to check it out for you."

"Another thing, dear."

"Yes?"

"Before your grandfather died, he set aside a few things he wanted you to have. Not really much, but maybe we can go through them sometime before you go back to San Francisco."

"I'd like that, Grandmother." Meg beamed. To think that Grandpa had actually thought of her before his death. It was a great comfort to know that. She leaned over and kissed Grandmother's cheek, something she'd never done before. She wondered if Grandmother would mind, but the old woman just smiled and closed her eyes.

"I'll be back tomorrow then, Grandmother."

"That'll be fine."

Nine

MEG TOLD ERIN ALL ABOUT HER CONFRONTATION with Cousin Abner as she peeled potatoes for dinner. "I cannot believe that man is actually related to us! He reminds me of a character in an old hillbilly movie; you know, the kind of guy who would meet you on his front porch with a loaded shotgun and spit a stream of tobacco on your shoe."

"I know what you mean, Meg. He's made it so uncomfortable that we hardly ever go out to see Grandmother anymore. We used to invite her over here, but then she became bedridden. I feel guilty for not going over more often, but the girls are terrified of Abner, and he's always popping in over there. I think it's like that for everyone. It's really sad. But all this time, Grandmother has never stood up to him once. She just lets him rule Briar Hedge as if he's lord of the manor. As if she's already dead and buried."

"But why?"

"Well, I think it has to do with his father."

"Really? How's that?"

"I don't know." Erin tore lettuce for a salad as she spoke. "But for some reason, I think Grandmother is carrying around a load of guilt about Bennie. Or maybe it's just displaced loyalty. I've

77

never been able to get to the bottom of it, but I know one thing: Bennie was no saint."

"How do you know?"

"Sunny told me a little bit about it once after she'd had a couple of drinks. She said that it hadn't been easy having Bennie as an older brother. It was almost as if being Bennie Lancaster's little sister carried some sort of awful shame with it. I felt kind of sorry for her."

"But what does that mean? How could Bennie make it hard for Sunny? Wasn't he about ten years older than her? Do you suppose he abused her or something?"

"No, I don't think so—not physically, anyway. Maybe verbally, though. It sounded like he was a real bully. That's probably why Abner is like that; it's some genetic thing." Erin sliced a tomato into wedges and tossed them onto the growing salad. "Apparently Bennie had a bad reputation that made it difficult for Sunny when she was a teenager. She didn't really go into much detail. She actually seemed a little uncomfortable talking about it. There are a few secrets in this family, Meg. It would sure be nice to get to the bottom of some of them before Grandmother is gone. There's no telling if we'll get much information from Sunny."

"Speaking of Sunny, I had quite an interesting lunch with her." Meg told Erin about the fiasco at the Beach House.

Erin laughed. "Oh, that's nothing. I could tell you a hundred stories that are that bad and worse." She paused. "Although, I have noticed lately that Sunny seems to be trying harder."

"Hmm. Now that you mention it, I was surprised that she didn't have anything to drink."

Erin turned down the burner under the bubbling pot of potatoes, then looked at Meg seriously. "All I can say is that our mother is a difficult person. There's a whole lot under the surface that we may or may not ever get to know. Whenever I pray for her, I get convicted just to love her."

"So, do you?"

"I wish I could say yes. I do try, but sometimes it's difficult. In fact, lately I've been asking God to love her through me. That seems to work better. Maybe now that you're here it'll get easier."

"I don't see how."

"Well, Sunny always seemed to relate to you better than to me."

"You've got to be kidding. I would have said just the opposite. I always felt like you two were always in sync and I was the odd one out."

Erin laughed. "That just goes to show you how tuned in we both were!"

The door to the garage suddenly opened. "Hi, ladies," called Tom. Behind him trooped in the three girls, dripping wet.

"Leave your muddy things in the laundry room," Erin told her daughters. "How was soccer practice, coach?"

"Wet and cold," said Tom as he pecked Erin on the cheek. Jennifer and Hannah streaked by in their stocking feet, arguing about who got the first shower.

"I think Ashley better not come with me next time," said Tom. "There's really not much for her to do, and I think she got pretty bored, not to mention cold."

"And soaked," said Erin, patting Ashley's wet curls. "Ash, you better go get those wet clothes off. And you can take a bath in Mommy's big tub, okay? That'll warm you right up. Can you help her, Tom?"

Ashley nodded and slowly plodded up the stairs, Tom following. On the third step, he swooped her up and carried her the rest of the way.

"That must be nice." Meg sighed.

"What's that?" Erin asked absently as she mixed salad dressing.

"Having a daddy like that. Do you ever wonder what it would have been like, Erin?"

Erin nodded slowly. "Yeah, I think about how lucky these girls are. Well, not lucky. More like blessed."

"Why weren't we blessed like that, Erin?"

"I don't know, Meg. But I think that God must keep a special watch over children without fathers."

"I hope so. I could sure use some watching out for."

Erin wrapped a comforting arm around her sister's shoulders. "And sometimes God uses people to watch out for the fatherless."

Erin was just setting the roast on the table when Tom and the girls came down. It was a pleasant dinner, with the older girls talking about soccer practice and the team they would play against on Saturday. Only Ashley remained quiet, her cheeks flushed.

"You look pretty worn out, Ashley," said Meg.

The little girl nodded slightly.

"Maybe you should go to bed early tonight, honey," Erin suggested.

"Can Aunt Meggie tuck me in?" asked Ashley.

"I'd love to," said Meg. Erin smiled, and Meg took Ashley by the hand and led her upstairs. Ashley's feet moved slowly, as if mounting each step were like climbing a mountain. Finally, they reached Ashley's room, and Meg tucked the little girl into her bed with the doll named Molly by her side.

"Would you like me to read a story or anything?" asked Meg.

"You can pray," said Ashley in a tired voice.

Pray? Meg used to pray back when she was a kid. But she hadn't prayed much in the last twenty years.

"Okay," she finally said in an uncertain voice. Ashley closed her eyes as if to signal she was ready for Meg to begin.

"Dear God," stated Meg. "Thank you for this good day. Thank you for letting me come to stay with Erin and her family. And thank you for letting me get to know my sweet little niece Ashley. Now, please give Ashley good dreams." Meg couldn't think of anything else to say. She peeked one eye open, and to her surprise, Ashley appeared to have already fallen asleep.

"Amen," whispered Meg as she brushed a stray curl from Ashley's forehead. Ashley's head felt warm, and her cheeks looked overly pink. Could she have a fever? But Meg had never been a mother; what did she know about these things? She clicked off the light and left the room.

"Thanks so much, Meg," said Erin when Meg came downstairs. "Do you want some tea or decaf coffee? Tom made a fire, and Jennifer has KP tonight. Let's go put our feet up and relax."

As they settled into the cozy living room, Meg had to fend off another unwanted wave of jealousy. Erin's life was so perfect. It just didn't seem fair. And yet, at the same time, Meg was very happy for her sister.

"I saw your pottery at Sunny's gallery. They look nice, Erin. Do you sell many there?"

"Not enough to quit my day job." Erin laughed. "It's mostly to make Sunny happy."

"Does Sunny paint anymore?"

"Not that I know of. It's too bad. She used to be pretty good. But she's such a tough art critic that it must be hard for her to allow her own work out in public. It's a shame; she used to enjoy painting."

"Where did she meet Sigfried? And what exactly is their relationship? He seems very protective of her."

"I'm never really sure. I used to think Siggie was pretty weird, but he's really a nice guy once you get to know him. He always speaks his mind, and if he doesn't like you, he'll be sure to let you know. But you're right; he is very protective of Sunny. He moved down here from Eugene the same time she did, about five years ago. He has his own apartment down by the waterfront. At first, I thought they'd live together, but it never happened. They do spend a lot of time together, though, outside of work."

"He looks quite a bit younger than Sunny, not that it's a big deal." Meg suddenly remembered that Jerred was almost ten years her junior.

"Sunny has never let age differences bother her." Erin chuckled. "Remember when she was going out with that college kid who was just a few years older than me?"

"Oh, yeah. Wasn't his name Ted, or Ed, or something like that?"

"Ned!" exclaimed Erin.

"That's right. Ned the nerd! Remember, we used to tease him about his pocket protectors and polyester pants. Boy, he sure didn't dress like that for long. He became a hippie right before our eyes."

"Do you ever wonder what his parents thought?" said Erin. "They send nerdy Ned off to college, and he comes back in tie-dyed T-shirts and love beads!"

"And with a girlfriend almost old enough to be his mother."

"Sad," said Erin.

"Very sad. It could almost make you never want to become a mother." Meg slowly shook her head.

Erin looked at Meg curiously. "Do you ever think about it?"

"What, you mean having kids? Don't you think I should get married first? Or did you forget the speech that you and Tom gave me just last night?" Meg grinned.

"Don't be smart. I'm serious—do you ever think about being a mom? Do you have any desire to have children? I mean, I hear about career women who have no intention of having children—ever."

"I thought about having kids when Jerred and I were engaged. It seemed like the natural thing to do then. But I'm not getting any younger. Sometimes I think about having kids at my age, and it's downright scary."

Erin smiled. "Oh, women are having babies clear into their forties these days. Don't worry. If God wants you to have kids, he'll work out all the details."

"Including the husband? Or did you think it might be immaculate conception?"

Erin rolled her eyes. "Very funny. But just for the record, I think you would make a great mom."

"And what do you base that wild assumption on?"

"I've seen you with Ashley. You have a way about you that children like. And I know Ashley likes you. She doesn't even let her sisters or the baby-sitter tuck her in at night. It's either Tom or me. You may have made Ashley-history tonight."

Meg smiled. "That's nice. I really like Ashley. If I ever do have children, I hope I have one just like her."

"Be careful what you wish for. Ashley can be a little devil when she wants to. She has quite the stubborn streak. In fact, she reminds me of another little girl I used to know."

"Well, good for her! A woman needs a bit of stubbornness in her." Meg leaned back and yawned. "Speaking of Ashley, she felt a little warm when I tucked her in. Do you think she could be coming down with anything?"

"Probably just all the excitement of the birthday party, and then getting wet at soccer practice—"

"Mommy," Hannah called from the den. "I need help with my math homework."

"I think I'll turn in early tonight," said Meg. "I picked up a new book that I can't wait to read."

"Sounds like a plan. Good night, Meg."

Meg slipped up to her room, grateful for a bit of solitude. As much as she liked Erin's family, she didn't know how long she would be comfortable here. There was definitely a lot more noise than she was used to. Meg had always had a low tolerance for noise. Maybe Erin was wrong about her. Maybe Meg would make a lousy mom. What if she always wanted to tell her children to be quiet? She knew that children couldn't help but make a lot of noise.

Meg pushed her thoughts aside when she climbed into bed and cracked open her book. Before she knew it, she was swept away into the cozy English mystery.

When she finally looked at her watch, it was past midnight. She realized with surprise that she was hungry. Must be this country air. She closed her book and tiptoed down the hallway. Just as she reached the stairs, she thought she heard the sound of a child moaning. She paused and listened again. It seemed to be coming from Ashley's room.

Meg crept down the hallway and peeked in the open door. The light from the hallway illuminated the room enough to see that Ashley was still tucked in just as she'd left her, and everything looked fine. But something drew Meg closer to the bed. She just wanted to make sure. She placed her hand on Ashley's forehead again. This time she was shocked by the heat that radiated from it. This couldn't be normal. Ashley moaned without moving, and her eyes remained closed.

Meg felt foolish as she knocked on Erin and Tom's bedroom door. Surely she was blowing this all out of proportion. Erin opened the door.

"I'm so sorry, Erin," whispered Meg. "It's probably nothing, but I heard Ashley moaning, and I went to check. And, well, she feels even hotter now than before. I hate to disturb you—"

Already, Erin was moving down the hall to Ashley's room. She flicked on a small lamp and pressed her hand to Ashley's cheeks, then against her forehead.

"She's burning up with fever," said Erin with a frown. In the brighter light, Meg could see that Ashley's skin was pale except for two bright red blotches on her cheeks.

"What's wrong?" asked Tom sleepily from the hallway.

"It's Ash, Tom. She seems to be sick. Do you think we should call Dr. McGregor?"

Tom came into the room and gently touched Ashley's arm.

"Wake up, Ashley, honey. Tell Daddy what's wrong." He gently shook her, but the little girl didn't open her eyes.

Erin gasped. "Something's wrong, Tom. I'm calling the doctor right now." She dashed from the room, and Tom turned to Meg.

"Can you get a wet washcloth? We'll see if we can start cooling her down," he said, peeling the quilt off. He fanned Ashley with his hands and spoke gently to her. Meg ran to the bathroom and quickly returned with a cold, wet cloth. As Tom placed it on Ashley's head, Erin came in with the cordless phone in hand.

"Yes, Doctor," she said in a trembling voice. "Tom is trying to cool her down right now. No, she isn't waking up. What does that mean?" Erin listened for a moment, then cupped her hand over the mouthpiece and spoke with urgency. "Tom? Meg? The doctor wants to know if she's had any other symptoms like headaches or soreness in her neck."

Tom's eyes grew wide. "She said it hurt to bend her neck when she was taking her bath. I wanted to rinse her hair for her."

Erin quickly relayed this information to the doctor, then listened silently. "Thank you, Doctor. We'll rush her right in." Erin hung up. "We've got to get Ashley to the emergency room. The doctor won't say what he thinks it is, but he wants her to come in right away. He said they'll probably want to run some tests."

"Oh, no!" Meg whispered. Erin's expression was tight with worry.

Erin grabbed the quilt and pillow from the bed. Tom already had Ashley in his arms and was heading out the door.

"Can you stay and watch after the girls?" called Tom.

"Of course. Don't worry about a thing."

"Say a prayer, Meg," pleaded Erin with fearful eyes.

Meg blinked back tears as she watched the red taillights pull out of the driveway, then disappear into the night. How quickly a perfect world could change. She wished she could have gone with them. She would have liked to hold Ashley's hand, to run cool fingers over the little girl's hot forehead. She had prayed once tonight. Now she would pray again.

Ten

AT FOUR O'CLOCK, MEG FINALLY GAVE UP ON SLEEP. Although it was still dark, she got up and quietly dressed, then tiptoed downstairs and sat in the dark kitchen, lit only by the small light above the range. She didn't want to do anything to wake the girls. She wasn't looking forward to telling them about Ashley. Several times she picked up the phone, but each time she replaced it, fighting the urge to phone the hospital. Why hadn't they called? Maybe they were waiting until they found out something definite. Perhaps in this case, no news was good news. She moved into the living room and paced back and forth across the carpet, looking out the window and watching and waiting for the dark gray sky to gradually grow light. After what seemed to be a lifetime, the sky became a paler shade of gray, and her heart whispered another prayer for Ashley.

She could see the hands on the mantel clock now. It was almost time to get the girls up for school. She had decided that it would probably be best to send them off on their regular routine. She wasn't sure why, but she didn't think it would help anything for them to stay home and worry.

"Mommy?" called Jennifer's voice from the top of the stairs.

Meg walked over and looked up. "Your mom and dad aren't here right now, Jenny."

"Where are they?"

Meg walked slowly up the steps. She still hadn't planned what to say to the girls. "Is Hannah up yet?" she asked when she reached the landing.

"Hannah!" yelled Jennifer. "Time to get up." She turned and looked at Meg with suspicion in her eyes. "What's going on? Is something wrong?"

Hannah stuck her head out into the hallway. "Did you say something was wrong?" she asked, sleepily rubbing her eyes.

Meg took Jennifer's hand and went into Hannah's bedroom. "Can we sit down?" she asked as she sat on Hannah's bed.

Hannah nodded absently. "Where's Mommy and Daddy?"

"Ashley got sick last night, and your mom and dad took her to the hospital."

"What's wrong with her?" asked Hannah.

"They don't know for sure, but I think they're running some tests on her."

"Is she going to be okay?" asked Jennifer.

"I'm sure she'll be fine." Meg wished she was as sure as she was trying to sound.

"When are they coming home?" asked Hannah.

"I don't know. But I think you two better get ready for school. You don't want to miss your bus." She tried to inflect her voice with a light tone.

"But how will we know if Ashley is okay?" asked Jennifer.

"I promise I'll let you know as soon as I find out anything."

"Maybe we can make Ashley a get-well card," said Hannah hopefully.

"Do you think she'll be back when we get home from school?" asked Jennifer.

"I'm not sure about that. But it's getting late. You two go get ready, and I'll fix breakfast."

Both girls helped Meg pack some hasty lunches with lopsided peanut-butter-and-jelly sandwiches. She was shoving the lumpy bags into their backpacks just as loud brakes hissed out in front of the house.

"Hurry up, girls," she called as she held the door open. "Remember to be praying for Ashley."

They hollered back that they would remember, then were swallowed up by the big yellow bus.

The house was silent now, but quiet and solitude were no longer welcome. Maybe her tolerance for noise had increased. She quickly cleaned the kitchen, then moved through the already tidy house, straightening the pillows, folding an afghan—anything to stay busy, anything to distract her from the fact that Erin still hadn't called from the hospital. Suddenly her "no news" theory felt all wrong. Shouldn't they know something by now? Finally, she could stand it no longer. She pulled on her coat and decided to join them at the Crandale hospital.

An elderly woman with a kind face, volunteering at the information desk, told Meg that Ashley was in the ICU. She patted her hand and smiled in a way that was neither comforting nor confirming. Meg numbly followed the woman's directions, trying not to consider the serious implications that the simple letters ICU seemed to spell.

She quickly found Erin and Tom huddled together in a corner of the intensive-care waiting room. They were harshly illuminated by a stark fluorescent light that had no regard for the human suffering going on beneath it. Tom's arms were wrapped around Erin's shoulders, and he appeared to be praying. Not eager to disturb them, Meg hovered by the nurses' station and waited, trying to avert her eyes from what should have been a private moment. But she couldn't help seeing the tears streaming down her sister's cheeks.

Meg bit her lip. What did this mean? Suddenly, she felt tears filling her own eyes, and she turned and ran down the hall until she came to the bathroom. Inside, her hands clutched the edge of the counter, and she stared into the sink. What was happening to her? How, in such a short time, had she come to care so deeply for these people? It was hard to believe that, except for Erin, she hadn't known any of them until a few days ago. Now it felt like their pain was her own. She shook her head back and forth, trying to shake away the pain. But it didn't work. She stared at her image in the mirror. Her face was pale, and her dark green eyes looked like they were sunk into two shadowy holes—the result of a sleepless night. The result of caring too much. For nearly twenty years she had managed to avoid this kind of pain.

Suddenly she wondered why she had come back. What good could come from loving people? It only meant you could be hurt when the people you loved were torn away from you. San Francisco was sounding better than ever to her. Her old job was still waiting. Even putting up with Jerred would be easy compared to this. She knew she didn't love him anymore, but perhaps that was a good thing, because he would no longer have the power to hurt her. Her old life seemed like a safe place. She could be free there. Maybe it was time to go back.

"Meg?" It was Erin's voice, but different. The warmth and color were gone. Meg turned to see her sister's red-rimmed eyes and grief-stricken face. She wrapped her arms around Erin's shoulders and whispered the words she was afraid to ask.

"Is Ashley—is she—okay?"

Erin sobbed. "It's meningitis. Dr. McGregor says it doesn't...doesn't look good. We might...we might actually lose her."

Meg held her sister for a long time, and they both cried. Meg didn't know what to say. She longed to comfort Erin, yet at the same time she too longed to be comforted. But no words came, and finally, they both pulled away. Meg picked up the box of tissues, probably placed there for times just like this. She handed several to Erin and then took one for herself.

"I don't know what to say, Erin," she said quietly. "I'm so sorry. I wish there was something I could do…."

"If only I'd paid more attention yesterday when Tom brought the girls home. And she'd even told me on the way to the party that her head hurt. I should have noticed that she wasn't well. And then she didn't even touch her dinner. Why didn't I figure it out? I'm a horrible mother—"

"No, you're not!" Meg said the words firmly as if scolding a child. "You cannot blame yourself for this, Erin."

"But I should have known. I should have been more aware. You even mentioned early last night that she had felt warm. But I just brushed it away. I'm such a fool—"

"Stop it, Erin." Meg grabbed her by the arms. "You can't blame yourself for this."

"But if I had—"

"Okay, Erin, if you're going to blame yourself, then you might as well blame me too. If I hadn't been here, distracting you, you might have noticed that Ashley was sick. Or if I hadn't put her to bed, you—" Meg broke into fresh tears now. Maybe it was her fault. Maybe Ashley would be okay if—

"Meg, it's not your fault!" Erin practically exploded. "We both better stop this nonsense, right now."

Meg blew her nose. "I suppose you're right. I'm sorry, Erin."

"I'm sorry, too. I started it." Erin took a deep breath. "Tom has the right idea. The doctors are treating her as best they can, so Tom says the only thing we can do now is pray. He's put Ashley on the church prayer chain. I'm going to go out there and pray with him some more. Do you want to come?"

Meg nodded and followed. Tom greeted her with a somber hug, and Meg explained to them that she had sent Jennifer and

Hannah off to school like normal, thinking it best to keep to routine. Tom and Erin thanked her for watching them, and for the next several hours, the three of them sat together with heads bowed. Meg didn't think their forlorn words would make any difference, but if it helped Tom and Erin to cope, then it was probably worth it.

Just before noon, Dr. McGregor came out and told them that it would be okay for Tom and Erin to take turns sitting with Ashley now. Everything possible was being done, but she was still unconscious. He said they would probably move her down to pediatrics—if she stabilized. But his face didn't look hopeful, and his eyes quickly glanced away as if he were afraid that they might guess the truth. Erin took the first shift, and Meg waited with Tom.

"I do believe that God can heal her, Meg," said Tom in a matter-of-fact tone.

Meg swallowed and nodded. She was not so sure.

"I know people who have been healed, Meg. There's a man in our church who had an inoperable brain tumor. He was given less than a year to live. The church prayed for him, and he's alive and well today. That was about seven years ago."

Meg looked up. "What did the doctors say?"

"They said it was a miracle."

In her heart, Meg wanted to believe that miracles were possible, but her mind rejected it as religious nonsense.

"I've never been that fond of children," she began, not knowing what she meant to say, or even why. "But something about Ashley just got to me from the very start." She tapped her chest. "Right here."

Tom nodded and wiped his nose. "I know what you mean."

"She showed me her bunnies—" Meg swallowed hard again. "And she let me hold them. It was so sweet. I just wish that I believed in miracles. Because if anyone deserves one, it's Ashley."

All afternoon, Tom and Erin took turns sitting with Ashley. Meg wished that she could see her little niece, but was afraid to ask. She knew that only the closest relatives were allowed in the ICU and that time with Ashley was precious, maybe even limited. She also knew it was getting close to the time when the girls would be getting home from school.

"Should I go and stay with Hannah and Jennifer?" asked Meg. "I told them this morning that I would let them know if I found out anything about Ashley, but I didn't tell them any details. I didn't really know what to say."

"No, maybe you could stay here with Erin," Tom suggested. "I'll go and talk to the girls. They need to know what's going on." Just then Erin came down the hall. They both looked expectantly at her face, the way they did whenever the shift changes occurred, but Meg could see by her expression that once again there had been no change.

"Maybe I'll pick up the girls and take them out for a burger or something," Tom said to Erin. "The cafeteria food is pretty bad. Then I'll bring them over here. Maybe the doctor will have moved Ashley out of ICU by then." His voice sounded hopeful. "And maybe they can see her."

"I hope so," said Erin, her quivering voice barely more than a whisper.

Meg placed her hand on Erin's shoulder. "Everyone is praying for a miracle."

Erin looked up. "Are you?"

Meg's cheeks grew warm. "I'd like to. I just don't know if I can. But I'm willing to try."

Tom turned to Meg. "Maybe you'd like to go sit with Ashley for a bit while Erin gets a bite to eat—"

"I'm not hungry," protested Erin.

"You need to eat," said Tom. "You haven't had a thing all day. It won't do Ashley any good if you collapse."

"I suppose you're right." She turned to Meg. "Do you mind sitting with Ashley for a few minutes?"

"Not at all. In fact, I was hoping for the chance."

"Thanks, Meg," said Erin. "I'm so glad that you're here."

Tom patted Meg on the back. "Yep, God had good timing in bringing you here. Thanks, Meg."

Meg headed toward the ICU doors, not knowing what to expect. But when she saw the tiny little body all hooked up to tubes, she sucked in her breath and felt her heart twist. The nurse glanced at her curiously, and Meg quickly sat down on the metal chair next to the bed. She didn't want to draw attention to herself, afraid that the nurse might make her leave.

She sat for several minutes just staring at all the machines and devices that appeared to be keeping this child alive. She knew that Ashley was on antibiotics to fight off the disease that was raging through her, but the doctor had said he still couldn't confirm that the drugs were helping. Tom had already explained to Meg that Ashley's white-cell count was so low that the doctor had been dismal about the medicines' effectiveness. Ashley truly did need a miracle. And although Meg was not a believer in miracles, she did believe in God. As she sat there, watching Ashley's chest rise and fall, she prayed that God would teach her to believe in miracles.

She had no idea how much time had passed when the ICU nurse tapped her on the shoulder and pointed to Erin, who was waiting in the doorway. She felt as if she'd been in some sort of time warp, because it seemed she had only just sat down. She glanced at Ashley as she left. She half expected to see the pale eyelashes flutter open, but nothing changed. She walked toward the door, amazed that she had honestly expected something to happen. Maybe that was faith.

"I prayed for a miracle," she whispered to Erin as they passed each other going through the door.

The corners of Erin's mouth curled up ever so slightly. "Thanks, Meg."

Meg went and sat down in the empty waiting room. For the first time, a strange sense of peace came over her. Her mind told her it was impossible, but her heart sighed. She closed her eyes and continued to pray.

After a while, she heard quiet footsteps and looked up to see Hannah and Jennifer come into the waiting room with Tom. Their red eyes and trembling chins revealed that they were aware of the serious nature of their sister's illness. They sat silently next to their dad, as if under a spell and afraid to speak, perhaps fearing that their words might make this bad situation even worse. She supposed it was the right thing for Tom to honestly tell the girls how sick Ashley was, but just the same, she pitied them and wished that childhood could be spared such pain and sorrow.

Her own childhood had certainly not been without suffering. As an adult she had learned to skillfully block out much of the unpleasantness. It was only when she spent time with Sunny that those bitter memories seemed to flood back, bringing with them all the old resentment for the way things had been.

Thoughts of Sunny made Meg wonder if she was even aware that her tiny granddaughter was hanging on the brink between life and death. She wondered if Sunny would care, then chided herself for being so coldhearted and skeptical toward her own mother. Of course she would care. Why wouldn't she?

"Is there anyone you'd like me to call?" Meg asked Tom. "I mean, it's none of my business, but I wondered if Sunny should know."

Tom smacked the heel of his hand against his forehead. "Of course. I called our pastor and asked him to put Ashley on the prayer chain, but I totally forgot about Erin's mother. You probably know that my parents have both passed on, but I can't believe that I forgot all about Erin's side of the family. And Grandmother

Lancaster should be informed, too. I know her health isn't the best, and you would probably want to tell her gently. But I'd feel horrible if they heard it from someone else in town, which is entirely possible. You know how Crandale is."

Meg stood. "Why don't I go and call Sunny? Perhaps she could let Grandmother know."

"Thanks, Meg. I'd appreciate that."

It wasn't yet five o'clock, and Meg hoped to catch Sunny at the shop, but it was Sigfried who answered.

"She's gone," he said in a cool, businesslike tone after she had identified herself.

"Well, this is urgent. Do you know if she went home, or if she'll be coming back?"

"Can't say that I do." His tone didn't change.

"Well, there's an emergency, and I don't have her apartment phone number. Do you suppose..." She paused, waiting for him to show some concern.

"You mean you don't even know your own mother's home phone number?" He made a scolding sound that was just like the sound Grandmother used to make when Meg was a little girl.

"Look, just give her this message." Meg was mad now, and she didn't care what he thought. "Tell her that her granddaughter is in the ICU at St. John's. She may not even make it through the night. You got that?"

His voice took on a concerned and helpful tone. "Do you want her number, or do you want me to call her for you?"

"Why don't you call her?" Without waiting for a response, she sighed and hung up. She leaned against the wall, suddenly feeling incredibly weary.

Eleven

SUNNY AND SIGFRIED BURST INTO THE ICU that evening laden
with bright Mylar balloons, a bouquet of flowers, and a giant
teddy bear. Meg thought it looked like they were staging the
beginnings of a circus parade.

"I got here as soon as I could," Sunny gushed in an overly loud
voice. She looked around with wide eyes, then glanced over at
Hannah and Jennifer as if taking a mental head count. "What's
going on? Is it Ashley? What happened? Tell me everything."

Tom had already stepped up and put a hand on Sunny's shoulder. He now quietly directed her past the gaping nurses at the
desk and over to the waiting area.

"Here. Sit down, Sunny," he said. "Let me explain." In a
hushed tone he proceeded to tell everything they knew, which he
admitted wasn't much.

"Are they doing everything they can?" asked Sunny. "Have you
gotten a second opinion? Are you sure that Dr. McGregor is the
best doctor to handle this?"

"Dr. McGregor has been our pediatrician since Jennifer was
born," Tom answered calmly. "He's always taken excellent care of
all the girls. I feel confident in his ability."

"Can I see her?" asked Sunny. "I brought some things to cheer her up."

Tom sighed and turned to Meg with a frustrated expression.

"Sunny," said Meg slowly, "Ashley is unconscious. She is in the intensive care unit. That means only immediate family, and there is certainly no room in there for this," she said, waving her hand toward the things Sunny had brought. She said the words as if the gifts were an insult and instantly regretted her tone, but it was too late.

"Well, I wanted to do something to cheer her up," Sunny said, and Sigfried put a protective hand on her arm. She looked to Tom. "Aren't I 'immediate family'?"

Tom nodded. "Sure, Sunny. That seems reasonable. And thanks for bringing these things. It was real thoughtful. You can give them to Ashley just as soon as they move her down to pediatrics."

Sunny smiled. "So they are moving her out of intensive care?"

Tom shook his head. "No," he said slowly. He started to explain again how serious Ashley's condition was, but Meg couldn't stand to hear any more.

She turned to the girls. "Jennifer and Hannah, do you want to come with me to get some cocoa?" They both nodded dumbly and went with her to the elevator.

In the cafeteria, the three of them sat around a Formica-topped table and sipped their cocoa. Meg wished she could think of something encouraging to say.

"Aunt Meggie," asked Jennifer in a tiny voice, "do you really think that God has everything under control?"

Meg blinked and looked down at her cocoa. "I'm not much of an expert on these things...." she began lamely.

"Well, Daddy says that God's holding Ashley in his hands and that everything will be okay." Jennifer looked at Meg with questioning eyes. "Is that true?"

"I think so." Meg returned her gaze. "To be honest, I hadn't given God much thought for quite a few years. But since Ashley got sick, I've been praying a lot. And just this afternoon, I got this reassurance, sort of a peaceful feeling, and it really seemed like God was listening."

Jennifer nodded thoughtfully, then sipped her cocoa.

"Daddy said that God can do a miracle," said Hannah. "And I believe it, too. That's what I'm praying for."

"Me, too," said Meg.

"Really?" asked Jennifer with big brown eyes, so much like her mother's. "Then I will, too."

"Great," said Meg. "Maybe the more people there are to pray for a miracle, the better the chance that it will happen."

"Do you think Sunny and Sigfried are praying for a miracle?" asked Jennifer.

"Maybe," said Meg, although she really didn't think so. Still, it would do no good to dampen the somewhat lifted spirits of the girls.

When they got back upstairs, Erin and Tom were both in the waiting room with Sigfried. Sunny was gone.

Meg lifted her brows in question. "Sunny?"

Erin nodded.

"We told her to stay for only five minutes," said Tom, glancing nervously at his watch. "I think it's about up. I haven't seen Ashley for quite a while." He stood and moved to the door and waited. He glanced around as if trying to spot a nurse to go in and let Sunny know her time was up, but no one appeared to be free. So Tom waited.

Meg tried to make small talk with Erin, but she kept looking at Tom, still waiting by the door. What was taking Sunny so long? Didn't she have a watch? Or did she think this was another instance where she could twist the rules a bit? It was so infuriating. Meg wanted to give her mother a piece of her mind, but she knew this was not the place for a scene.

"Would you like me to take the girls home?" she asked Erin.

Erin looked at her with an absent expression, as if she had become incapable of making simple decisions.

"What do you think, Meg?" Erin finally asked, although the words sounded empty.

"Maybe it would be best if they got home and stayed in something of a routine. You can always call me and tell me otherwise." She glanced at the girls and said in a quiet voice, "If things change or we need to come back..."

Erin's chin quivered. "Sure. That sounds like a good plan. Thanks, Meg."

Meg gathered the girls, trying not to look at Tom still waiting by the door as she herded them toward the elevator. She was relieved that she wouldn't be here when Sunny finally came out. If she ever came out. Perhaps a nurse would have to go in and drag her away. It was even more irksome to consider Sunny's behavior since Erin had told her how often Sunny had missed birthdays and other important occasions over the years. Maybe Sunny's act tonight was inspired by guilt.

Finally, they pulled into the driveway, and Meg told herself to let go of this bitterness toward Sunny. She knew it wasn't healthy, and right now the girls needed her.

"Daddy took care of the dog," Jennifer informed her as they walked into the house. "But I don't think anyone has checked on Ashley's bunnies."

"Ashley showed me how to do that," said Meg. "You two had better go get ready for bed. I hope you didn't have any homework."

"I have a little," said Jennifer. "But it won't take me long."

Meg found a flashlight by the back door and made her way to the bunny hutch. She fumbled for a while, trying to open the latch and hold the flashlight steady enough to see. Finally, she set the flashlight down. It was a clear night, and the moon was shining bright. She allowed her eyes a chance to adjust to the dark until she could see well enough to open the latch without the flashlight.

The bunnies still had enough water for the night, but were without food. She filled the bowls and watched them gobble it up hungrily. She reached in and petted the fur of one of the rabbits. She wasn't sure which one, because it was so dark, but the feel of soft, warm fur between her fingers was soothing.

"Ashley is very sick," she told the bunnies quietly. "She would probably want me to tell you hello for her. And I'm sure you would want to send back your best bunny regards." She removed her hand and fastened the door shut. "I hope she'll get to see you again soon." Meg turned in the darkness and wiped a tear from her cheek. "Please, God," she whispered desperately. "Please, do a miracle."

The next two days passed slowly, each one nearly the same as the one before. Meg took care of Jennifer and Hannah and kept the house in order. She stopped in to see Grandmother and informed her of Ashley's progress, or rather lack of progress. Grandmother was very concerned, and she told Meg there was no loss on earth so great as the loss of one's own child. She said she was praying for Ashley.

Erin continued to stay in the hospital, sleeping when she could in a room they allowed her to use. But each day, Erin looked more worn and pale. Meg worried that Erin might get sick too. She tried to get her to eat and drink, but Erin's only interest was sitting by Ashley's side whenever she could. Sometimes Meg took turns sitting by Ashley's bed while Erin rested. She would try to chatter cheerfully to the still girl, telling her about the bunnies, the weather, and whatever else came to mind. Finally, she discovered a subject that was easy to go on and on about. She began telling Ashley all about the cranberry bog, and how she'd started helping Grandpa when she was about the same age as Ashley. She described in detail how the bog looked and smelled at various times of the year, telling what fun it was to harvest the shiny red berries as they floated in the flooded bogs.

On the third evening of Ashley's stay in the hospital, Tom decided to take the girls home himself, asking Meg to remain with Erin. He, too, was getting concerned about Erin's health. But no one knew what to do. Erin refused to go home. She had even lost interest in her other two daughters. Meg could see that Tom was almost at his wit's end.

That night, just before midnight, Erin came away from Ashley's room, sank into a chair beside Meg, and began to talk. Her words were slow at first, spoken in a monotone, and Meg wasn't sure what she was trying to say. But she gradually became more upset, and Meg tried to stop her, afraid that Erin might later regret her words. Her intense tone frightened Meg; it was rambling and almost delirious. Finally Meg gave up. Stopping Erin was like trying to flag down an overloaded freight train as it thundered down the mountain. Instead, Meg just sat back and listened as her sister poured out her story.

"I'm an awful person, Meg. You have no idea. Horrible. You should be ashamed to call me your sister. You see, when Ashley was born, I wanted a boy. It wasn't just for Tom's sake, either. No, selfish me, I just wanted to have a son. Anyway, I was mad when I found out I'd had another girl." She wiped tears from her eyes and continued. "I've never told anyone this, Meg. But when I saw Ashley's wrinkled red face and kinky red hair, I felt nothing for her. No love at all. Nothing."

For some reason, this admission was worse than if Erin had admitted to being a hit-and-run driver or a bigamist. Meg felt as if someone were twisting a dull steak knife right into her heart. She could almost hear Sunny's voice saying the exact same thing about her. Had she? Meg shook her head to disperse the crazy thoughts and brought herself back to Erin.

"But surely, Erin, that was only for a moment. After that, you must have felt something—"

"No, Meg." Erin's voice grew calmer now, as if this outpouring had begun to work its therapy. "The sad truth is, for a long time I felt nothing. I took care of her, fed her, changed her. But I never really bonded with her. Of course, I know I loved her. But it was an odd, almost crippled kind of love. Nothing like what I felt for Jennifer and Hannah. And it didn't help that Ashley looked so different from them. You must understand, Meg. She's not a beautiful child...." Erin looked at Meg with tears flowing freely down her cheeks now. "You must hate me for saying this."

"No, I don't. I just feel sorry for Ashley."

"It's breaking my heart, too, Meg. I feel so horribly guilty about the past. I keep wondering if somehow she knew in her heart, if she knew that I didn't love her like I loved her sisters. If I could change the past, I would. The good part is that I feel totally different now. Now, I love Ashley so much. I keep telling her how much I love her. I don't know if she can hear me. I would gladly die if she could just live. I really would, Meg." Erin collapsed into wracking sobs, and Meg held her tightly.

"I know you would, Erin." Meg paused. "I would too," she added softly.

Erin pulled back and looked at Meg. "You would?"

Meg nodded with tears in her eyes. "Yes, that little girl feels like the closest thing to my own daughter. She and I hit it off right from the start."

"It's funny, isn't it? She even looks enough like you to be yours. And she really likes you."

Meg nodded. "I really want to see her grow up, Erin."

"Me, too."

They prayed together for Ashley. It was the first time Meg had actually prayed aloud with anyone. She had sat in on their prayers, listening and agreeing in her heart, but she had always been too uncomfortable to speak herself. Even now her words were not flowery or poetic, and she didn't know all the words to use, but what she said was from her heart.

"Amen," said Erin, squeezing Meg's hands. "I'm so glad you're here, Meg. I honestly don't know what we would have done without you. I hope you never leave."

Meg looked away. This was a decision she had not settled on yet. At times, she felt a crushing urgency that she needed to get back to her old life, back to the big city. She imagined herself back in her little apartment, going back to work, going shopping and out for dinner. Then in weaker moments, she wasn't so sure. Part of her felt strangely at home in Crandale. More at home than she had ever felt anywhere else.

"Mrs. Edwards?" called the ICU nurse. "Can you come here right now?" Erin leaped up and disappeared behind the doors that led to Ashley. Meg leaned over and buried her head in her hands, pleading silently with God.

It seemed like hours before Meg heard Erin's footsteps emerging from the room. Meg looked up slowly, almost afraid to know. She stared into her sister's face.

"She's come back to us, Meg." Erin's face broke into a glowing smile. "She spoke to me. She even asked about Aunt Meggie."

Meg jumped up. "Can I see her?"

"In a few minutes. They are doing some things right now." The two sisters hugged and cried and thanked God, right there in front of the nurses' station. Soon the nurses joined in. Everyone in ICU had come to care deeply for Ashley in the short time she'd been there.

"I've got to call Tom," said Erin. A nurse handed her the phone from the desk and told her to go ahead.

Meg listened as Erin filled Tom in on all the medical details. It seemed the ICU doctor wasn't ready to admit that Ashley was out of the woods yet, but he was amazed that she was recovering at all. Then a nurse came out of ICU and motioned for Meg to come over.

"You can go in now," said the nurse. "Just don't tire her out. She's been through quite an ordeal, poor little angel."

Meg slipped into the chair next to Ashley. All the same tubes and machines were hooked up, and Ashley's eyes were closed. Just as Meg began to grow worried that Ashley might have lost consciousness again, the little girl's eyes opened. Meg stood up so that Ashley could see her without moving her head.

"Hi, Ashley," said Meg quietly. "I'm sure glad to see you. I've been taking care of Peter and Flopsy. They're both doing just fine, but they miss you."

Ashley smiled. "Did you give them a carrot?" she whispered.

"Yes, and some broccoli, too." Meg reached over and touched Ashley's hand. "I'm so glad you're better, Ashley. I've been missing you, too."

"Aunt Meggie?"

"Yes?"

"I want to see Grandpa's cranberries."

Meg laughed. Ashley had actually heard what Meg said during those long hours of waiting. "Well, then you shall. Just as soon as you get all better, I promise to take you to see Grandpa's cranberries!"

Ashley smiled and closed her eyes.

Twelve

ERIN CALLED EARLY THE NEXT MORNING to report that Ashley was doing even better, and Tom headed straight for the hospital. Meg was glad to help get the girls off to school this time. It was a pleasant change to see their happy faces as they boarded the bus. The final prognosis wasn't in yet, but in her heart, Meg believed that Ashley was going to be okay.

She rummaged through Erin's closet in search of warm outdoor clothes. Erin had given her borrowing privileges when she'd learned that Meg hadn't brought much with her from San Francisco. Meg smiled as she pulled on some jeans. As a teenager she had never been able to squeeze into her sister's things, but now the jeans were loose and comfortable, and Erin was as slender as ever. Meg pulled a wool sweater over her head and searched for a pair of sturdy boots. Her goals were to get to the bog this morning so she could take some photos to show Ashley what the bog looked like, and to pay Grandmother a visit to tell her the good news.

She checked on the dog and fed the bunnies, then grabbed her camera and headed for town. The sky was clear and blue today, with the promise of spring in the air. It was a good day to be alive.

And for a change, she felt alive and glad to be in Crandale. As she drove toward town, she realized she would need to buy some film, and since she would be stopping anyway, the decent thing to do would be to stop by Sunny's and tell her about Ashley's progress.

The little bell jingled on the door of the gallery, and she quickly spotted Sigfried opening some boxes in the back room.

"Hi, Sigfried," she called. "Is Sunny around?"

He looked up and pushed his wire-rimmed glasses back on his nose. "Nope. She doesn't usually come in this early. You know Sunny; she's not much of a morning person."

"That's right, I forgot." Meg smiled, hoping to win his approval. They hadn't gotten started on the right foot, but she wanted to fix it now, although she wasn't quite sure why. Maybe they all just needed a fresh start. "Well, I do have some good news."

"Is it Ashley?" His eyes lit up as he leaned a big frame against the counter and gave her his full attention.

"Yep, she regained consciousness late last night. We think she's going to be okay now. Of course, the doctors aren't saying anything for sure yet, but her pediatrician will be in today to check on her."

"That's great. Sunny will be so pleased." He walked over to Meg and stuck out his hand. "Sorry about that little episode on the phone the other day. Don't know what comes over me sometimes."

"That's okay." She said, taking his hand. He gave it a little shake and a friendly squeeze. "I know I still have some fences to mend with Sunny." She released his hand and looked down at her feet. "It's just not easy...."

"Never is. But that's no reason to give up. Right?"

"Sure, I guess so. Anyway, tell Sunny the good news."

"You bet I will. Thanks for dropping by."

She picked up several rolls of film and found out where the

one-hour photo shop was located, then headed over to Briar Hedge. She drove past the familiar old house and down the road, then stopped, deciding to walk the remaining distance. It was a beautiful morning, and the sun would be at a perfect angle to get some shots of the bogs. She remembered the year she and Grandpa had planted dozens of daffodil bulbs around the bogs, and wondered if they would still be around. If so, they should be in bloom about now.

The land where the bog was situated was up on a slight incline from the house, at an elevation that couldn't be more than sixty or seventy feet above sea level, but high enough that the bog wasn't visible from the house. For that reason, Grandpa had built a little cabin where he could camp out and watch out for frost in the late spring and occasionally even into the summer. She walked until the cabin came into sight, then pulled out her old camera and took a couple shots. It looked a little run-down, but she supposed that was to be expected. She knew that Abner had been neglecting the bog in recent years. She reached the top of the rise, took a deep breath, and looked expectantly out over the bogs.

A sick feeling washed over her when she saw what had once been one of the best cranberry farms in the area. It was only mid-March, and the bogs already were choked by all kinds of weeds. It was plain to see that this was not the result of only one season of neglect. It was normal to have some weeds every year; she had spent many a spring break out here weeding the few stragglers that popped up. But now the weeds were so thick that they were all she could see. Even the wild blackberries, long neglected, had slithered down the hillside and were reaching their greedy fingers toward the bogs.

She walked closer, staring in horror at the hopelessly overgrown bogs. How could any of the cranberry plants have possibly survived this kind of abuse and neglect? She hopped down the incline and right into the bog, remembering how Grandpa had told her that many people thought the bogs were a wet and soggy place, when in fact their soil had to be kept somewhat dry to protect the plants. He had explained to her that a layer of peat was laid beneath the bog to hold just the right amount of moisture for the plants, since they didn't like to sit in water. Grandpa used to fret about a few weeds; she hated to imagine what he would think about this horrible mess.

Meg got down on her knees and pushed the stubborn weeds aside until she could finally see what lay beneath. To her relief and amazement, she discovered the tiny reddish green leaves of cranberry plants. Not healthy and thick like they should have been, but alive just the same. She began pulling weeds with her bare hands. At first she tugged cautiously, afraid to disturb the brave plants rooted beneath, but before long she was pulling with force and determination, and then with fury. How dare Abner allow Grandpa's bogs to deteriorate into such a state! It was a horror, an abomination. Unforgivable.

After a short time, her hands were throbbing in hot pain, and she climbed out of the bog and flopped to the ground. It was hopeless. Totally and completely hopeless. She looked at her stained and blistered palms, then down to the tiny patch she had weeded. At last her eyes settled on the remaining twenty bogs—two acres each, and all equally full of weeds. Was she going mad? Did she actually think she could weed forty acres of weed-infested bogs? Besides, this was Abner and Grandmother's business. Not hers. And not Grandpa's—not anymore.

"I'm so sorry, Grandpa," she said aloud. "I'm sorry this place has come to such ruin. If there was anything I could do, I would." Her voice choked, her chest tightening. Why did it hurt so much? It wasn't as if the bog was a living, breathing thing. But just the same, it felt as if something was dead. Or dying...

She stood and picked up her camera. There was nothing here she wanted to photograph. Nothing here she wanted to show

Ashley. Poor Ashley. She would never know the thrill of seeing bright red cranberries floating like glistening jewels on the water as they were corralled for harvest. Ashley would never be able to appreciate the magical wonders of her great-grandpa's cranberry farm. Of course, Ashley had other things to look forward to. But it was sad to lose a heritage. As a child, Meg had always lived for the times when she could be with Grandpa out on the cranberry bog. Having grown up on a liberal college campus in the crazy seventies with a mom who cared nothing about mothering, Meg had always been able to count on this one thing. It was her haven. A place to come home to.

Today, she felt like she had come to a funeral. She turned and walked away. Well, at least it wasn't Ashley's funeral. That was something to be thankful for. She would much rather lose a cranberry bog than a niece. As she walked away, she noticed a scrap of yellow, half hidden by blackberry vines. She walked over to take a look, and there, poking its sunny head between the vines, bloomed a daffodil. Meg pushed back the vines and found more daffodil plants, some with blossoms just ready to open. She gingerly pulled back the thorny vines, bent them away from the flowers, then stomped on them. One by one she pulled them back, anchoring some with large rocks to keep them from popping back into place. There before her bloomed about a dozen yellow daffodils. She knelt, pulled out her camera, and took several shots. Then she noticed the tall stand of firs along the edge of the property and took several shots of that.

She began to see more and more lovely pictures. The little apple orchard that Grandpa had planted and carefully tended, and where she used to pick apples by the bushel, was about to burst into bloom. The trees looked like they hadn't been pruned in ages, but their round buds glowed like pearls in the morning sun. She took about a dozen shots of the ocean not too far off in the distance. Before long, she had used up two rolls of film.

Before she left, she returned to the part of the bog she had weeded in such a frenzy. She stood on the bank and studied the plants below her. Was it just her imagination, or had those sturdy plants perked up their little light-deprived heads to get a glimpse of the sun? She climbed down and adjusted her camera to take a few close-ups of the plants, then studied them again. Grandpa had always said that cranberry plants were hearty, and she figured he was right. But even so, they probably couldn't survive another season of this kind of neglect. She replaced her lens cap and stood sadly. Well, at least she could show Ashley what her great-grandpa's plants looked like while they were still alive.

She stopped by Grandmother's to tell her the good news about Ashley before she headed back to the hospital. She had decided not to worry Grandmother by mentioning her disappointment in the bog. The poor old woman had been so worried about her great-granddaughter, Meg didn't want to spoil her relief.

"Good morning," Meg called as she came into the room. Rosa was just removing a breakfast tray of mostly untouched food. "Looks like you weren't very hungry this morning, Grandmother."

"She eats like a bird," hissed Rosa as she passed by.

"I come with good news, Grandmother." Meg pulled up a chair and smiled.

"Is it about Ashley?"

"Yes. She's better, Grandmother. Isn't that great?"

Grandmother sighed. "Oh, I'm so relieved. I was lying here thinking that it wasn't fair for an old thing like me to go on living when my little great-granddaughter was slipping away. It's more than a body can bear. I'm so relieved. Please tell Erin and Tom how glad I am for them." She leaned back and closed her eyes for a moment.

"Maybe you'll feel like eating then?" asked Meg hopefully.

Grandmother smiled. "Well, now, I just might."

"I'll get Rosa on my way out. I really can't stay long; I just wanted to pop in and share the good news."

"And I thank you, Meggie." Grandmother peered at Meg's dirty clothes curiously. "Been up to the bogs, have you?"

Meg nodded.

"So, how do they look?"

Meg swallowed. "Well, uh..."

"Be straight with me, Meggie."

"Not so good."

Grandmother nodded. "I was afraid of that. Just how bad are they?"

"They're pretty bad, Grandmother." Meg stood and began pacing. It was too late to keep it a secret, and like the floodgates at harvesttime, the words gushed out. "It's deplorable. An abomination. They have gone to complete ruin. Totally overgrown with weeds. I don't know if they can ever be brought back. It makes me so angry I could—" Meg stopped and turned. She was shocked by how carried away she had gotten, especially after her resolve not to burden Grandmother with these worries.

"I'm sorry, Grandmother. It's just that I loved them so." Meg sat down again and stared at the floor. "I guess it's an emotional issue with me. I'm still in shock."

Grandmother made an odd choking sound, and Meg looked up in surprise, afraid that she had finally given the woman a heart attack. To her amazement, Grandmother was chuckling.

"What is it?" asked Meg. "What's so funny?"

Grandmother smiled and slowly shook her head. "You are, Meggie. Just like your grandfather, you are! Oh, how he could go on about his berries. I used to think that cranberry juice ran through his veins, and now I think it might run through yours, too."

Meg smiled. "Thanks, Grandmother."

"Don't thank me. Some folks wouldn't take that as a compliment."

"Well, I do. At least you understand why it irks me so. But I don't understand why Abner doesn't care. I guess cranberry juice doesn't run through his veins."

Grandmother's face grew cloudy. "No, I don't suppose it does."

"Well, I hope I didn't worry you with my little fit, Grandmother. I really should go. I want to get to the hospital to check on Ashley. I'll call and let you know how she's doing."

"I'd appreciate that, Meggie. But can you stay for another minute or two?"

"Sure."

"Go on over to my dresser, Meggie. There's a bunch of envelopes on it, but I think it's the long blue one on top. Bring it over here."

Meg stood and moved to the old cherry dresser. It was the only piece of furniture in the room from the original set. "What happened to the rest of the cherry furniture, Grandmother?" asked Meg as she handed her the envelope.

"What?" Grandmother said absently. "Oh, that. Abner and Phoebe took them. They needed furniture. They want the dresser too, but I'm hanging on to it." She grinned mischievously. "Hand me my glasses, Meggie. There on the table."

Meg handed her the glasses and waited while the woman situated them just so on her nose and then finally began to open the envelope. Her gnarled fingers trembled as she attempted to remove the letter from inside. Meg suppressed the urge to reach over and help, wondering as she waited why the contents of what looked like an ordinary water bill could be of any interest to her. Grandmother silently read over the letter, and Meg impatiently glanced at her watch.

Finally Grandmother spoke. "I won't read you the whole letter. You can read it later if you want. But the gist of it is that Briar Hedge is on the verge of losing its water rights."

"You mean for the bog? Why? I thought Grandpa's water rights were supposed to last forever. How can they do it?"

"Seems there's some new law in Oregon that says if you don't use your agricultural water for five years, they can take away your water rights."

"Do you mean to tell me that Abner hasn't used water for five years?"

"Well, this would be the fifth. This letter is a warning."

"So how has he harvested for the last four years? Don't tell me he does a dry harvest. Hardly anyone does that anymore."

Grandmother shook her head. "No, I don't expect he has. I remember as a girl, when they used to do dry harvests, I went out to pick cranberries by hand one fall. I wanted to make some spending money. But it was backbreaking work, and I figured there had to be better ways to make money. Anyway, what I'm trying to say is, in order to preserve the rights, we have to use water for agricultural purposes."

Meg shook her head in disbelief. "Abner must not even have irrigated. I don't know how the plants could still be alive."

"I don't know either, Meggie. Maybe it's a miracle or something." Grandmother's forehead creased as if she were deep in thought.

"Well, I am starting to believe in miracles."

"The question is, Meggie, do we want to preserve those water rights?"

"Why are you asking me? Shouldn't you be having this conversation with Abner?"

"Apparently I should have had this conversation with Abner several years ago. For nearly twenty years, I've left this business to him. And until recently, I thought he was handling things just fine."

"Well, I suppose you know that he thinks it'd be smart to sell Briar Hedge." Meg wasn't sure how much Grandmother knew about Cousin Abner's scheme, and Meg wasn't eager to be the one to fill her in.

"Oh, he does? Well, he might be right about that. I always told your grandpa there had to be better things to do with perfectly good land than to grow bitter old berries."

Meg frowned.

"Oh, I know, Meggie." Grandmother waved a wrinkled hand in the air. "You have cranberry juice in your blood, and you believe that cranberries are perfectly wonderful. But think about it—what are they really good for? Have you ever eaten one right off the plant?"

"Sure. I sort of like them raw. Besides, they're one of the few native fruits of North America. And they're good for lots of things. You remember all the stuff Grandpa used to concoct out of his cranberries."

Grandmother smiled with a faraway look in her eyes. "Yes, I do."

"So, Grandmother, why are you telling me about all this water rights business anyway? What can I do about it? Or do you even want anything done?"

"I thought you could see about saving our water rights, Meggie. It's a shame to just let them go like that. It seems downright wasteful. And you know how I hate seeing anything going to waste."

"What exactly do you mean? Do you want me to try to save the bog?" Meg laughed at the absurdity, imagining herself frantically weeding all twenty bogs the same way she had done today. It was ridiculous. It was impossible.

"I thought you loved them."

"I do, Grandmother. And if I honestly thought you were, just for one moment, serious—I would do everything in my power to save them."

"I am serious."

116

"But what about Abner?"

"What about him?"

"Well, aren't the bogs—well, don't they sort of belong to him?"

"Every square inch of Briar Hedge belongs to me. And it will continue to belong to me until the day I die, which shouldn't be too far off. And which I'm sure will make some people very happy."

Meg leaned over and grabbed Grandmother's hands in hers. "Not me, Grandmother. I want you to stick around for a long time. I wasted a lot of years not knowing you. And now that I know you, I like you."

Grandmother smiled. "Well, I'll stick around as long as I can, but don't expect much. The doctor said—"

"Oh, I don't want to hear what the doctor said. Just think what the doctor was saying about Ashley." Meg stood up. "Speaking of Ashley, I really ought to go."

"So you'll look into it, then?"

"The water rights?"

"Yes, and the bog."

"Are you really telling me to do this? Can I do it on your authority?"

"That's what I'm saying, Meggie."

Meg smiled widely. "Well, then it would be my pleasure, Grandmother. Consider it done."

Thirteen

MEG WENT TO CRANDALE FEED AND SEED while her film was being developed. Not much had changed here in twenty years. It still smelled musty and sweet, a mixture of grain and seed and fertilizer. She walked around and looked at the large sacks of various farm materials. The labels meant nothing to her, and she didn't have a clue as to where she should begin. All she remembered was that Grandpa used to come in here from time to time to pick up things for the bog.

She walked up and down the aisles of the barnlike store, finally ending up in a corner where work clothes were displayed. Denim overalls and work shirts were neatly stacked across from the heavy-duty gloves hanging on pegs. She stared blankly at the tough-looking garments and marveled that only two weeks ago she'd been shopping for a new business suit at Ann Taylor. She grinned to herself and began searching for the smaller-sized overalls, rubber boots, and denim work shirts, as well as several pairs of gloves. At the last minute, she grabbed a handful of heavy cotton socks and piled them on top of her stack. On her way to the cash register, she found a good selection of heavy barn coats that looked perfect for cool, wet days.

She flopped her selections onto the counter and was met by a somewhat familiar face. The man appeared to be in his sixties and had a smooth-featured, round face with sparkling blue eyes. The eyes were what stopped her.

"Don't I know you?" she asked, pulling out her checkbook.

He studied her intently, then shook his head. "You seem a bit familiar, but I don't think I can place you."

"I'm Meg Lancaster, and my grandfather, Stewart Lancaster, owned—"

"Well, I'll be!" The man extended a calloused hand and gave hers a hearty shake. "I'm Cal Logan. Your granddad gave me my first job out at Briar Hedge more than fifty years ago. It was during the war, when I was too young to fight, but too old to sit around twiddling my thumbs. Sure, I remember you, Meggie. I can still see you skedaddling after your granddad all over that bog. He used to say that you were his right-hand gal."

Meg smiled. "That'd be me."

He looked down at her pile with a puzzled expression. "Well, looks like you're planning to go to work, little lady. Or is this for someone else?"

Meg grinned sheepishly. "It's for me. I'm going to work on the bog, and I needed a few work clothes."

Cal's brows lifted. "You don't say? Well, you're sure going to have your work cut out for you."

"That's an understatement. I went out and looked at the bog today."

"Pretty bad?"

She nodded. "I'd hate to think what Grandpa would say if he could see it now."

Cal shook his head. "Darn shame, too. That used to be the best-looking bog in the county. Your granddad took better care of it than a mother takes with her newborn babe. Darn shame. I've been out there a couple of times, even offered to give your cousin some advice...." She could tell by the tone of Cal's voice that he probably hadn't been very well received by Abner.

"Grandmother has asked me to see about bringing it back."

"Well, it'll be a tough job, Meggie, but those are McFarlin berries, and they are the heartiest. You might be able to bring them back, but you'll probably need to get some herbicides and fertilizers going. Although it's a little late in the season for some of the more effective herbicides."

"Herbicides? Grandpa always tried to stay away from chemicals. I was hoping I could do something a little more organic. I hate the idea of dumping a bunch of chemicals in the bog."

Cal laughed and held up a pair of her gloves. "Well, then I suggest you get a couple dozen more pairs of these."

Meg frowned. "Is it hopeless, Cal?"

"No, not at all. But it's going to take a lot of time and work. Did you plan on getting any help, or are you taking it on single-handed?"

"I hadn't really thought about it. To be honest, it was only this morning that Grandmother asked me to do this."

Cal nodded. "I see. Well, it takes a lot of commitment to restore cranberry bogs that have been let go like this. Are you going to be sticking around for a while? Do you expect to see any profits this year?"

"I'm not in it for the money, if that's what you mean. Of course, if I stick around, I'd need enough to live on, but I have some money set aside."

"It's none of my business, Meggie, but since your granddad was one of my best friends, I'm going to give you a little advice, if you don't mind."

"Sure. I'd appreciate anything."

"Well, I'm not sure what Alexandra has in mind, but everyone in these parts thinks that bog is going to Abner when she passes on. And goodness knows, she must be close to a hundred,

Meggie. She can't hold out forever. What I'm wondering is, why are you getting yourself involved in this? It could turn into a big mess."

"I know. It doesn't make a whole lot of sense to me, either. All I can say is that Grandpa loved that bog, and I love it, too. It makes me sick to see it this way. Grandmother just learned that this is her last year to retain water rights to the property, and she made it very clear that the property still belongs to her and that she wants to preserve those water rights. Working the bog is the only way to do that. And I offered to take it on. Do you think I'm crazy?"

"No, not at all, Meggie. I think your granddad would be proud of you. I just would hate to see you get hurt. But it sounds like you're going in with your eyes wide open." He totaled the amount of her purchase, and she wrote out a check, noting that it wasn't as much as she'd paid for that business suit at Ann Taylor.

"And Meggie?" said Cal as he handed her two very full bags. "I'd be real glad to help you out in any way I can. You probably didn't know that I owned my own bog for nearly thirty years. It was your granddad who helped get me started. I had to sell out a couple years back because of my health—that's when I bought the Feed and Seed here. But I'd be real glad to see Briar Hedge up and running again. Real glad."

"Thanks, Cal. You can bet that I'll take you up on that offer. See you later."

"Good luck, Meggie."

She stopped at the diner for a bowl of clam chowder, then went over to pick up the photos. They weren't half bad, and Meg hurried to the hospital, eager to show them to Ashley. It seemed like ages since she'd seen the little girl, when in reality it had been just over twelve hours.

She asked at the information desk and found that Ashley had been moved to pediatrics that morning. Meg quickly found the room and pushed open the door to see Sunny and Erin sitting next to Ashley's bed, quietly visiting. They both looked up to greet her. Meg smiled and looked over to the bed where Ashley was sleeping.

"And hence comes my prodigal daughter," said Sunny in what Meg supposed was meant to be a humorous greeting, but somehow it didn't strike her as such. Meg, deciding to ignore it, pasted a bright smile on her face. Sunny would not be getting the best of her today.

"Hi, Meg," said Erin, quietly scooting a third chair close to the bed. "Here, come and sit down. Ashley's having a little nap right now."

"What in heaven's name have you been doing?" asked Sunny, frowning at Meg's muddy jeans and boots.

Meg had forgotten all about her clothes. She turned to Erin. "Maybe I should go change. As you can see, I took you up on your offer to borrow some clothes. I've been out at the bog."

"The bog?" asked Sunny. "Whatever for?"

"I wanted to check it out."

"You're just fine, Meg," reassured Erin. "And don't worry about the clothes. Ashley asked about you this morning. She's so much better. Dr. McGregor couldn't believe it. He said it must be a miracle."

"Well, we knew that, didn't we?" Meg looked at Ashley. There was a little color back in her cheeks, and she seemed to be resting comfortably. Meg glanced around the flower-and-balloon-decorated room. "Looks like the carnival's back in town."

"I just wanted to brighten up my granddaughter's room," said Sunny defensively. "Bring in some color and life."

"Yes, and Ashley appreciates it." Erin's eyes moved from Sunny to Meg as if in warning that she didn't want to play referee. Suddenly Meg felt ashamed. Why did she act like this around Sunny? It was so childish. The three sat in silence, and Meg felt as if she had spoiled their visit. Maybe she should leave.

Just then, Ashley stirred and opened her eyes. Erin moved closer, fluffing the pillows behind her so she could sit up and see her visitors. Several stuffed animals were perched around her bed, and Ashley looked like a little princess of the animal kingdom.

"Hi, Aunt Meggie," she said in a quiet voice.

"Hi, Ashley. Are you feeling better?"

Ashley nodded.

"You look beautiful," said Meg. "I'm sure glad you're getting well. I brought you some pictures of your great-grandpa's cranberry bog. It doesn't really look like much right now, but I thought you might like to see it."

Meg handed her niece the photos, and Ashley carefully studied each one as Meg told her a little about it.

"May I see them?" asked Erin.

"Sure." Meg handed her sister the stack that Ashley had already seen.

"These are lovely shots, Meg. Do you think I could get some prints made, too? I'd love to have something to remember the bog by."

Sunny laughed. "Yes, you better get your pictures while you can, girls, before Cousin Abner plows it all under for condos and an eighteen-hole golf course."

Meg wondered about telling them her plans to restore the bog. She was eager to tell Erin but had no idea what Sunny's reaction might be, and she didn't need anyone to shoot down her ideas right now.

"Where's all the cranberries, Aunt Meggie?" asked Ashley after she'd laid down the last photo.

Meg laughed. "Sorry, Ashley. It's the wrong time of year to see the cranberries. Right now there are only the little plants that the berries will grow on."

Ashley nodded sadly. "Can I see the cranberries when they grow up?"

"I think so, Ashley."

"Don't hold your breath," said Sunny.

Meg turned and looked directly at Sunny. "Grandmother has asked me to help bring the bog back."

Sunny cocked her head to one side. "She asked you to do what?"

"To bring the bog back," answered Meg evenly. "As you know, Abner has let it go to ruin, and Grandmother would like it restored."

Sunny lifted her brows. "Is this the same grandmother who has never given a hill of beans for cranberry bogs?"

Meg smiled a placating smile. "The same one."

"Meg, she must be losing her mind, then. Abner is always insinuating that she has Alzheimer's. Do you think it could be possible?"

"She seems perfectly fine to me. By the way, Erin, she said to tell you and Tom how glad she was about Ashley's recovery. She was really quite worried about her." Meg gently squeezed Ashley's hand. "We all were."

"I hope you're not taking your grandmother seriously about this cranberry business, Meg," said Sunny. "It sounds like a formula for disaster. Everyone knows that Abner has his fingers wrapped so tight around that property that it would take a major earthquake to pry him out of there."

"Well, I'm not taking anything away from anyone. I'm just trying to see that Grandpa's cranberry bog isn't lost forever. If it's not used this year, Grandmother will lose her water rights."

Sunny nodded. "Ah. I knew that woman wasn't senile. She's just smart. Very smart."

"Why do you need to make such a big deal about it? Maybe Grandmother has finally come to appreciate the land and all that Grandpa did—"

"Maybe." Sunny laughed. "Now, let's not talk about this anymore. I think we're disturbing my granddaughter."

Meg agreed for Ashley's sake, but it was a long while later before she was calm again.

Fourteen

ASHLEY WAS RELEASED FROM THE HOSPITAL after another day of observation. The doctor said it was a remarkable recovery—something that possibly could be written up in a medical journal. By the weekend, the family was back into their normal routine, and Meg felt that her presence would not be so greatly missed. On Sunday night, she explained to them how much she appreciated their hospitality but that she had decided to live at Briar Hedge in order to be closer to the bog. They all pleaded for her to stay, but Meg promised them that they would still see each other often and that they were all invited to come over and visit at Briar Hedge anytime they wanted.

Grandmother said she was pleased as punch to have Meg move in, and Meg was excited finally to have the freedom to seriously begin the restoration of the bog. As much as she had enjoyed being able to help Erin and her family in their time of need, she was thankful to be on her own again. She liked her independence. She supposed she was like Grandmother in that sense.

Meg had called Cal Logan and scheduled an appointment for a field consultation. On Monday morning, she was already down at the bog when his old pickup came rumbling down the road. She noticed a shaggy blonde head bobbing up and down beside him.

"Hi there, Meggie," called Cal. "This is my granddaughter, Clive. She wanted to come along and see your bogs. She's never quite forgiven me for selling ours." He poked the pretty teen with his elbow.

"That's not true, Granddad." Clive blushed and pushed a lock of bangs off her forehead. "I know you had to sell them after your heart attack and all. I just wished you could have kept them."

"Well, it's nice to meet you, Clive," said Meg. "And I can relate to how you feel. But shouldn't you be in school today?"

"It's spring break," said Cal. "The fact is, I told Clive about your plan to try and bring the bogs back without chemicals. I said you might be needing some manpower—or shall I say person power?"

"You'd be willing to pull weeds?" Meg eyed the slender girl skeptically.

"Sure. I used to help Granddad all the time. He can vouch for me. I practically grew up in the cranberry bogs."

"She's one tough cookie, all right. Works like a horse—eats like one, too, I might add."

"Granddad!"

Meg smiled. "I'd love to have help, but I probably can't pay much more than minimum wage."

"That's more'n I ever got working for him." Clive poked her grandfather in the middle. "I've got gloves and overalls in the truck." She trotted off to get them, and Cal and Meg began to walk around the edges of the bog.

"It's bad, Meg," said Cal. "Does Alexandra plan to put some money into the place?"

"You mean like a lot of money? More than just the average yearly maintenance costs?"

"Yep, I mean like a lot of money."

"No. She hasn't indicated that she wants to do that." Meg bit her lip and tried to push from her mind how concerned Grandmother had seemed just that morning about what the restoration might cost. Meg had tried to reassure her that it would be minimal.

"Well then, you've really got your work cut out for you. It seems to me the big goal here will be to preserve water rights by having at least two or three working bogs."

"Just two or three? What about the rest?"

"I don't even know if you can manage to restore two or three, Meg. If you had access to any kind of cash, I'd suggest that you tear everything out and start over—maybe even with a different berry. Like a Stevens; they're getting real popular in these parts. They're a high-yield berry that can be harvested a whole lot sooner than these McFarlins you got here."

"But I thought you said McFarlins are good."

"Sure, they're good—good for surviving this kind of neglect. And they're good for some other reasons, too. They have real nice color. And they are frost-resistant. In your case, you should probably keep them. But do you want to know what I'd do if I were you?"

"Of course, other than an extensive use of chemicals." Meg looked over and saw that Clive was already hard at work on the bog Meg had been weeding. "Thanks for bringing Clive, Cal. She seems like a good kid. How old is she?"

"She just turned sixteen. And she's not a bit like a lot of other teenagers these days. She's real mature and sensible for her age." Cal watched his granddaughter for a moment, then turned and continued talking as they walked. "Okay. For starters, I'd pick out your three best-looking bogs with the fewest weeds." He pointed toward the center. "See those three in that same terraced line, but on different levels? They don't look quite as bad as the ones on the perimeter. And by keeping them in the same terrace you can recycle your water by draining it down from the top one to the next."

Meg nodded. "Yes, I see what you mean. But only three?"

"It may be that you can do more than that. But why don't you start with three and see how it goes."

"I guess that makes sense." But she was thinking she might as well go for the whole row of five.

"So you get those three under control, or at least try. In the meantime, you go ahead and irrigate everything, weeds and all. And then, if it was me, I'd put some on a good dose of norflurazon in the middle of winter to knock out some of these weeds."

"Do you really think it will take chemicals to do that?"

"Depends on how long you want to take in bringing those cranberry plants back. You might just lose them altogether and have to replant anyway, if you let them go much further. Fact is, you don't have to make that decision now. Just wait until you've had your war with the weeds this year. You might be singing a different tune come fall."

"I suppose you're right."

They continued to walk around the bog, Cal talking the whole time about fertilizers and herbicides, when and how much to irrigate, and so many other details that Meg felt certain she'd never remember them all. Finally they returned to his truck, and he opened the door and pulled out several booklets and timetables.

"Here." He handed her the stack. "I don't expect you'll be remembering everything I just told you, although you always were a smart little whippersnapper."

"I don't know how to thank you, Cal. Do you have a consultant fee? I know I never could have learned all this without you."

"And just who do you think I learned it all from in the first place? I say it's like casting your bread upon the waters; in due time it comes back to you."

Meg smiled. "Well, Grandpa would be glad to know how you're helping me now."

"Don't get discouraged, Meggie. You've got a lot going for you here. Everything your granddad did, he did right. He built these bogs just as level as can be. The peat beneath the plants still looks real good, and all your drainage pipes look to be in good order. The only thing you're not up-to-date on is the frost-detecting equipment, but heck, the old boys got along without that, and I expect you can too this first year. But you'll have to keep an eye on things once those berries start to blossom. I'll help see that you do. I don't know what the harvest equipment is looking like, but seems I remember your cousin sold off a few pieces of the newer machines a year or two back. When the time comes, we'll figure something out." Cal climbed into his truck. "Say, do you mind dropping Clive by the Feed and Seed around five?"

"Not at all. Thanks again, Cal." She watched his old blue pickup rumble away and then went back to join Clive.

The two of them worked quietly all morning. When the sun was high in the sky, Meg stood and looked around. It looked like they'd hardly made a dent on the two-acre bog.

"It's slow work," said Clive.

"I'll say." Meg tried not to show her disappointment; she didn't want Clive to think she was unappreciative. "You're doing a great job, Clive. I'm sure glad you're available. Do you think you'll want to work all week?"

"Sure, and I can come on weekends, and maybe even sometimes after school—at least when I don't have track practice." She stood up and stretched, looking around. "I love it out here."

"Me, too. But I think we'd better go get some lunch if we want to survive the afternoon." Meg pushed the wheelbarrow up the road and dumped her load in the spot they had designated for the weed pile.

"Can you believe how huge that is?" said Clive. "You'd think that whole bog would be clean by now."

"I know. It's incredible, isn't it?" Meg rolled the wheelbarrow to one side and removed her gloves. Her hands, even beneath the gloves, were red and irritated.

"Yeah, it's hard to believe anyone would let it get this bad."

By the time they reached the house, Rosa had a lunch of roast beef and all the trimmings laid out, and even though she hadn't expected Clive, there was plenty for both of them.

"Mrs. Lancaster said for me to make you a good lunch, Meggie," said Rosa as she set the mashed potatoes on the table. "It's so nice to cook for more than just two."

After lunch, Meg and Clive sat on the porch drinking hot cocoa. A fog had begun to roll in, and Meg decided to take her camera back with them. She thought some shots of Clive working on the mist-covered bog might be interesting.

By late afternoon they had cleared about an eighth of the bog. Or maybe less, thought Meg, as she stood and looked from a higher vantage point. But at least it was enough to tell there was work in progress. She had used half a roll of film on Clive weeding in the white mist. If the photos turned out, she would get some reprints made for Cal, and Clive too, maybe in a nice frame.

Meg heard the sound of an engine to the south. She looked up to see a vehicle coming over the rise in the opposite direction of Grandmother's house and the main road. She didn't recognize the dark-colored Suburban, and the tinted glass made it impossible to see who was inside, but she suspected it might be Abner. She had been dreading this moment and was surprised that it hadn't happened sooner. She bent over and continued to weed, looking over her shoulder to see if anyone got out. Finally, she heard the creak of a door opening, and then another. Then they both closed. *Bang. Bang.* The sound made her jump. She stood and saw Abner and Jason walking toward her, and even from this distance she could see the dark scowl on her cousin's puffy face.

"Who's that?" asked Clive, standing and brushing the hair from her eyes. "Hey, isn't that Jason Lancaster? I've seen him at school. Is he related to you?"

"His dad, Abner, is my cousin, but let me warn you, Abner's not a real nice guy." Meg spoke quietly, keeping her eyes on Abner as he approached.

"What the devil are you doing out here?" demanded Abner when he and Jason were within shouting distance.

"Weeding," answered Meg calmly.

"What the heck for?" Abner kept walking, with Jason just a couple steps behind.

"Because it needs to be done."

"Says who?" Abner placed both hands on his hips and glowered down at her. The bottom of the bog was three feet below the level where Abner and Jason now stood, and their height advantage had an intimidating effect on Meg.

She took a deep breath. "Grandmother has authorized me to do this."

Abner laughed. It was a deep, howling laugh that seemed to echo through the bog, but there was no trace of humor in it. As quickly as it had begun, it stopped. His brows drew together into one dark line.

"So you mean to tell me you're out here weeding these bogs because some senile old woman told you to? Well, Meggie Lancaster, you are dumber than you look!" He spat into the bog.

Meg glared up at him but said nothing. She looked over to where Jason stood. His gaze was downcast, and his lips were pressed together tightly, making a thin white line of his mouth. His cheeks were blazing red, even redder than his curly hair, and she saw his eyes flicker to where Clive was standing with her blue eyes opened wide. Poor Clive, she'd come out to help and had ended up in the midst of this family feud.

"For your information," Meg began in a tight, angry voice,

"Grandmother is not senile. And furthermore, she happens to own this property."

"Just look at you!" Abner snarled as he pointed his finger at her. "Who are you to tell me whether that old bat is crazy or not? Here you are, out groveling in the dirt like an old sow. I don't know which of you is the craziest. But I'm telling you this: I don't want to see you up here again. C'mon, Jason." He grabbed the boy roughly by the arm and pulled him away. Jason turned and looked over his shoulder with an expression that looked half apologetic and half humiliated.

"Poor Jason," said Clive as the Suburban roared down the road, followed by a cloud of dust. "How would you like to have him for a dad?" She looked at Meg. "Oh, I'm sorry. I forgot he's your relative."

"Don't be sorry about that. I'd like to forget he's my relative, too. And I'm sorry about his lack of manners. I don't know what his problem is. But I'll have another talk with Grandmother; maybe she can set him straight." Meg glanced at her watch. "We'd better get you into town. You may not want to come back and work now that you know what kind of kooks I have for relatives."

Meg drove silently to town. The scene with Abner had rattled her considerably. She dropped Clive off at the Feed and Seed and started to turn around. Just then, Sunny popped out of the gallery and ran into the street, waving her arms frantically. Meg rolled down her window, afraid something was horribly wrong.

"Oh, Meg, I'm so glad I caught you," called Sunny breathlessly. "Sigfried left a message with Rosa inviting you to join us for dinner tonight. I know it's last minute, but Sigfried made reservations at the Osprey Inn—"

Meg cut her off. "I don't think so, Sunny. I'm filthy and tired, and it's been a very long day. I'm just not up for it. How about another time?"

"Oh, well, sure. Okay." To Meg's surprise, Sunny didn't argue.

She just stepped away with a sad face and waved. Meg waved back and continued driving down the street. Great. Now on top of everything else, she felt guilty. But the last thing she needed tonight was to have dinner with Sunny. Was it so wrong to decline a last-minute invitation?

By the time Meg had cleaned up for dinner, Grandmother had already eaten and was asleep for the night, and Rosa was parked in front of the TV intently watching *Wheel of Fortune*. Meg's dinner of leftover roast beef was neatly arranged on a plate, and she popped it into the microwave and sat down to wait. Suddenly the idea of dinner at the Osprey Inn sounded pretty good. Maybe she shouldn't have been so hasty. Or so stubborn. On the other hand, it might have been another disaster. She took the plate out and began to eat. Part of the meal was too hot and part of it was still cold. After a few bites, she tossed the remainder into the garbage and put the kettle on for a cup of tea.

"Meggie," called Rosa from the front room. "Did you see my note about the dinner tonight?"

"You mean with Sigfried and Sunny?" Meg moved to the doorway as she waited for the kettle to boil.

"Yes. Did you decide not to go? I thought you would want to go and celebrate your mother's birthday."

"Sunny's birthday?" Meg asked weakly.

"That's right. Tom and Erin were going, too. Why did you not go, Meggie? Are you feeling okay?"

"Just very tired, Rosa. Thanks for the message." Meg looked at her watch. It might not be too late to join them. But then again, she didn't want to walk in while they were in the middle of dinner. Besides, with her luck, she and Sunny would probably end up in a fight, and that would be some great birthday surprise. No, it was better to sit this one out. She would think of some way to make up for it tomorrow.

Fifteen

THE NEXT MORNING, MEG GOT UP EARLY and crawled painfully out of bed. Every muscle in her body screamed in protest. She hurt in places she didn't even know she had muscles. Maybe Abner was right. Maybe she was crazy.

Feeling slightly better after a long, hot shower and some aspirin, she went downstairs, grabbed a cup of coffee, and dashed for the door.

"You need some breakfast, Meggie," said Rosa.

"I'm okay for now, but I'll see you at lunch," Meg called as she shoved her feet into her boots on the back porch. She considered driving up to the bog, but that seemed ridiculous. She thought it was ironic that she'd always wanted a Jaguar but now that she had one it seemed totally inappropriate. Fine for a marketing executive, but useless to a farmer. It was all wrong. Or maybe she was just trying to live the wrong life. As she passed the car, she saw her cell phone inside. At least that might come in handy. She tucked it into her coat pocket and headed for the bog.

She walked up the hill slowly, allowing her muscles to stretch and adjust. Birds were singing; it sounded sweet, almost as if they were welcoming the day or celebrating spring. Today the sky was clear, and she didn't see any fog banks looming on the ocean. She breathed the cool, fresh air and knew deep within her that this wasn't the wrong life. It couldn't be.

She had been worried that Cal might have dropped Clive off before she got there, but there wasn't a soul in sight. She thought about Abner's nasty fit yesterday and figured it was entirely possible that Clive would not be back today or ever. Meg wouldn't blame her, either. She got the wheelbarrow and headed toward the bog that they'd been working on. She slowly bent over and began pulling weeds. Before long, her muscles began to loosen up. She hoped by the end of the week she wouldn't even be sore anymore. She just needed to pace herself. There was no sense in trying to rush it; she could only work so fast.

She had been working quietly for almost an hour before she heard the sound of a vehicle coming up the road. Fortunately it was from the north, so she knew it wasn't Abner. When she spied the blue roof and hood of Cal's old pickup, she waved happily.

"Howdy!" called Clive as she jumped from the rig. "Thanks, Granddad."

Cal waved at Meg. "Heard you had some trouble," he called. Meg climbed out of the bog and walked over to the pickup. She figured she had better do some fast explaining about Abner; she owed that much to Cal.

She leaned against the door. "Abner's not too happy about my working on the bog. I told Clive I'd understand if she didn't feel comfortable coming back."

"She's not worried, Meggie. And neither am I. Abner might be a bit of a loose cannon, but I never heard of him hurting anyone. If I thought different, I wouldn't bring Clive, and I would warn you as well."

"Thanks, Cal."

"You girls have a good day," said Cal before he backed up and drove away.

She went back and joined Clive, but after a few minutes she heard the sound of another engine. This time she got worried, but once again it was coming from the north. A moment later, Erin's green Volvo pulled to a stop. Meg climbed out of the bog and ran up to the road. She hoped everything was okay; she worried that maybe Ashley had had a relapse.

"Hi, Erin," Meg said breathlessly. "What's up?"

Erin and the three girls climbed out of the car. They all had on overalls and boots.

"We've come to help pull weeds, Aunt Meggie," said Hannah.

"Yeah, we're gonna help the cranberries to grow," said Ashley with a big grin.

"You're kidding! I can't believe it. You all came out here just to help? That's so sweet of you."

"Sweet has nothing to do with it. It's spring break, and we needed something to do," said Erin. "And don't you remember how we used to help Grandpa during spring break, Meg? This is our history. Our heritage." Erin and the girls marched down to the bog, and soon everyone was working hard.

Meg used her cellular phone to call Rosa and tell her to expect Erin and the girls for lunch. Hannah and Jennifer turned out to be good workers, and Ashley found a frog to entertain her. At noon, they had nearly a third of the bog cleared, and they all piled into the Volvo and rode down the hill.

Rosa had set up their lunch in the dining room, and to everyone's surprise, Grandmother was seated in a wheelchair at the head of the table.

"Well, don't just stand there gawking," chided the old woman. "Come on, everyone, get washed up and sit down."

Before long, they all were cleaned up and seated around the same long table that Meg remembered sitting at as a girl. Grandpa had always sat at the head then. Today, Grandmother had saved a special spot beside her for Ashley, and she invited Erin to say a blessing.

When Erin finished, Grandmother looked up with glistening eyes. "Now, this is how it always should be," she said in a trembling voice.

Soon they were all chattering and eating, and somewhere midway through the meal, Meg remembered Sunny. She felt bad for forgetting Sunny's birthday, but even more than that, it didn't seem right that Sunny was not here to share in this unexpected gathering. A wave of guilt swept over her. Meg told herself it wasn't her fault; she hadn't planned this little impromptu lunch. Who could have known that Grandmother would get out of bed and sit here with them?

Meg decided to take photos of the group. She got shots of the three girls with their great-grandmother, and Clive offered to take ones of Erin and Meg with Grandmother. Finally, it was time for Grandmother to retire to bed and for the rest of them to return to work. Erin put Ashley down for a nap on the couch, and Rosa promised to watch her so Erin could go back to the bog.

"Are you sure you don't want to stay here and take a nap with Ashley? This kind of work is tough," teased Meg as they headed toward the bog.

"No problem," said Erin. "I do aerobics three times a week. I'm in great shape."

"Tell me that in the morning," said Meg as they plodded up the hill. "How was the dinner for Sunny last night? I didn't find out until too late that it was her birthday. I would have come if I'd known."

"I would have warned you, but it caught us by surprise, too—what with Ashley's illness and all, I blanked out on Sunny's birthday. But we really had a nice time. We ended up taking the girls because we couldn't get a sitter, but it was fine. It was sweet of Siggie to plan the whole thing. I just wish you could have come. In some ways, it was really quite amazing. Sunny was getting very reminiscent and nostalgic. It was a whole new side of her."

"Well, it's probably better that I wasn't there," said Meg as she pulled her gloves out of her coat pocket. "I might have spoiled the whole evening by getting into it with Sunny."

"It's funny, Meg. Lately, Sunny and I have been getting along a whole lot better. I have to admit, it's nice. I'm just sorry to see you having such a hard time with her. But I think maybe she's changing."

"Maybe," said Meg. She wondered if she would ever be able to change, too. It seemed she was always getting stuck in the past when it came to Sunny. Why couldn't she let go of all this old bitterness?

"Who's that?" asked Jennifer, pointing to a lone figure by the bog.

"Oh no," said Meg as they got closer. "It's Jason. I hope this doesn't mean trouble." Clive was walking ahead of the rest, and Meg watched warily as the girl approached Jason. It looked like the two were talking normally.

"I don't see Abner around," said Erin. "Maybe it's okay. You know, Jason's not a bad kid."

"Yeah, I know," said Meg. "I'm just not sure how much influence his dad has over him. And after yesterday's fireworks I'm feeling a little skittish when it comes to that family."

The rest of the group approached Jason and Clive. They might all be females, but they had him outnumbered five to one. Clive turned and smiled.

"Jason came to help out in the bog," she called out.

"Really?" Meg stepped up and looked into Jason's eyes. His cheeks were reddened slightly, but nothing like yesterday. "You really want to help us weed?"

"Yep." Jason looked from Meg to Clive and nodded his head.

"Does your dad know about this?"

"Nope." A slight frown creased his forehead.

"Aren't you concerned about that?"

Jason rubbed his chin as if giving the question serious thought. "I guess so," he finally answered.

"Hmm." Meg sighed. She could certainly use a couple more hands. "Well, I'd love to have your help, but I don't want your blood on my head."

"I don't think there's gonna be any bleeding going on." Jason grinned. "My dad might yell pretty loud, and he can sure make a big stink, but that's about all that comes from it."

Meg stuck out her hand, and Jason shook it firmly. "Well, I'm glad to have you on board, Jason."

"Okay, troops," Erin ordered. "I suggest we break up into pairs and divide the remainder of this bog into thirds. Hannah and Jennifer, you take the east side. Meg and I will do the center, and Jason and Clive can work the west side."

Meg grinned at her sister and saluted. "Yes, sir! We shall divide and conquer."

Soon they were all working in their designated areas. Jason had brought another wheelbarrow, along with an old garden wagon that he said he'd found in the toolshed. Each group now had its own cart to haul the weeds out.

"What do you suppose got into Jason to make him come and help like this?" whispered Meg as she and Erin worked side by side.

"I'd guess it's Clive."

"Ah, I think you may be on to something. Well, whatever it takes to increase the labor force. I just hope Abner doesn't drop by." Meg impatiently shoved a stray lock of hair back from her eyes. She'd forgotten to wear Grandpa's old cap to keep it out of her face.

"Here, let me help," said Erin, pulling a coated elastic hair band from her pocket. "I always keep these handy for the girls. I think your hair's long enough to make a French braid—that should keep it out of your eyes." Erin quickly began weaving

Meg's hair until it was off her face and out of her eyes.

"You have beautiful hair, Meg," said Erin. "What I wouldn't give for that perfect amount of wave and curl. My hair is still as straight as a board. And you should see how the color shines in the sun. It looks just like this old burnished copper kettle that I have."

"Thanks, I think."

Erin twisted the band several times around the end of the braid. "There you go. Lovely."

"And much better," sighed Meg. "That's great, Erin."

Erin plucked several purple asters and stuck them artfully into Meg's hair. "Now it's perfect. Truly a work of art."

"Well, I'm glad those weed flowers are good for something." Meg grinned. "And now back to the grindstone."

The afternoon turned out to be unseasonably warm, and before long they stripped off jackets and sweatshirts. Fortunately, Erin had brought along sunscreen for her girls and shared it with everyone else.

In the middle of the afternoon, Rosa and Ashley came up the hill bearing lemonade and sugar cookies. Ashley proudly carried a stack of paper cups.

"I hope you don't mind, Erin," said Rosa. "She begged for me to bring her out, and she did take a nice long nap."

"Not at all, Rosa. Thank you for bringing her," said Erin. "The fresh air and sunshine will do her good."

"And thanks for the cookies," said Jason as he took another.

They returned to work, and by four o'clock they were closing in on having the entire bog cleared.

Erin looked at her watch. "I hate to go when we're so close to finishing this up, but Jennifer has Awana tonight."

"No problem, Erin. I can't thank you enough for coming out. Can you believe how much we got done? It's really encouraging, especially after yesterday."

Erin rounded up the three girls, and Meg thanked them all again.

"Can we come back, Mommy?" chirped Ashley, and the other two girls chimed in.

"Sure, if you want to," said Erin. "And if Meg doesn't mind. Although you girls got a little silly this afternoon; Meg might not think you're very good workers."

"Of course, I'd love to have you come back. And if I remember right, Erin, we used to get a little silly sometimes, too."

Erin laughed. "I guess we did."

"Can we play in the cabin tomorrow?" asked Jennifer. "It looks like a playhouse."

"I don't see why not," said Meg. "We'll have to check it out and make sure it's safe, though."

"Sounds great," said Erin as she herded the girls up toward the road. "We'll see you tomorrow, then."

"Thanks again," called Meg.

Jason worked for another hour, then announced that it was time for him to go. He promised to be back the next day, and Meg told him that she would pay him the same wages she had offered Clive. He accepted her offer, then waved and took off walking toward the south.

As Meg watched him disappear around a curve, she realized that she hadn't seen their house yet. She knew it was on Briar Hedge property, but there were at least twenty acres beyond the bog that were still undeveloped. She remembered the land being pretty brushy and covered with timber. A few spots held brackish water and could get smelly in the summertime. She supposed Abner must have built a home back there some time ago, but she had no desire to go visiting.

"Looks like quitting time, Clive," said Meg reluctantly. There was still a corner that hadn't been weeded yet, but it was past five o'clock, and she didn't want to keep Clive too late.

"My dad's picking me up today," said Clive as she heaped a pile of weeds into the wagon. "I might as well work until he gets here."

"Okay," Meg agreed as she reached for another clump of tussocks. She had come to hate this cane type of grass that grew so prolifically. But she reminded herself that Cal had said it was one of the easiest weeds to get rid of. She was probably lucky that there seemed to be more of it than anything else.

Clive returned with the empty cart and began pulling tussocks beside her. "You know, Meg, pulling these weeds makes me think of this story in the Bible."

"Oh?" said Meg. Somehow she hadn't thought of Clive as a religious person. But then, why wouldn't she be? It was when Meg had been Clive's age that she had become a Christian, and only when she'd become an adult that she strayed. She hoped she was finding her way back home to God now.

"There's a story about God's Word being like these seeds that are supposed to get planted, but some seeds end up on this really hard, dry ground, so they don't get a chance to grow roots, and soon they blow away or get eaten by birds."

"I sort of remember that story," said Meg as she pulled out a stubborn weed. She stopped to examine the cranberry plant growing below, pushing the loose soil back down around it.

"Yeah, then in the next part of the story, some of the seeds actually start to grow roots, but then the weeds come up and choke the seedlings out."

"Sort of like this?"

"No, not really, because with that part of the story, the weed roots are all mixed into the good plants' roots, and you can't pull out the weeds without pulling up the good plants, too. You know what I mean. It sort of ruins the crop."

"Uh-huh, I think so. Then doesn't the story end with the good seeds going into the good soil? And the plants turn out to be healthy."

"Right. But I think we can add on to this story."

"I thought you weren't supposed to add anything to the Bible," teased Meg.

"I'm not talking about adding anything to the Bible. But listen. See, your granddad did it all right—he prepared the soil and got rid of all the weeds, and then he planted his good seeds, or seedlings, or whatever he used. Anyway, the weeds didn't come until later, but because his plants had good soil and good care, most of them were strong enough to withstand all these weeds. Now look," Clive said, pointing to the cleared bog behind them. "See, they're still there. Of course, they wouldn't have lasted much longer without help. But do you know what I mean?"

Meg nodded slowly, staring at the cranberry plants and trying to let Clive's lesson sink in. "Clive?" she said finally.

"Yeah?"

"Are you thinking about going into the ministry?"

Clive threw back her head and laughed. "No, it's my dad's influence. He's always telling stories to make points. I guess it rubs off after a while."

"Well, it's a nice thing to have rub off—" Meg broke off when she heard a vehicle coming. She listened quietly until she was sure it was coming from the north.

"That sounds like my dad's Blazer," said Clive. She looked to the tiny unweeded patch that still remained. "Too bad I have to go. We almost got this one all done today."

"Don't worry. Before sunset, that corner will be clean," Meg said with resolve.

"Come take a break and meet my dad," called Clive as she picked up her jacket and tennis shoes. Meg followed Clive up to the white Blazer parked in the middle of the road. A tall blonde man climbed out, and Meg squinted toward the sun as she looked up at him. He smiled and waved, then started down toward them. Something about him reminded her of someone she had briefly

146

known once. But of course, he couldn't be the same—

"Meggie Lancaster," he said as he held out his hand, "you probably don't remember me, but—"

"Matt? Matt from Camp Waneema?"

"Wow, you do have a good memory."

"Not that good. I never remembered your last name. Or maybe I just never knew it. So you're Cal Logan's son, and Clive's dad. That must make you Matt Logan."

"Actually, I go by Matthew now. It sounds a little more impressive, I suppose, and in my business, that's important."

"What's Camp Waneema?" asked Clive.

Matthew chuckled. "It was an old run-down camp that the church used to send kids to every summer, until about twelve years ago when the property was purchased for a subdivision. I'd guess it was over twenty years ago that I was a counselor and Meggie here was a reluctant camper." He grinned with a mischievous twinkle in his blue eyes.

Meg turned to Clive. "I was sixteen, and Grandpa decided I should go to church camp. I was furious! I thought summer camp was for babies. Of course, I never let on to Grandpa. But when I got to camp, well, have you ever heard the expression 'Not a happy camper'?"

Clive nodded.

"That's where the saying originated," said Matthew with a wink, and they all laughed. "What Meggie didn't know was that her granddad had asked me to keep an eye on her, without her knowing it, of course."

"You're kidding!" said Meg.

"Nope, it's the truth."

Meg shook her head. "I can't believe it."

"Hey, Dad, come see how great it looks," said Clive, and she pulled him by the hand toward the bog. Meg followed at a short distance. The idea that Matt, from Camp Waneema, was Cal

Logan's son and Grandpa's spy and that they should meet again after all these years.... It was too much. That helped to explain why Clive was such a sweet girl, though. She obviously took after her dad. Of course, that wasn't very fair to her mom. Her mom was probably a wonderful person too.

"This bog looks pretty good," said Matthew, but Meg could hear the question in his voice as she joined them in front of the weeded bog.

"But you're thinking that the rest is incredibly bad," Meg said.

"Well, they've certainly gone downhill." Matthew surveyed the other bogs with a creased forehead. "Too bad."

"Yes, but if we keep this up, we might be able to get several of the bogs into shape before they start to blossom."

He nodded skeptically. "That's quite a job."

"I know." Meg sighed. "But we had a great work crew today. Another few days like this, and you just never know...."

"Well, I have to hand it to you—you've sure got the right attitude. Are you looking for any more workers?" asked Matthew.

"Sure. Do you know anyone? I can't pay much."

Matthew grinned, and his face looked just like Clive's. "I wouldn't expect pay."

"You mean you?" Meg quickly inventoried his expensive suit, neatly striped shirt, and designer tie, and frowned. Clive had already mentioned that her dad was an attorney. Somehow Meg couldn't imagine this man who looked like he'd just stepped out of *GQ* magazine wanting to get his hands dirty.

"Sure, I mean me. Don't judge a book by its cover, Meggie. Remember, my pop ran a cranberry bog for thirty years. I'm pretty sure there's still cranberry juice pumping in these veins."

Meg looked at him in surprise. She'd never heard anyone say that besides her grandparents, but then, Grandpa had spent a lot of time with Cal, and probably Matthew as well. She grinned.

"You're more than welcome to come and lend a hand

anytime you like, Matthew Logan. I have no doubt that you know your way around a cranberry bog."

"That's right, and sometimes I really miss it."

"May I ask why you didn't consider taking over for your dad when his health became a problem?" Meg instantly regretted her intrusion, but Matthew didn't seem to be offended.

"I thought about it. At the time, I wished I had the money to buy him out, but my practice was still barely holding its own, and Pop had a cash offer that would allow him to buy the Feed and Seed. It seemed selfish on my part to try and hang on to the bog under those circumstances. It's been great for Pop, owning the Feed and Seed. Now he gets to share all his knowledge about agriculture without the backbreaking work."

"That makes a lot of sense. I'm sorry, it was none of my business to ask. It's just that Cal feels like an old friend to me, and I just wondered."

"No problem." Matthew looked out over the ocean. "Pop thought the world of your granddad, and so did I. And just for the record, Pop's thrilled with what you're doing out here. I expect he'll be out every few days to check on your progress, as well as to give you some advice."

"Well, I would appreciate that a lot."

"Hey, I'm starving, Dad," said Clive, tugging at his arm.

"Okay. I guess we'd better get going. Nice to meet you again, Meggie."

"Dad," said Clive in an exasperated tone. "Only her family calls her that. Her friends call her Meg." She turned to Meg. "Right?"

"It's okay; you guys are like family. He can call me Meggie if he wants to." Matthew shot her a warm smile. After they drove away, Meg returned to work, thinking fondly of Camp Waneema.

Sixteen

"HELLO, MEGGIE," ROSA SAID FROM THE KITCHEN as Meg deposited her boots and jacket on the back porch.

"Hi, Rosa. I think we should post a warning out here. These porch boards feel so rotten, I'm sure a person could go right through if they stomped their feet too hard."

"I know. I am always very careful when I walk out there, but one of these days I will probably fall right through. And it's a sure thing that Mrs. Lancaster will never hear me screaming. I'll probably be stuck there until the meter man comes and finds me."

Meg laughed. "Hopefully not. Just the same, I think I'll ask Tom about fixing it."

"Wouldn't that be nice."

"Something smells pretty good in here, Rosa."

"It's chicken. Mrs. Lancaster wanted to wait up and have her supper with you tonight, if you didn't come in too late."

"Am I too late?"

"No, but you may want to hurry and get cleaned up. Mrs. Lancaster likes to be all done with dinner and ready for bed by seven."

Meg grinned. She knew that seven o'clock was when *Wheel of*

151

Fortune came on. "Sure, I'll be back down in about ten minutes. Will that be okay?"

"Perfect." Rosa glanced at the little clock on the stove. "I'll set you up a TV tray in your grandmother's room."

Meg showered and got dressed in just under ten minutes, then raced downstairs.

"Whoa," said Rosa as she carried a tray of food from the kitchen. "I didn't really believe you could be ready so fast."

"Well, I'm not usually this quick. Can I help you with anything?"

"Sure. You take this, and I'll go get the teapot."

"Hello, Grandmother," said Meg as she set down the tray. "Rosa said I could join you for dinner."

"Good, good. You're here at last. I was starting to get tired. This has been a long day, Meggie. But how I enjoyed seeing Erin and the girls. They haven't been out here for ages."

"They had a great time. And we got one whole bog weeded. It was amazing. We ended up with a work crew of six people, which really speeded things up."

Rosa brought in the rest of the meal. As they ate, Meg told Grandmother about funny little incidents that had happened during the day and how the girls wanted to come back tomorrow and maybe use the old cabin for a playhouse. It was a pleasant meal, and Grandmother was in good spirits. Meg thought she seemed to be improving.

"Well, it sounds like things are going well, Meggie. I was hoping that you weren't having any problems." The way her voice trailed up ever so slightly at the end made Meg think that Grandmother suspected Abner might cause trouble. Meg wondered if Abner had been by to see her. But then, Meg hadn't seen him pass by on the road. Of course, he could circle around on the main road to get to Grandmother's house.

"No, we didn't have any problems today. In fact, Jason even

came and joined us. He helped out all afternoon." Meg took a sip of tea.

Grandmother smiled. "Oh, that Jason. He's such a fine boy. I'm so glad to hear everything is working out."

"Well, I wouldn't say that everything is working out, Grandmother. I think we might have a few things that need to be ironed out yet. Yesterday, Abner stopped by."

Grandmother set down her cup and looked at Meg.

"He wasn't very happy to see me working on the bog, and he made it pretty clear." Meg studied Grandmother's face closely. She seemed to be considering Meg's words carefully.

"Abner told me that I had no business being up there," continued Meg. She would spare Grandmother the details about what Abner thought of her mental state, not to mention his opinion of Meg. "I told him it was your property and that you were the one who told me to work on it."

Grandmother's thin brows shot up and her pale blue eyes opened wide. "Oh, my. What did he say to that?"

"I don't think you'd like to hear what he said."

Grandmother chuckled. "No, I don't suppose I would. But tell me, Meggie, did you stand up to him?"

"Of course I did."

"That's my girl."

"You haven't changed your mind or anything? You still want me up there, right?"

"Of course. Why would I change my mind?"

"I don't know. I just wanted to make sure."

Grandmother sighed and leaned back. "I'm awful tired, Meggie. Do you want to tell Rosa that I'm ready for bed?"

Meg looked at her watch. It was quarter past seven, so Rosa would be in the middle of her show. "How about if I help you get started, Grandmother?"

"You?"

"Sure. Don't you think I'm able?"

Grandmother chuckled again. "Well, I don't doubt you're able. I'm just surprised that you're willing."

By the time Meg had brought Grandmother a warm soapy washcloth and gotten her dentures soaking, Rosa scurried in.

"Bless you, Meggie," said Rosa. "Now you run along. I'll take care of Mrs. Lancaster."

"Watch out, Rotha," lisped Grandmother with a puckered toothless mouth. Meg tried not to smile. She had never seen the old woman without her dentures. "Meggie will get your job."

Rosa laughed. "It's all hers anytime she wants it."

"Good night, Grandmother," said Meg.

"Good night, dear. Thleep well."

Meg choked back giggles as she closed the door. It was fun seeing this side of Grandmother. Such a contrast to the stern-faced grandmother of Meg's childhood. What had become of the pompous, self-important woman who had seldom smiled and never approved of Meggie?

After dinner, Meg went through the box of mementos Grandpa had left her. There were some old photographs and books, but the thing that brought back the best memories for her was a small, tattered notebook filled with all of Grandpa's cranberry recipes. Meg could almost smell the fragrance of cranberry bread and cranberry cake and cranberry muffins as she leafed through the pages. She piled everything back into the box and took it back to her room, vowing that one day soon she would try out some of those recipes.

It wasn't until Meg was in bed that she realized she had forgotten to call Sunny and apologize for missing the birthday dinner. She felt as if she were accumulating guilt about Sunny every time she turned around. She glanced at the little tin alarm clock by her bed, the same one that had been in this room when she was a child. In fact, almost nothing in the room had changed.

It was only ten o'clock. Early for Sunny. Meg could easily go out in the hallway and use the wall phone there to call Sunny. But she was so tired, and the bed with its old feather mattress seemed to pull at her. She knew it would take only moments to lull her to sleep. Meg flicked off the light and rolled over. In the morning she would call and see if she could arrange to get together with Sunny. In the morning.

Seventeen

IN THE MORNING, MEG WOKE to the sound of the phone jangling. She jumped out of bed and dashed to the hallway to answer it.

"Hello?" she said groggily, wondering who in the world would be calling so early. It was barely even light outside.

"Meg? This is Sigfried."

"Sigfried? What is it?"

"Meg, Sunny is dead."

Meg didn't answer. Her head began to buzz, and her stomach rose and fell. No, it could not be true. She was having a bad dream. This was not happening.

"Meg? Are you there?" His voice was urgent. "Did you hear me, Meg?"

"I don't know." She leaned against the wall and felt her knees grow weak beneath her. "Did you say—" She couldn't repeat the words. She must have heard him wrong.

"Meg, Sunny died early this morning. I found her. I've called Erin already—"

"No." She opened her mouth to scream, but the words came out in a hoarse whisper. "No. No, it can't be! It just can't be." She slid down the wall into a squatting position, wrapping her arms around her knees. "It can't be," she whispered. "It's not fair. Not fair." Sunny couldn't die, not yet. The phone slipped from her hands, and she crumpled over and began to sob uncontrollably.

She didn't know how long she sat on the hallway floor. The next thing she knew, Rosa was there, drawing her gently to her feet and untangling the phone cord from her arms and placing the receiver back on the hook. Meg watched her as if from a great distance and felt numb. Then Rosa wrapped an arm around her shoulders and guided her back into the bedroom. She heard Rosa muttering softly in Spanish as she tucked Meg under the covers. Her mother had never tucked her in like that before. And now her mother was dead. Meg curled into a tight ball and cried silently until she went to sleep. She didn't care if she ever woke up. Ever.

It was the sunlight that woke her, filtering in through the dusty curtains, shining stark and bright without feeling, and right into her face. She tried to brush it away, but it was no use. Finally she got up and stared out the window, despising the sunshine and blue sky. It was profane.

"How could you do this, God?" she demanded. "How could you take her like that, when you know that—" Tears filled her eyes again. "You know that I never got to make things right with her. I never got to say—" She couldn't make herself say it. Not even now. "It's so unfair, God. It's just so unfair. Just when I was beginning to trust you. How could you allow this to happen?"

She tugged on jeans and a sweater and slipped down the stairway and out the door, breaking into a run toward the beach steps. She felt guilt pangs of a different kind now, heaped upon the mountain that was already crushing her. Perhaps she should comfort Grandmother and call Erin. But how could she comfort anyone? What comfort was there? She remembered how Grandmother used to say there was "no comfort for the wicked." Now she knew exactly what that meant.

On the beach, she ran and ran, as if to escape. Finally, she felt as if her chest were caving in, and her legs refused to go any farther. She fell to her knees in the wet strip of sand at the water's edge, where the surf was flowing back and forth, and looked up to the sky with tightly clenched fists pressed against her sides.

"Why?" she screamed into the air. A lone gull answered her with a haunting cry, and the ice-cold seawater washed across her knees and over her feet, soaking her jeans and shoes, but still she didn't move. She didn't care. She continued to whisper the hideous word again and again. "Why? Why? Why?"

Finally her legs grew numb from the stinging surf, and she stood up stiffly in the now ankle-deep tide and started to walk straight out into the ocean. She couldn't feel the coldness anymore. She couldn't feel anything. She kept walking until the waves rose above her chest and she felt her feet gently swept off the ocean floor. And even that did not alarm her. She felt as if something were calling her. Something lonely and cold and unfeeling. It felt kindred. Like her own heart.

It wasn't until a wave slapped her in the face, forcing salt water into her mouth and nose, that she came to her senses and turned around. Afterward, she didn't recall swimming to shore, but she figured the tide had done its job, carrying her back like a useless piece of debris that even the ocean didn't want.

It wasn't until she collapsed on the beach, gasping for breath, that she began to see something. She had heard of people who witnessed their lives flashing before their eyes after a close brush with death, but she didn't think that's what this was. She didn't see any sweet scenes from her childhood or even a bright light at the end of a tunnel. No, what she saw was a woman consumed by bitterness, resentment, and unforgiveness. And the woman was her.

It was then that she prayed a different kind of prayer. No questions this time, no demands. Just three words—again and again. *Help me, God. Help me, God.* It was all she knew to say. And oddly enough, it comforted her some. It felt like a beginning.

As she walked slowly back to the house, a strange sense of peace enveloped her. It was as if she could feel God's hand upon her, giving her comfort. It made no sense, but it felt stunningly real. She wanted it to be real—but was her faith strong enough to hold on to it?

"God, I need you," she prayed, out loud this time. "I need you to show me how to believe in you again."

Back at the house, she changed into dry clothes and went down to Grandmother's room, knocking lightly on the door. She grew concerned when there was no answer. Perhaps the news had been too much for Grandmother's weakened heart. Or perhaps she was asleep. Meg quietly opened the door and peeked inside. Grandmother held up her hand and motioned Meg in. The old woman looked tired and gray. Her eyes were dull and rimmed in red. Her hair, which was usually kept neatly in a hairnet, now hung in wisps, giving her an even more haggard appearance.

"Come sit with me, Meggie." She said the words slowly as if speaking were painful, and Meg scooted a chair close to the bed and sat down. Grandmother stretched out a hand, and Meg reached over and held tightly to it.

"I know how it feels to lose a mother, Meggie." She dabbed her eyes with a lace-trimmed hankie. "It's almost as hard as losing a child."

Meg nodded. She didn't know what it was like to have a child, let alone lose one. But she knew this wasn't easy. A dull ache had rooted itself in her chest. Although she tried to think of words that might comfort Grandmother, none would come.

"Meggie, I know you and Sunny had your differences, but I also know that she loved you."

Meg turned and looked into Grandmother's face. "Really?" she said in honest surprise. "How do you know that? I don't even know that."

Grandmother sighed. "I just know, child."

Silent tears streaked down Meg's face again, and she tried to speak. "But I don't think Sunny knew that I loved her." It was the first time Meg had said it, but she knew it was true. She did love Sunny. Sure, there were many times when she couldn't stand her. But wasn't that sometimes a part of love? Why had she never told Sunny? That was the part that ached.

"She knew, Meggie."

"How do you know these things, Grandmother? How do you know for sure? Or are you just saying all this to make me feel better?"

"If I didn't believe them, then I would have died long ago. I don't know exactly how I know, Meggie. I just hope I'm not wrong." Fresh tears poured down Grandmother's cheeks, and Meg was sorry she had questioned the old woman. What right did she have to disturb what might be the only peace that Grandmother could find at a time like this?

"I'm sorry, Grandmother. It's just that I'm still in shock."

"So am I, Meggie."

"Do you know? What happened, I mean? How she died?" Meg was almost afraid to find out the answer. Already suffocating in guilt, she wasn't sure how much more she could take.

"Erin called about an hour ago and filled me in on the details. She only just learned them from Sigfried herself. It seems that Sunny had been diagnosed with ovarian cancer some time ago. Apparently the cancer had already spread by the time she went to the doctor. You know how she is—I mean—was…. She never liked going to doctors. I'm sure she always thought I was a hypochondriac." Grandmother leaned her head back. "If only it could have been me instead of her. That would make more sense."

"No, Grandmother. Don't say that."

"I know, I know. These things are not for us to decide."

"Was Sunny getting treatment? She was pretty thin, but she

didn't look sick. I had no idea—" Meg choked on the words. Every single memory that came to her about Sunny was tainted with recollections of Meg's own selfish bitterness and hostility. If only she had known that Sunny was dying. Why couldn't Sunny have told her?

"No. Erin said that the chances of treatment curing a cancer as advanced as Sunny's were not very good, and Sunny decided not to bother. You know how she was. Such a free spirit. She was such a happy child. Do you know where the name *Sunny* came from? Daddy used to call her Sunbeam. Before long, that got shortened to Sunny. I can still remember her as a little girl. When she was three or four, I made her a little yellow dress from a Shirley Temple pattern. I can still see her skipping around; she did look just like a little sunbeam. Pretty and bright and gay..."

Grandmother closed her eyes, continuing to talk as if she were going back in time. "Oh, Sunny, such a happy-go-lucky girl. Never afraid of anything. Always ready to try something new. Daddy's little sunshine. I'm so sorry I was so busy, Sunny. Too busy to appreciate my little sunbeam. Too busy to notice. I'm sorry...." Grandmother quit talking, but her lips kept moving as if she were trying to communicate something. Meg felt this was a moment she shouldn't be witnessing. She rose and quietly slipped out of the room.

Rosa was sitting in the kitchen, but got up quickly when she saw Meg start for the stairs.

"Meggie?" called Rosa. "You should have something to eat. You need to keep up your strength."

Meg looked at the kind woman who had so gently helped her off the floor and put her to bed earlier. Rosa's eyes and nose were red. Of course, she too had known Sunny. Perhaps even better than Meg had.

"I'm not hungry, Rosa. I just want to rest for a bit. I'm fine, really."

"Well, I am going to bring you up some tea and toast anyway," said Rosa firmly.

"Okay. Thanks, Rosa."

Meg nibbled a corner of toast and drank a cup of tea. She couldn't sleep, and being alone with her thoughts was frightening. She knew that Grandmother would probably need to rest this afternoon. And after all the emotional upheaval of the morning, Meg wondered if Grandmother's doctor should be called. Perhaps this stress was taking its toll on her heart. She would have to check with Rosa.

And what was the family supposed to do when someone died? Weren't there arrangements to be made? Decisions about how and who and where. Had Meg, by falling apart and then running away, left Erin to deal with these unpleasant things alone? Poor Erin.

Meg dialed Erin's number and waited as the phone rang again and again. Just when she was about to hang up, Erin answered breathlessly.

"Hello, Erin. This is Meg. Did I interrupt something, or wake you? I just wanted to—" Again her voice broke and her hands began to shake.

"No, you didn't interrupt anything. We were all sitting outside. The girls are so upset, and we were sitting in the garden, talking. Why don't you come over, Meg?"

"Could I?"

"Of course. Do you want Tom to come pick you up? You sound pretty upset."

"No, I can drive. Actually, I think it might do me good to drive. I'm coming right now. Is that okay?"

"It's better than okay—" Erin's voice broke this time.

"See you."

Meg didn't remember the drive, but she pulled into the driveway safely, and even before she climbed out of the car, her sister

163

was running to meet her. They hugged and cried for a long time.

"Tom and the girls are picking flowers. I know it's probably early, but the girls wanted to pick them for Sunny's grave. Come on inside and have a cup of coffee. Sigfried is coming over in about an hour."

They sat in a corner of the living room and talked about Sunny. It was a relief to hear Erin remembering some of the good times, and Meg listened intently, trying to memorize each one and paste it into her own memory like a photo album. Meg wondered why she didn't have memories like that of her own. Was it because Erin was older? Or because Erin was more creative and imaginative? Certainly Erin wasn't making them up. And even if she was, and Meg was sure that she wasn't, it didn't matter, for when Erin spoke it was like a soothing balm on a burning, open wound.

"Hello," called Sigfried as he came down the hall and into the living room. His face looked tired and much older. "I saw Tom out back, and he told me to let myself in. He thought it might be better if I spoke to you two about the...the details. Without the girls listening."

"Come sit down, Siggie," said Erin. "Can I get you some coffee or anything?"

"No thanks." He sat down on the edge of the sofa and held his hat in his lap. It was olive green with a little feather in the band; it reminded Meg of something a Swiss yodeler might wear. He cleared his throat and began to recite what sounded like a well-rehearsed speech.

"As you both now know, Sunny was well aware that she was dying. And in a Sunny-like fashion, she was determined to live life to the very end as if nothing was the matter. It was her desire that no one be aware of her struggle. Other than me, of course. However, in her final months she did take time to get her affairs in order, and she has left me a rather detailed list of instructions."

164

He went on to explain that Sunny's wish was to be cremated and that she had already made this arrangement with the local funeral home, and it had, in fact, already taken place. Erin and Meg looked at each other with wide eyes. It was all so sudden, so shocking.

"But what about a service?" exclaimed Erin.

"Just wait, I'm getting to that." Sigfried took a paper out of his pocket and unfolded it, then silently read it and folded it again. "Sunny wanted to have a brief memorial service at Briar Hedge, up by the bog. She said that was where she'd had some of her happiest childhood memories. She also wanted to have a small evening showing at her gallery the following night, and she gave me specific instructions for how to set this up."

"Isn't there anything for us to do?" asked Erin. "This all feels so cut and dried, so impersonal. The girls wanted to put together flowers for her funeral—" Big tears began to pour down her cheeks, and Meg put an arm around her shoulder. She felt the same way.

"I know, I know," said Sigfried in a soothing voice. "But believe me, Sunny thought she was doing you all a favor by taking care of everything like this. She thought that would leave you free to remember who she was, and she hoped that might help you to be able to celebrate her life."

Erin sat up straight. "I'm sorry. I'm just being selfish. Go on, Siggie. I know this is hard on you, too."

He nodded solemnly. "Just a couple more things. Sunny has arranged for you two, along with me, to fly out over the ocean and sprinkle her ashes. And then she has some things packaged up for you in her apartment that I'm supposed to give you after the show in the gallery. And just so you'll know, she has left the gallery and everything in her apartment to both of you, fifty-fifty. It's all written up legally. You'll find that she had next to nothing in the bank, but no major debts, either. Everything she had went into the gallery. Her only stipulation for the gallery was that you keep me on as manager."

"Of course," said Erin. "We wouldn't have it any other way. Right, Meg?"

Meg nodded dumbly. This was too much for her to take in right now. It still seemed unreal that Sunny was gone, and to be talking about all these plans felt wrong. She tried to focus and listen as Erin and Siggie ironed out a few more details, but none of it made sense to her.

As soon as Sigfried left, Meg turned to Erin and blurted, "I know it's stupid and old-fashioned and probably, like you said, selfish, but I want her to have a regular funeral. I want her to have a grave so I can go there. I need to take her flowers. I need a place to go to where I can tell her I'm sorry."

"I know, Meggie. I know exactly how you feel."

Eighteen

FRIDAY WAS SET AS THE DAY THEY WERE TO GATHER at the bog to remember Sunny. The service was at one o'clock, but Meg walked up early to look around. The sun was hidden behind a thick curtain of fog, and she was grateful for the gloom. She knew Sunny would probably have preferred clear blue skies, but the gray mist better suited Meg's heavy heart.

She walked around the weeded bog and, to her dismay, spotted new weeds already coming up. Maybe it was all a useless battle. She picked up a dead weed lying on the road that had probably escaped from an overloaded wheelbarrow, and walked over to toss it in one of the dump piles. She dusted her hands off, trying not to get her dark wool pants dirty. She and Erin had discussed what would be appropriate apparel for a memorial service in a cranberry bog and had finally agreed that nice pants and jackets were sufficient. Grandmother would probably think that black dresses would be more fitting for a funeral, but then, this wasn't a funeral.

Suddenly Meg remembered her reason for coming up here early. It was probably foolish, and it wasn't as if she believed in ghosts, but she had truly hoped to communicate with Sunny. Somehow. She picked a bunch of daffodils and laid them next to the podium that Sigfried had set up that morning, along with several rows of white folding chairs. He decided to forgo the canopy because it didn't look like rain.

Meg had no idea what Sigfried's memorial program would consist of, but he seemed to have everything under control. Meg gazed toward the horizon and sighed. The firs on the far side of the bog were shrouded in mist, giving them an eerie, yet beautiful, look. Maybe Sunny's idea to be up here was a good one after all.

"Sunny, can you hear me?" she whispered. The question reminded Meg of the many times when as a girl she would poke her sleeping mother to see if she were still alive. Sunny had always had a penchant for parties. For Sunny, a party could consist of merely herself and someone else, it never mattered who, and a bottle of cheap booze. They would laugh and drink through the night, and more often than not, Sunny would go to sleep wherever she landed. Usually it was the couch or an easy chair. Occasionally it was the kitchen floor, and once it had been on the front porch steps.

That was the time that had scared Meg the most. Erin had been gone by then, living in the commune, and Meg had found Sunny splayed across the front porch, face ashen and mouth gaping open. Meg almost called an ambulance, but first she poked Sunny. When Sunny finally moaned and rolled over, Meg knew it was nothing more than another hangover. By that time, Meg was almost beyond embarrassment at such displays because she had plenty of problems of her own. But it hurt her enough to make her resolve to get out. That was the night Meg decided to drop out of high school and get her GED. She thought that might be the best way to get on with her life and out of Sunny's. And a few months later, Grandpa died, severing Meg's last tie to her family. After his funeral, she had left, planning never to return.

But here she was, back in the midst of her family. Somehow, this time she felt more tightly bound to them than ever before.

Meg spied Erin's green Volvo creeping up the hill. The others had been asked to park at the house, but Erin and Tom were bringing Grandmother up. Everyone had been surprised when Grandmother insisted on getting out of bed and coming, but they all knew better than to argue with the old woman. Tom pulled the car close to where the chairs were set up, and he and Erin helped Grandmother slowly out and into her wheelchair. At first Grandmother had told them she would come without the wheelchair, but on this point they had insisted. Her balance was not dependable after all the time she had spent in bed, and they knew her strength was minimal.

Tom wheeled the chair over to the front row where Sigfried had left a space, and parked it, carefully setting the brakes. People were coming now, winding up the hill like a solemn parade. Meg was surprised by the number. It didn't look like Sigfried had rented enough chairs. Some would probably have to stand.

"Should we sit down?" asked Erin as she and her daughters approached.

"Yes, Grandmother would probably appreciate not having to sit alone," said Meg. They walked over and sat down in the front row. Ashley sat next to Meg, and after a few minutes, she reached out to take Meg's hand. Meg held the soft, tiny hand in hers and thought this was perhaps the best comfort she had known since Sunny's death. A tear slipped down Meg's cheek, cooling in the slight ocean breeze.

Soon all the chairs were filled, and at least twenty or thirty people were still standing. Meg shouldn't have been surprised. Sunny had always been an outgoing person with a large circle of friends, and even after she gave up her drinking parties, she still enjoyed people—and people enjoyed her. What caught Meg off guard was that she knew hardly any of these people who were apparently her mother's good friends. But then, why should she? They had lived separate lives for the past twenty years.

The only people Meg recognized, besides her own family and Rosa, were Cal, Clive, and Matthew. With Matthew was a pretty blonde woman with a small, turned-up nose just like Clive's. She had to be the girl's mother. For some reason, the thought made Meg frown. She glanced around the rest of the crowd. Abner and his family hadn't arrived yet. Surely they would come. But then, Abner was such a strange man; maybe the memorial for his aunt meant nothing to him.

Sigfried hurried around, trying to greet people and make sure that no chairs were left empty in a standing-room-only crowd. He had placed up front a large wreath of pink chrysanthemums that had been delivered at the last moment, probably sent by someone who hadn't heard about Sunny's request that donations be sent to the homeless shelter in lieu of flowers. Just as Sigfried began to make his way to the podium, the sound of an engine roared from the south, and a moment later, a dark Suburban pulled up.

Out climbed Abner, wearing a blue three-piece polyester suit with cowboy boots. His vest buttons strained across his front, and Meg was sure that his pants had once been bell-bottoms, or at least flared. Jason wore clean black jeans and a white shirt tucked in and buttoned up to the neck. But the strangest member of the threesome was a woman Meg knew must be Phoebe. She was nearly as wide as she was tall, and her lilac polyester tent dress swayed back and forth as she huffed towards them in wobbly spike-heeled shoes that kept getting stuck in the dirt. It seemed incredible that she didn't tip over and roll down the hill. But when the woman was close enough for Meg to see, her face looked sweet and kind. Meg instantly liked her and felt sorry that she was stuck with a man like Abner.

Sigfried graciously greeted the three and invited Phoebe to take his chair, apologizing that Jason and Abner would have to stand. Abner made a sound of disgust and shuffled off to the back of the crowd.

Sigfried looked at his watch, then made his way to the podium again. He cleared his throat and began to speak.

"As you all know, we have gathered today to remember our dear friend, Sunny Lancaster. Sunny was an unconventional woman in many ways. She told me once that she had made it her goal in life to break all the rules. And I'm sure many of you will agree that Sunny managed to break a lot of rules. But the rules that Sunny most often broke were ones like 'never talk to strangers' or 'proceed with caution' or 'watch your step.'

"Sunny was seldom careful. At the age of fifty, she took up sky-diving, and just last year she went bungee-jumping off a bridge." Sigfried paused and took a breath. "Sunny asked that one of her favorite songs be played today. Like Sunny, it's unconventional. In fact, I doubt if it's ever been played at a funeral before." He bent over and pushed a button on a portable stereo. The guitar chords of the Beatles' "Fool on the Hill" penetrated the silence of the misty bog.

When Sigfried pressed the stop button on the stereo, Meg was certain there were few dry eyes left in the crowd, including her own. She heard sniffling and throat clearing, and even Grandmother, who surely had no idea who the Beatles were, had tears running down her powdered cheeks.

"Now, Sunny didn't want that song to make you sad. She just wanted to remind you that it's okay to be different. It's okay to chase your dreams, even if people think you're crazy, think that you're the fool on the hill. But Sunny also wanted me to make it very clear today that she was never completely proud of, or even pleased with, her life. She said if she could live it over again, she would do some things differently. There were a lot of things she wouldn't change—she told me that just a few nights ago, on her birthday. She said she would rather live her life all wrong, with a passion for living and an honest and searching heart, than live it properly and flawlessly, and constantly afraid of making a mistake."

Sigfried looked over to where Matthew Logan was sitting and

nodded. "Sunny asked that another good friend of hers might share today. She met Matthew Logan through her dear friend Abby." Sigfried smiled at the woman next to Matthew. "A lot of you know Abby Logan by her beautiful oil paintings that hang in Sunny's gallery. But what you might not know is that Matthew and Abby have a fellowship group that meets in their home, and Sunny had been attending it for the past couple of months. Sunny said that it was because of what Matthew and Abby shared that she was finally ready to go home. Come on up, Matthew."

Meg could hardly see for the tears in her eyes. But she listened as Matthew explained how Sunny had only recently come into their lives, yet would leave an impression that would change them all forever.

"Sunny was never afraid. She was a mover, a shaker, a seeker. Never content to settle for status quo. Some of you may remember her fighting with the chamber of commerce to get hanging flower baskets. Some of you may remember how she worked on the downtown commission to clean up the waterfront and bring more tourism to what had recently been a dying mill town. But what you may not know, and what Sunny most wanted me to share with you today, was that Sunny had finally found the ultimate answer to her lifelong search."

Matthew proceeded to share a simple gospel message, not unlike the one Meg had heard him share so many years before at Camp Waneema in front of the big, crackling campfire. What stunned Meg was when he said that Sunny had accepted this message and that she'd become a Christian just weeks before her death. Meg felt the tears, cool and wet, on her cheeks. Sunny, a Christian? It seemed too incredible to be true. And yet, she and Erin had both noticed some changes in Sunny.

Matthew finished by praying a simple prayer. Then people began moving around, visiting briefly, and finally heading slowly back down the hill.

Sigfried and the Logans had been invited by Erin to share a meal at Briar Hedge with the family. Meg knew that Abner's family was also invited, but she hoped they would decline, or at least that Abner would. Unfortunately, it looked as if that was not to be as they piled into their Suburban and rumbled down the hill, causing people to scatter off the dirt road in order to let them by.

Rosa already had almost everything laid out and ready for the meal, but Meg volunteered to help with the last-minute details. She needed something to distract her from her thoughts, and she wanted to keep a safe distance from Abner. The kitchen provided a good refuge. As she worked at keeping the buffet table laden with food, Meg wished she could meet Abby. She wanted to see what kind of woman Matthew's wife was, and it intrigued her that Abby had been an artist friend of Sunny, and a Christian, as well.

"Meg, you go get yourself something to eat, before it's too late," said Rosa when things finally slowed down in the kitchen. Meg peeked in to spy where Abner had settled, and saw that his back was to the buffet table. She slipped in and quickly filled a plate, then went over to an old deacon's bench nestled beneath the stairs. She sat down and began to pick at the Waldorf salad, not really hungry, but not knowing what else to do.

"May I join you?" Meg looked up to see Abby Logan standing before her with lifted brows.

"Of course." Meg scooted over to make room. "Actually, I was hoping to get to meet you, Abby."

"Me, too." Abby smiled and sat down. "Although I feel like I already know you. Sunny told me a lot about you. It was so nice that you got to come back before...well, before Sunny had to leave."

Meg nodded. "I guess so."

"Have you been to her apartment yet?"

"No. Why?"

"I think Sunny left some things there for you. But I imagine

Siggie will take care of that. I wanted you to know that Sunny told me quite a few things about her life. In fact, if you ever want to talk about anything...I mean, if you have any questions, I'd be happy to talk. Even though Sunny was a lot older, we got to be very close. We were sort of like kindred spirits, if you know what I mean."

Meg didn't know. She couldn't understand what this nice woman, who must be about the same age as Meg, could have possibly had in common with Sunny. But Meg just nodded numbly and took a bite of ham.

"I don't want to intrude, Meg. I know that grief is a very personal thing. But sometimes it helps to have someone to talk to."

"Thanks." Meg laid down her fork and looked at Abby. "I'll probably take you up on that offer. It's just so hard to think right now. But I really appreciate it." She paused. "There is one thing I can't quite understand. Is it true—did Sunny really become a Christian?"

Abby nodded. "It's true."

"I'm so surprised," said Meg. "I never would have guessed."

"Well, I'm sure you've heard it said, and I've seen it happen, that God works in mysterious ways."

Meg slowly shook her head. She felt fresh tears burning in her eyes, and couldn't think of anything else to say.

Abby smiled and squeezed her hand. "Say, it sounds like you've made some good progress on the bog, Meg. Clive has been thrilled to be involved. I hope she can keep helping you."

"I hope so, too," said Meg, grateful for the change in subject. "She's such a good worker, and a delightful girl."

Abby looked over to where Clive and Matthew were sitting, talking to Tom. "Yes, we certainly think so."

"Did I hear Sigfried right, Abby? Are you an artist?"

Abby nodded.

"I've only been in the gallery a couple of times," Meg continued. "I'm trying to remember if I saw your name. What type of paintings do you do?"

"Mostly oils. And usually safe subjects like seascapes and lighthouses, and an old house or building once in a while."

"I remember a number of really large paintings, done from different perspectives. There was one of an old house, and it looks like the house is really tall. Are those yours?"

Abby nodded. "Those are mine."

"They're beautiful. They were my favorite group of paintings in the gallery. For what you call a safe subject, they sure have a lot of feeling in them."

"Thanks. I'm trying a few new things. Sunny really encouraged me not to dwell in the safety zone forever. But I can only take one little step at a time when it comes to my art. I don't know how I'll move any faster without Sunny to prod me along, although Matthew may pick up where she left off. He has become a huge fan of your mother."

"Really?"

"Yes, everything he said today was completely true. As much of an influence as he had on her, she had quite an impact on him as well. He keeps talking about living life to the fullest and taking risks. I think God used Sunny in an amazing way with Matthew."

"Really?" Meg knew she probably sounded like a broken record player, but what Abby was saying was incredible. "I have to admit that it boggles my mind to think that Sunny could have an influence on someone so together as Matthew."

Abby looked puzzled. "I didn't know that you knew Matthew."

"I don't know him that well. In fact, all these years I didn't even know he was Cal's son."

Abby still looked confused. "I thought you'd been gone for the past twenty years."

"Right. You see, I met Matthew at a summer camp eons ago.

175

In fact, I had quite a crush on your husband. Well, he wasn't married then, of course. In fact, I was only sixteen, but my crush lasted a whole summer. Of course, he barely knew who I was."

Abby chuckled.

"I guess it is sort of funny," Meg said with a wry smile.

"No, it's not that. It's just that Matthew is not my husband."

Now Meg was puzzled, and embarrassed, and at the same time, glad for some reason. "But what about Clive? And isn't your last name Logan?"

Abby nodded. "Yes. I'm Matthew's sister. I moved back to town to stay with him and Clive after his wife died nine years ago. I needed a place to live where I could paint, and Matthew needed someone to help him with Clive."

"Oh, I feel so stupid."

Abby reached out and touched her arm. "Don't. It's an understandable mistake. How would you know?"

"The three of you just looked so much like a family. And Clive looks so much like you."

"Thanks. And we are a family."

"Abby," called Matthew as he walked over to them. "I hate to interrupt you, but I have an appointment at four."

Abby turned to Meg. "Well, unless I want to walk, I'd better go. I look forward to getting to know you better, Meg. Please call me, anytime, if you need someone to talk to. I assume we'll see you tomorrow night?"

"Tomorrow night?"

"The gathering at the gallery."

"Right," said Meg. "I almost forgot."

Nineteen

THE NEXT MORNING, Meg and Erin both agreed that Sigfried should have the honor of scattering Sunny's ashes as they flew out over the Pacific in the small single-engine plane. Meg wouldn't admit that the thought of handling Sunny's remains made her uneasy, but she suspected Erin felt the same. They both watched as Sigfried held the urn out the window with a straight arm, then ceremoniously turned it upside down, holding it there for several seconds as they watched the powdery white ashes get swept up in the wind. The pilot circled back around, and Meg thought she saw a small white cloud drifting down, but then decided it was probably just the sunlight reflecting off the window.

Sigfried kept his face turned to the window as the pilot headed toward shore, looking back to the place where he had let the ashes fall. When he finally turned around, there were two lines of tears streaming down his face. It was the first time Meg had seen him cry. Trying to respect his privacy, she looked the other way, studying the line of pale sand bordering the blue of the water. It was obvious that Sigfried had loved Sunny very much, whatever their relationship had been.

After they landed and climbed from the plane, Sigfried gave

Erin and Meg a hug right there on the tarmac.

"Sunny was a beautiful woman," he said. "You two should be very proud to be her daughters." As they walked back to their cars, Sigfried reminded them of Sunny's final exhibit at the gallery that night.

"I know you've made it clear that you won't fill us in on any of the details, but can you at least tell us who might be there or what we should wear?" asked Erin. "And can I assume it's okay for the girls to come?"

"Certainly. The girls will enjoy it, I think. As far as people, it's just some of Sunny's closest friends," Sigfried explained. "And I think Sunny would like it if you considered it a festive occasion. Dress as if for a grand party. That's what Sunny intended it to be."

When Meg got back to Grandmother's house, she was surprised to find Grandmother sitting on the porch in her old rocker. Her aluminum walker was parked close by.

"Grandmother?" said Meg. "Did you walk out here all by yourself?"

Grandmother nodded her head smugly. "I'm tired of being an invalid, Meggie. I've decided if I'm going to die, then I might as well have a good time on my way out." She rocked gently back and forth. "This chair feels grand, Meggie."

"Just be careful you don't trip over any of these loose floorboards," warned Meg as she sat down on the top step and looked toward the ocean.

"You get her ashes all taken care of, then?" Grandmother's voice was tight, as if the words were painful. Meg knew the idea of cremation went against the grain with the old woman.

"Yes." The ashes were probably settling into the water as they spoke.

"I saw a little plane out there. I wondered if that might have been you folks." There was a slight wistfulness in her voice, and Meg wondered if she might have wanted to come.

178

"It probably was us. It was a just quick flight; we went up and out over the water, then back to the airstrip."

"Ashes to ashes, dust to dust...."

They sat quietly on the porch, the only noises the gentle creak of the old wicker rocker and the roar of the ocean in the distance. In some odd and unexplainable way, it felt like an eternal moment to Meg. Like something that would be etched into a corner of her memory forever. Meg wasn't sure how much time had passed, but finally Grandmother stirred. She began to reach for her walker, and Meg got up, asking if she needed any help.

"Well, it might not be smart for me to overdo right away," said Grandmother as she pulled herself slowly up to the walker.

"No. You should pace yourself and build up your strength." Meg walked beside her, watching carefully in case Grandmother needed help. But the old woman slowly plodded along, her slippers making a swishing sound as she moved across the hardwood floor to her bedroom.

"You were supposed to call me," cried Rosa as she came running from the kitchen. "Oh, Meggie. Thank goodness you're there."

"I'll help Grandmother to her bed, Rosa. I think she's due for a rest. Isn't she doing well, though?"

"Yes, but I do not want her to fall."

"Don't you worry, Rosa," said Grandmother. "I'm just fine."

It took a while to get Grandmother settled into bed, and when Meg finally pulled the covers up, Grandmother looked exhausted.

"Are you planning on coming to the exhibit tonight, Grandmother?" asked Meg as she adjusted the blinds.

"I don't know. I think I'll wait and see how spunky I feel later on."

"That sounds like a good idea. I'll be out at the bog today. I'll have my cell phone if you or Rosa need me for anything."

"I still can't get over the idea of those phones with no cords," said Grandmother sleepily as Meg slipped out.

Meg spent the rest of the day up at the bog. She started weeding the bog that was a level lower than the one they had finished a few days ago. When she quit in the early evening and looked over her work, it didn't look as if she had made any progress. She sat down on a rock and studied the weedy bogs. Was this a hopeless task? At first she had been driven by the desire to save Grandpa's bog and preserve Grandmother's water rights. But what if it couldn't be done? Perhaps she was like Don Quixote, tilting at windmills.

A breeze swept up from the ocean, and she lifted her gaze to look out over the water. The sun was starting to go down, and a cluster of clouds was huddled at the horizon, catching the last rays of light in brilliant bursts of pink and orange. She stared at the sky as one color shifted into another. If only she had brought her camera. But there was no time to run back down and fetch it and still be able to enjoy this incredible sight.

Suddenly she recalled the song at Sunny's memorial service yesterday. The Beatles sang about the fool on the hill who lived in his own world, never paying attention to the real world around him. Maybe that song had been for Meg. Maybe she was the fool on the hill.

According to Sunny, that was supposed to be a good thing. Still, Meg wasn't so sure she wanted to be that fool. Then again, she wasn't sure that she didn't. In fact, she didn't feel very sure about much of anything anymore. All she knew was that she was searching for something, for a place to belong and a purpose for her life, and she hoped that God was leading her. She had prayed a desperate prayer on the beach the other morning, pleading for God to help her. Somehow she had survived the past few days, and she didn't think that was a coincidence. But her heart still felt like an iron fist was clamped around it, and she knew she still needed, would always need, God's help.

There among the freshly weeded cranberry plants, Meg knelt and prayed. "God, I don't know what I'm doing, but I'm hoping you know. Please show me what to do. Show me how to live. Please help me...."

The sun had dipped down behind the sea when Meg finally lifted her head. The clouds had turned to mauve and the sky to a dusty shade of periwinkle. Meg rose stiffly to her feet and took in a deep breath. The cool air smelled of sweet musty earth and vegetation, and she felt another tiny flame of hope flicker within her.

She looked out upon the dark ocean where her mother's ashes had been scattered. "Good-bye, Sunny," she whispered into the breeze.

She walked slowly down to the house in the dusk. Every bit of her felt tired and worn. All she wanted to do was fall across her feather mattress and sleep and sleep, not caring if she ever woke up. But tonight was Sunny's exhibit, and Meg would not miss it for anything. She had missed Sunny's birthday dinner, and who knew how much else. Tonight, she would be there at eight o'clock sharp when Sigfried opened the doors.

Meg made it to the gallery with five minutes to spare. Tom and Erin and the girls were just pulling up as she climbed out of the car, but the gallery looked dark and deserted. A few other cars pulled up, and people stood on the sidewalk, talking uncomfortably in hushed tones. Was something wrong? Where was Sigfried?

Suddenly the gallery burst into life as garlands of tiny white lights came on, shining in all the windows as if it were Christmas. The interior lights began to glow, and Sigfried unlocked the door, turning on the outside light as well. Dressed in a stylish gray suit, he stepped out on the sidewalk and graciously welcomed everyone in. Rich strains of classical music poured out the door and onto the street, and Sunny's friends entered the gallery with an air of excitement. A linen-covered table was set up in the center of the front room of the gallery, adorned with a huge bouquet of fresh

181

flowers, and flickering candles illuminated bountiful platters of cheese, fruit, bread, and wine.

Under normal circumstances, it would be a tempting feast, but Meg moved woodenly past the table without touching the food. Was Sunny's goal to simply throw a big party for her friends? If that was the case, perhaps Meg would just make an appearance and then leave—

"Meg," gasped Erin. She grabbed Meg's arm and pointed to the back wall of the gallery. "Look at that."

Meg turned to see a collection of old photos, enlarged and nicely matted, hanging on the far wall of the next room. As she looked more carefully, she realized that they were old pictures of Sunny, Erin, and herself. She walked into the back room, staring at the pictures in wonder. Some looked faintly familiar. Some she couldn't remember having seen before.

She stared at an old photo of Sunny as a gawky-looking teen wearing a plaid shirt and hip waders. She was pouring a bucket of cranberries into a wagon. And although the photo was black and white, the cranberries had been tinted a bright, sparkling red. The amazing part was the expression in Sunny's eyes; she looked so innocent and full of life. So sweet. Meg had never thought of Sunny as innocent or sweet. Her eyes wandered over other photos of Sunny in her younger years. She felt as if she were looking upon a stranger, yet the stranger seemed like someone Meg would have liked to know. Sunny's face was always more vibrant in the tinted shots on the cranberry bog, as if she were completely in her element. Her expressions mirrored Meg's own feelings of time spent at Briar Hedge.

Finally, Meg moved on to the pictures of Sunny and her two girls. There was one on the beach from the time when Erin and Meg had buried Sunny in the sand, with only her head showing. They had placed shells and rocks around Sunny's face like a frame, then lay down next to their mother and smiled up at the camera while Grandpa took the picture. There were other seaside shots: one around a fire after crabbing, one on a picnic with their grandparents, and a later one with Sunny and Erin and Meg holding hands and kicking their bare legs up like showgirls as they stood in the ankle-deep surf. By that time, Erin had been as tall as Sunny, and their legs were both nice and long while Meg's were still short and chubby, but they were all laughing. It was good to be reminded that they had had some good times. Meg noted sadly that none of the later photos ever showed that same innocent expression on Sunny's face, but still she looked happy.

Meg moved slowly along the wall, taking time to study each shot, trying to stir up some good memories that she seemed to have replaced by the bitter, ugly ones. Of course, those would not be exhibited here tonight. Those were pictures that had never been documented by photos, and would remain hidden in the darkroom of Meg's mind.

She turned a corner and saw that she had come to the end of Sunny's memory-lane exhibit. But the next set of photos she saw, enlarged and neatly mounted, looked familiar. Very familiar. She stared at the card next to the first one and read the graceful calligraphy listing the photographer as *A. Megan Lancaster*. She read her name and looked again to the photos. They were the ones she had taken over twenty years ago when Grandpa had given her the camera. Sunny had kept them all this time and had even gone to the trouble to enlarge and frame them.

Tears filled Meg's eyes, and she could no longer focus on the photographs. The iron clamp around her heart constricted even tighter, and she turned and slipped past the blurred, crowded room and out the door. She crossed the street and continued toward the waterfront, eager to escape the lights and warmth and music, walking quickly until she found a bench down by the dock. Sitting down, she took a deep breath and willed herself to relax. In an attempt to block out her thoughts, her emotions, she focused on the rhythmic sound of the water lapping against the fishing boats and the far-off, mournful sound of the foghorn. She looked up at the sky. No moon, no stars. Just a thick blanket of slate-colored clouds loomed overhead. She bent over, buried her head in her hands, and wept.

After a while, she heard footsteps on the wooden walk that led to the docks and waterfront. Probably a fisherman checking on his boat or turning in for the night. She knew that some of them lived and slept on their boats, and she wasn't afraid. But instead of turning toward the dock, the steps continued directly toward her, and just as she began to feel uneasy, she heard a male voice call out.

"Meg, it's just me."

She couldn't recall who the familiar voice belonged to and vaguely wondered how anyone knew she was out here.

"Can I join you?" he asked. She peered up and saw Matthew Logan in the faint wash of light from a streetlamp.

"Sure, if you want. But I should warn you that I'm pretty bad company just now."

"I figured as much." He sat down on the bench, and she wiped the tears from her face with the back of her hands, then sat up straight, thankful that the darkness didn't allow them to see each other very well. She had never liked anyone to see her when she cried.

"I don't mean to intrude," he began with apology in his voice, "but I thought you could use a friend right now."

She didn't answer. The truth was, she didn't think she could offer much in the way of friendship.

"I know this is really tough on you, Meg. It's hard letting someone go."

"How do you let someone go when they were never really yours? Even if they were supposed to be."

He didn't answer at first, and she wondered if he would want to be her friend if he could see all the darkness and bitterness inside her.

"Maybe you just don't realize that Sunny was yours." His simple words surprised her. He spoke as if he actually understood.

"That's just the point. I don't know. I don't know anything about her. Except what I remember from twenty years ago, and that's not anything I care to recall."

"And now you feel like it's too late."

She laughed, but the sound was humorless. "Well, isn't it?"

"It depends."

"On what? Are you suggesting we can communicate with the dead?"

"No, nothing like that. But I know that Sunny went to a lot of trouble before she died so that you could get to know her after she was gone."

"But why couldn't I have known her before she went? And you don't need to answer, because I know that it's my fault. She tried to get me to spend time with her when I came back to town. But either I fought with her, or I was too busy. I never even gave her a chance. If only I had known she was ill, I would have done things differently."

"Like what?"

"I would have spent time with her, and I wouldn't have been so impatient. I would have told her that I love her."

"How differently we would live if we knew what was down the road...."

"But Sunny knew what was down the road. Why couldn't she have told me?"

"I don't think she knew that her time was so near, Meg. She probably thought she would still have a chance to spend time with you."

"But she knew she was dying. Why couldn't she have told us? It seems so selfish that she would keep it a secret and then just slip away without even giving us a chance to—to—" Meg's voice broke, and she dropped her head, trying to hold back the tears.

"It's okay to cry, Meg."

"I know." She took in a breath and sat back up. "And believe me, I've done more than my share lately."

"It's always hard when someone dies unexpectedly. There are so many regrets."

Abby had said he'd lost his wife nine years ago. Maybe he knew a little bit about what it was like, but he couldn't possibly know what Meg was feeling right now. "Losing someone is one thing, but when you lose someone who was supposed to be close to you, someone you're supposed to love, but aren't sure if you do because there's all this awful baggage attached..."

"It makes it hard to grieve, because you feel angry and bitter and robbed."

"Exactly. How did you know?"

"I know." The way he said the words sounded as if they came from a deep place. Perhaps a place she had no right to ask about.

"So how do you go about grieving when you're angry and bitter?"

"Maybe you take the grieving back a ways."

"What do you mean?"

"You go back and grieve for what was lost long ago. You allow yourself to acknowledge all the pain and the hurt that have induced the anger and bitterness."

"Then what?"

"Then you forgive."

Meg thought about that. It made sense to her, but how could she make herself forgive someone whose actions had so impacted, even impaired, her entire life?

"What if you can't forgive?" The words came out in a barely audible whisper.

"Then you'll regret it for the rest of your life."

It sounded like a pretty harsh judgment to Meg, yet she had to admit she was miserable right now, and at this point, she couldn't imagine ever feeling better.

"The thing is, Meg, most of us are not very good at forgiving. I think it's one of the hardest things that God asks us to do. But the fact is, he asks us to do it for our own good. I've found that once I'm willing to forgive, if I ask God to help me, he always does."

Meg felt a small ray of hope. "I'd like to believe that's true. I really would." She shivered and wrapped her arms around her middle. The cold, damp fog had penetrated her thin silk dress.

"It's getting cold out here," said Matthew. "Maybe we should go in."

"You go ahead," she said. "I'm not ready yet."

He stood and removed his jacket, slipping it over her shoulders and pulling it together in front. She started to protest, but the warmth of it began to seep through immediately, and she couldn't quite make herself give the coat back.

"See you inside, then?" he asked.

"Yes, I'll be in soon. Thanks."

She listened as his footsteps disappeared into the night. Part of her wanted to go with him. But she knew she had unfinished business to take care of. Maybe she couldn't take care of it all in one night, but she could make a good start. What he had said about forgiveness seemed right. It felt like the key that she was looking for. And although it sounded amazingly simple, she knew it would not be easy. But if what he said about God helping was true, then it might be possible.

She closed her eyes and asked God to help her forgive Sunny, to help her wipe away all the bitter memories of childhood and erase them with forgiveness. She confessed that part of her wanted to cling to those horrible things and to shake her fist at Sunny and shout that it wasn't fair, but she knew that wouldn't help anyone.

Finally, she asked God, once again, to forgive her. Then she thanked him for helping her.

She headed back to the gallery and was relieved to see that the lights were still on. She slipped to the rest room in back and splashed cold water on her face, then looked up into the mirror.

"I'm trying, Sunny," she whispered. She applied a little lipstick and blush and attempted a smile. For Sunny's sake she would go out there and meet her mother's friends and look at the rest of the exhibit. And maybe she would even eat something now that she didn't feel so knotted up inside.

Twenty

ERIN INVITED MEG TO GO TO CHURCH with them on Sunday, but Meg had already decided she wanted to go to Grandpa's old church. At breakfast, Meg asked Grandmother if she would like to join her. Although she wasn't surprised when Grandmother declined, Meg nearly choked on her toast when Grandmother said that perhaps by next week she would be strong enough to go. Even in Grandmother's healthier and younger days she had never gone to church with Grandpa.

Meg drove to church with a lighter heart than she had had in days. She hadn't been to Grandpa's church for over twenty years, but she had always enjoyed the peaceful quiet of the old brick building and the rich mellow sounds of the organ. She hoped that everything was still just the same, and, like a child, she looked forward to seeing the jewel tones of the old stained glass windows.

She had checked in the religious section of the small town newspaper, found that the service began at eleven o'clock, and arrived a few minutes before the hour. She didn't want to have to talk to anyone today; she only wanted to slip into the back, sit through the service, and then slip out again, unnoticed.

The church looked just the same. As she entered the foyer, she could hear the comforting sounds of the organ, and as planned, she slipped into an empty back pew. Just as she set down her purse and opened her bulletin, someone else slid in beside her, and Meg looked up to see Clive Logan grinning at her.

Meg smiled back, surprised and yet glad to see the girl. The service began before they could say anything more than hello. Although the pastor was new to her, everything else was very much as she remembered from childhood. Grandpa had always been an usher, and now she almost expected to see his tall, lanky frame coming down the aisle with an offering plate. But when the offering was taken, it was Matthew Logan who handed a plate down their row. Their eyes met, and she smiled up at him.

She hadn't had much chance to speak with him again last night after she'd returned to the exhibit. She had only discreetly handed him his jacket before she was pulled into a conversation with a bearded man who displayed metal sculptures in the gallery and wanted to make sure that nothing would change in his commissions and contracts. She hoped that Matthew knew how much she appreciated what he had shared with her, and perhaps someday, hopefully when she was further along in this forgiveness process, she would have a chance to thank him. She watched his back as he returned to his seat near the front, and saw that Abby and Cal were seated up there as well. Had they gone to church here when she was a child and she hadn't noticed? She wondered if Clive would normally be seated with them and, if so, appreciated that the thoughtful girl had joined her.

After church, Meg visited with Clive briefly, then began to make her way toward the door.

"Don't leave yet, Meg," said Clive, pulling on her arm. "I want to ask Daddy something."

Meg waited uncomfortably by the door, fearing that Clive, out of pity, might be begging her father to invite Meg to join them for Sunday dinner or something like that.

Matthew and Clive walked over to where Meg was standing, and Matthew shook her hand. "Say, Meg, Clive has come up with a really terrific idea. It's a beautiful day, perfect for sailing. And I just got our boat all cleaned up and ready to go out last weekend." The way his blue eyes lit up reminded her of a young boy about to play with his favorite toy. "Anyway, we wondered if you would like to go out with us. Have you ever sailed? Or do you already have plans for today?"

"My only plans were to go out and weed the bog."

"Oh, that's right, Meg," said Clive. "I almost forgot about the bog. We made such good progress last week, and then—" She stopped in midsentence, her face red, but Matthew graciously jumped in.

"I have an idea. How about if we make a deal with you, Meg? You come with us today, and we promise to help you out at the bog to make up for this lost time. We could come out next week if you like. Okay?"

Meg smiled. "It sounds like a pretty good deal for me. But I don't think you have much to gain."

Clive put her arm around Meg. "We get to take you with us." She looked over her shoulder. "Abby," she called. "We're taking the boat out, and Meg's coming. You want to come, too?"

"Sounds great," called Abby. "Can I bring a guest?"

"Sure," said Matthew. "The more the merrier."

"What time shall I meet you?" asked Meg.

"Can you be ready in about an hour?" Matthew glanced at his watch.

"Sure. Anything I can bring?"

"Nope, but plan on eating lunch on deck. And dress warm," he said with a smile. She wondered if he was referring to last night.

"Aye, aye, Skipper."

"I can see already that you'll make a good sailor."

191

"I hope so. I've never been sailing before."

Within the hour, Meg was at the docks, where she found Matthew and Clive already at work on the boat, removing the heavy canvas mooring cover and untying ropes. Matthew looked younger in his faded Levi's, sweatshirt, and deck shoes.

"This is a beautiful boat, Matthew," she said as he gave her a hand to help her aboard.

"Thanks. She's called the *Regina.*"

Meg figured that must be his wife's name but didn't comment. "What can I do to help?"

"Well, I don't want to come across as a chauvinist, but if you wouldn't mind getting those groceries into the galley, that would help."

"No problem." She gathered the bags and headed below, relieved to have such a simple task. She'd been worried that she might have to understand sailing terms, which would be a problem since she didn't know a fore from an aft. The galley was cozy, with a gas stove, sink, refrigerator, and all the other comforts of home in miniature sizes. She quickly stowed the food and checked to see that the refrigerator was running before she returned to the deck.

"We're here," called Abby from the dock. She had Sigfried with her, and Meg waved to both of them, glad to see that he was the other guest.

"Meg already put the food away," said Matthew. "I didn't mention to her that you were the official galley slave."

"Slave?" said Abby indignantly. "Ha! You mean the galley queen. I rule down there, Meg. Be warned."

"That's fine by me," said Meg. "But I'm happy to help, and I know how to take orders."

"Good," said Abby. "In that case, I'll let you help." She turned to Sigfried. "You said you know how to sail, right?"

He smiled. "Sure do."

"Well then, here's your captain."

"This is one nice-looking boat, Matthew," said Sigfried. "How long have you had her?"

"Just a couple years. I couldn't really afford it, but then I decided that Clive and I weren't getting any younger. Here, can you handle this for me?" Matthew handed him some loose rope, and Meg followed Abby down the steep, ladderlike stairs that led to the galley.

Abby put Meg to work making a tossed salad, and before long they heard the engine rumbling and felt the swaying motion of the launch. At first there was barely any movement, but before long the boat began to rock up and down. Meg had almost finished with the salad when she started to feel woozy.

"Good grief, girl," said Abby. "You look like you're going to toss your cookies right into our salad. You'd better get on deck fast and get some fresh air."

"Okay," said Meg. She climbed the stairs weakly. She desperately hoped that she wasn't going to be seasick. That would spoil it for everyone.

Matthew was at the top of the ladder, looking down. "Meg, you're looking a little green around the gills." He reached down and pulled her up out of the hold. "Come sit in the cockpit and get some air." He led her over to the padded bench seat and set her gently down.

"Thanks," she muttered.

He reached into a cooler next to the bench seat and pulled out a cold club soda. He popped it open and handed it to her.

"Here you go. This and some good sea air usually does the trick. I forgot that being down below isn't the best way to get someone used to sailing. And it does get a little rougher here when we cross the bar."

Meg nodded and breathed in some fresh air, then cautiously sipped the soda. To her relief, she quickly began to feel better.

"Looks like my remedy is working," said Matthew with a

warm smile. "If you'll excuse me for a minute, we need to get some canvas up."

Before long, Meg felt back to normal. She leaned back and looked across the horizon. The sky was mostly clear, with just a few wispy clouds passing by from time to time. The ocean was calm and blue. Clive, wearing a crew hat, manned the helm like a pro, while Matthew and Sigfried hoisted the mainsail.

Meg watched the two of them working together. Matthew was taller and probably ten years younger, but Sigfried was holding his own and appeared to know what he was doing.

"Cut the engine, Clive," yelled Matthew as the sail whipped into place and gently filled with wind. The sound of the engine died away, and a peaceful quiet followed as the boat seemed to glide like a bird across the water. It was amazing how just the wind could propel a large boat with such power and speed across the water. Meg felt exhilarated.

Matthew came over and sat down. "You like it, don't you, Meg?"

She nodded.

"I could tell."

"It's beautiful. Almost like we're flying," she said in wonder.

"That's what I thought the first time I sailed."

"How about some help carrying this food?" called Abby from below. Meg started to get up, but Matthew stopped her with a gentle hand on her arm.

"I think you should stay on deck this time around. It takes a while to get your sea legs, and we don't want to spoil this trip for you."

"Okay, but I don't like feeling like a useless piece of baggage."

Matthew laughed. "Don't worry about that. By the way, didn't I see your camera around here?"

"It's in my bag."

"How about getting some shots of the boat and everyone?

That's something I haven't taken time to do. Not to mention that I usually cut off heads or hold the camera cockeyed. After seeing your photography talents at Sunny's last night, I think a few pictures would be a pretty fair exchange."

Sigfried and Matthew each carried up two plates loaded with grilled chicken strips on pasta, salad topped with fresh crab, and big wedges of sourdough bread.

"How can you balance coming up those steep stairs with your hands full?" said Meg.

Matthew grinned as he handed her a plate. "Just naturally graceful, I guess."

Sigfried handed a plate to Clive, then tried to talk her into taking a break, but Clive insisted on eating at the helm.

"Yeah, you'll be lucky if you ever get your hands on that wheel, Siggie," called Abby as she sat down with her own plate of food.

The four adults sat down on the curving bench seat of the cockpit, and Matthew said a blessing over their food.

"Abby, this looks delicious," said Meg, thankful that all signs of her earlier nausea were gone now. "This is the first time I've felt hungry in days."

"The sea air will do that to you," said Abby. "I'm glad you're feeling better."

It was quiet and peaceful as they ate, with just the sound of the water swishing alongside the boat and the occasional snap of the sail. Before Meg had finished her last bite, Abby ducked down into the galley again and emerged with a pan of steaming blackberry cobbler and five bowls.

"Can you dish this up, Meg?" said Abby. "I'm going to brew some coffee."

"You bet," said Meg. "It looks fantastic."

"And don't forget this." Abby pulled a can of whipped cream out of her jacket pocket and held it proudly in the air. "The galley queen thinks of everything."

Meg dished out generous helpings of cobbler but couldn't get the whipped cream to squirt out of the can.

"Here, let me try," offered Sigfried. He fiddled with the top and finally gave it a firm push, which sent an explosion of whipped cream into the air and all over Meg's face and sweatshirt.

Sigfried looked so horrified that Meg began to laugh. He seemed confused for a moment but soon started to chuckle. Matthew joined in, and when Abby returned from the galley, all three were laughing hysterically over the silly incident.

"So this is what happens when I leave you kids unattended," Abby teased as she handed out mugs of coffee. Matthew pulled a blue bandanna from his pocket and carefully began to wipe Meg's face.

"There," he said with a smile as he dabbed one last spot on her nose. "That should do it."

"Thanks," said Meg, looking into his clear blue eyes. She suddenly felt self-conscious and took a step away from Matthew. Returning her attention to the cobbler, she topped each dish with whipped cream and handed them all out. She took the last one over to Clive and remained by the girl's side for a few moments to regain her composure.

"So, Clive, do you know which way you're going?" asked Meg as she took a sip of coffee.

Clive looked down at the compass. "Yep. We're going south-southwest. Pretty soon I'll have to turn her around to tack back north."

"Uh-huh," said Meg, although she didn't know what the girl was talking about. Clive had a beautifully confident look in her eyes as she stood tall before the helm. Meg abruptly set down her coffee, pulled out her camera, and began snapping shots of Clive, trying to get just the right angle on that look. If she could capture that expression on Clive's face, it would be a picture worth framing. She couldn't wait to see the prints.

"Hey, your cobbler's getting cold, Meg," called Abby. Meg returned to the group, feeling more relaxed now. She ate her cobbler, and they all lingered over another cup of coffee.

Meg leaned back and looked out over the ocean. "What a way to live," she said. "I can understand now why some people set sail and keep going all the way around the world."

"Sure, on a day like today," said Sigfried. "But if you sailed through some real weather, you might not think so."

"You're probably right," she said, remembering how she'd felt down below earlier. "Have you sailed in bad weather, Siggie?" It was the first time she had called him Siggie, and it surprised her that it had slipped out so naturally. She had heard Sunny and Erin call him that, but she had never felt comfortable with the nickname before.

He smiled. "Yep, I've sailed through some weather all right. Back in October of 1970, I sailed with a friend from Auckland, New Zealand, up to Brisbane, Australia, in a boat smaller than this. When we hit a storm in the Tasmanian Strait, I thought we were goners for sure. That was one heck of a trip...."

Just as Siggie finished recounting the adventure, Matthew said it was time to turn around and tack back. Matthew explained to Meg that she would need to be very careful to avoid getting hit in the head as the sail swung across the deck from time to time as the boat changed direction.

"We sort of zigzag back and forth, catching the winds to take us back up the coast in a northerly direction," he explained.

"So that's what tacking means."

"Right. If you here someone yell 'coming around!' and you're anywhere near the sail, then you'd better duck quick."

"Okay."

"It would probably be safer for you to stay in one place. You can go up front to the bowsprit, if you like. But you need to be careful up there; it gets a lot of motion. It might be better to stay back here, although you could probably get some good shots from the bowsprit."

Meg chose to go up front. It was fun being right at the tip of the bow. The front of the boat rose up high, then went down, again and again, as they went over the waves. It really felt like flying. She didn't mind being splashed by the sea from time to time as the boat changed course, and she managed to get quite a few good shots. After a while, Matthew joined her.

"Everything going okay up here?" he asked.

"Great. I think I like sailing."

He grinned. "I think we figured that out already."

She smiled back, then paused for a moment, becoming serious again. "Matthew, I wanted to thank you."

"What for?"

"For what you shared last night. I really needed to hear what you said. It was perfect timing."

"Well," he said, squinting out toward the horizon, "I think God must've told me to go out there."

"I'm sure glad you listened."

"Me, too."

Meg studied his profile as he stared out to sea. His sandy eyebrows were drawn together as if he were looking for something, and his deep-set eyes were the same shade as the waves. She had always considered him handsome, but in that moment she saw something more attractive than his physical appearance, something she wanted to capture in her camera lens, but suspected she could not.

When he turned back toward her, she averted her eyes, embarrassed to be caught staring. She sucked in a quick breath. What was she getting herself into?

Twenty-One

THE NEXT MORNING, MEG REPLAYED SAILING SCENES through her mind as she started to weed the bog. She knew she couldn't expect any help today since spring break was over, but she didn't mind working alone. It gave her time to think. Time to work things out.

She thought about what Matthew had said about grieving for the things that had gone wrong in her childhood with Sunny. But as she tried to consider the earlier days of her life, she kept thinking about that photo of Sunny in the cranberry bog—the one where she was pouring out the cranberries with the look of innocence and excitement on her face. When had that all changed? What had become of that wonder-eyed, sweet-faced country girl? What had turned her into the woman Meg recalled from her childhood?

Sunny had never told the girls much about their father. Meg had never even seen him. Her parents had divorced when Sunny was pregnant with Meg, and any photos that had, at one time, included their father's face were blackened out by the time Meg saw them. Erin said she remembered very little about their father and had never cared to talk about him. Even now, she would just brush away the subject if Meg brought it up, saying, "Why worry about the past?" Consequently, Meg had grown up with the conclusion that her father was not a very nice man.

In the fifth grade, Meg's class had traced the ethnic origins of their last names, and Meg asked Sunny why their last name was the same as Sunny's parents' instead of their dad's. Sunny had told Meg that after the divorce she didn't want to have his name anymore and didn't think that Erin or Meg would either. Meg wasn't so sure. She asked Sunny what his name was, and after much pestering, Sunny had finally told her. John Gibson. That was all Meg ever learned about him, other than that he lived in California and that he occasionally sent a birthday or Christmas card in care of her grandparents. Even Grandpa would not talk about him when she asked. "Some stones are better left unturned," he would say. And that was the end of the discussion.

When Meg was a teenager and feeling rebellious against Sunny, she created her own fantasy of what had happened with her father. In this version it was Sunny who played the bad guy. Meg decided that her father must have been a good man, but simply couldn't stand the way his wife drank and carried on, and finally she drove him off and told him never to return.

Meg suspected now that her fantasy had been wrong and that perhaps Sunny had been hurt by her husband. Maybe that was why Sunny made so many bad choices back in those days. Why hadn't that ever occurred to Meg before? She ripped a weed out of the ground angrily. For a change, her anger was directed not at Sunny this time but at herself.

An electronic beeping shook her from her thoughts, and she realized that her cell phone was ringing. She jumped out of the bog and ran to pick it up, hoping that nothing was wrong with Grandmother. Erin's voice greeted her.

"Hi, Meg," she said. "How are you doing?"

"Better," said Meg. "What's up?"

"Siggie just called and wondered if we could meet him at Sunny's apartment tonight. He wants to talk to us about some gallery business and give us the stuff that he told us about. You know, the things that Sunny put together for us. Can you meet there at seven?"

"Sure."

"Are you out in the bog right now?" asked Erin.

"Yep. And it looks pretty hopeless."

"That's too bad. But don't give up, Meg. I'd come over, but Ashley has a bit of a cold, and I'm still a little cautious about her health. Maybe if she gets better, I can leave her with Rosa tomorrow and come help."

"Don't worry about it, Erin. I'm thinking about hiring some regular workers."

"Can Grandmother afford that?"

"I'd pay for it myself."

"You shouldn't do that, Meg. You never know what's going to happen to that land. How would you feel if you put a bunch of your own money in it and then Abner turned it into a golf course?"

"I know. But it's so frustrating."

"I don't know what to tell you, Meg. Tom and I were talking, and we think that any work you put into that place has got to be with the understanding that it might be for nothing—just a labor of love for the land."

"I know, and that's how I started this whole thing. But the more I work on it, the more bound I feel to protect and save it. Sometimes I think I should pack up and go back to San Francisco."

"Don't say that, Meg."

"I haven't made up my mind about anything. I just don't know what I'm doing."

"Well, here's some good news," said Erin. "Tom is going to

work on Grandmother's porches today."

"At least that's encouraging."

"Don't work too hard, Meg."

"I won't. See you at seven, then."

Meg continued working past noon. She decided to skip lunch and try to quit by the middle of the afternoon. She had brought up a bottle of water and a granola bar, and that would have to sustain her.

The weather was clear and dry again, and Meg thought it might be a good day to burn the weeds. She gathered all the piles and heaped them into one large mound, throwing some dry brush and pieces of wood debris on top. She then struck a match to the driest part of the pile and watched with pleasure as it slowly began to burn. There was something very primal and satisfying about a good burn pile. The flames leaped up and gradually grew hotter. Meg picked up a stick and poked at the fire, lifting up the smoldering areas to let the air flow underneath.

Soon she heard a vehicle roar up the road and looked up to see Abner's dark Suburban pull to a stop. He leaped out and began charging down the bog toward her. When she saw the expression on his face, she was glad he didn't have a weapon in his hand, or she might have been terrified. As it was, she felt more than a little concerned.

"What do you think you're doing?" he thundered, his blotchy red face twisted in anger.

"Burning the weeds and brush." She tried to answer evenly without showing her fear. She had learned long ago, in the world of advertising, how to conceal emotion and in turn get the upper hand with your adversary.

"I saw smoke and thought you were burning the whole place down." His face was close to hers now, and she could smell alcohol on his breath. "I thought I told you to stay out of here!"

"You know, Abner, I don't really care what you told me.

Grandmother owns this property, and she—"

He cut her off, sticking a stubby finger in her face. "Don't you go telling me about Grandmother. Everyone knows she's batty. And for that matter, so are you."

She took a few steps back, placing the fire between them. She derived some security from the fact that she still held the smoldering stick in her hand. But she was angry now, and ready to give him a good-sized chunk of her mind.

"Well, Abner," she said calmly, "you may be right about me. I just might be crazy to be up here fighting a battle with these stinking weeds that you've allowed to take over what was once a thriving cranberry bog. But you have absolutely no right to say that about Grandmother. In fact, she's doing better than ever right now. She's getting out of bed every day, and she's even planning to go into town and get her hair done this week."

Abner's brow furrowed deeper, and it was plain to see that this wasn't good news to him. His hands curled into fists as he seethed. But Meg didn't care. Maybe it was time to have it out. If she could give him a display of strength, perhaps he would back down once and for all.

"And," she continued, "I don't know what you have in your thick head about this place, but it's about time you realized that you are not the only person in this family. Erin and I both care a great deal about these cranberry bogs. Our grandpa poured his whole life into this place, and we think it's a heritage that's well worth preserving. I don't understand why you're so bent on destroying that. You've let these bogs go nearly to the point of no return, but I am not going to give up." She jabbed the smoking stick into the air as if to drive her point home.

He stared at her for a long, silent moment, and Meg thought he looked as if he'd like to punch her. Then he threw back his head and laughed.

"I was right!" he sputtered. "You are crazy. And the sooner

something is done about it, the better." He turned on his heel and marched back to his vehicle. Just as he took off down the hill, another rig pulled up. Meg thought it looked like Matthew's Blazer and sighed in relief. But what was he doing out here?

"Hi, Meg," called Matthew as he walked over. He wore jeans and a light blue denim shirt, not his normal work clothes. "I stopped by the house, and Rosa said you were down here. She was a little worried since you didn't come back for lunch." He stopped and looked at her. "Hey, are you okay? Your face is white. Maybe you should sit down." He took the stick from her hand and laid it by the fire, then led her over to a fallen log and gently pushed her down. He sat beside her.

"So what's up, Meg? That looked like Abner's rig that just disappeared over the hill. Is something wrong?"

She nodded. "He thinks Grandmother and I are both crazy."

Matthew chuckled. "I hope you didn't take him seriously."

"No, not really. But I do wonder about my mental state sometimes." She paused, then turned and looked at him. "Do you realize that just a few weeks ago, I had a top position in one of the biggest advertising firms in San Francisco? Actually, I still do; I've just taken a leave of absence." She wondered why she was telling him all this; then she couldn't even remember what they'd been talking about to start with.

"I see," he said slowly. But his eyes said that he didn't really understand.

"Now I'm spending all my time up here pulling these weeds. Does that make any sense at all?"

"Depends."

"On what?"

"On what you want to be doing."

She nodded. "Maybe that's the crazy part."

"How's that?"

"I don't have the slightest idea." But even as she said the

words, she wondered if they were true. With each passing day she seemed to feel more and more at home.

"Meg, you're being too hard on yourself. I don't know where you'll be a month from now, but I think for the time being you are right where you should be. And you are not crazy. Sometimes we need seasons like these in our lives. We need to give ourselves time to take stock and realign our lives with what's really important."

"How did you get to be so wise?" she asked, staring at him curiously.

He grinned. "It wasn't easy. I did come up here to lend a hand with these weeds, but my great wisdom suggests that you may be more in need of food than free labor. So, if you don't mind, I'll take you into town for a bowl of chowder or something. Come to think of it, I had a pretty skimpy lunch myself. What do you say?"

"Sounds good. But what about my burn pile?"

"It looks like it will be out soon. Maybe we can hurry it along a little."

Matthew poked the fire, igniting new pockets and sending orange flames licking up into the air. "I always liked a good burn pile," he said. "I think the smell of a bonfire in the fall is about one of the best smells there is."

"I know what you mean," she said with a smile. "But that's nothing compared to the smell of a really good cranberry harvest."

"You're right about that. Do you think Briar Hedge will get that far?"

"Not if Abner has his way. Matthew, can I ask you a legal question?"

"Sure, go ahead."

"Well, Abner seems pretty determined to try to stop my restoring the bogs. I'm afraid he might try to get Grandmother's power of attorney, or something like that. He keeps saying she's crazy. Could he really do that?"

"I wouldn't go so far as to say that it could never happen. Almost anything can happen in our legal system. I don't think it's likely, but I've seen stranger things."

"Do lawyers tend to hear what's going on around town? If you heard that Abner was trying to do something like that with another attorney, would you be able to tell me? Ethically, that is."

"Sure, I would."

Meg smiled. "Thanks. That makes me feel a little better. The way he carries on sometimes, I just don't know what he might do."

"Do you think he's dangerous?"

"Probably not, although I think he might have a drinking problem. Even your dad said he thought Abner's bark was a lot worse than his bite. But he's so full of anger and bitterness; it's scary."

"Really makes you want to stay away from those things, doesn't it? And you know, it probably stems from some deep-rooted unforgiveness."

Meg nodded slowly. "Do you think I could have become like that?"

"I think anyone could, at least to a certain degree."

"I think you're right. I was probably heading there myself before God opened my eyes. I don't remember ever giving the idea of unforgiveness much thought, but now that I look back, I'm starting to see how crippled it was making me."

"I know what you mean," said Matthew. "Some of my hardest lessons about forgiveness have come from when I had to forgive myself."

Meg nodded. She still struggled with that one. It was easier to forgive Sunny than to let herself off the hook.

Before long, the fire had burned to the ground, and Matthew found a shovel and buried the cinders with dirt until the smoke was gone and the dirt cold.

"Do you mind if I run into the house for a couple of minutes to wash up before we go into town?" asked Meg as they drove down the road.

"Not at all. I'd like to say hello to your grandmother." When Matthew pulled up in front of the house, Meg noticed Tom's truck was parked along the side, and the sound of hammering was coming from the back porch.

"Good afternoon, Mrs. Lancaster," said Matthew.

"Well, hello, Matthew Logan," said Grandmother brightly from the front porch. "Hello, Meggie. We missed you at lunch."

"Sorry, Grandmother. You know how it is up there. Those bogs grab hold of you, and you just can't get away."

Grandmother laughed. "Just like your grandpa."

Meg went into the house and dashed upstairs. She scrubbed her hands with a fingernail brush, but the stains from weeding were becoming more stubborn each day, even with wearing gloves. She brushed her hair and applied a little lip color and some blush, then changed into a fresh shirt. She tucked it into her jeans and tightened her belt. She could tell that she had lost a few pounds in the last two weeks, and she really didn't need to take off any weight. Matthew was probably right; she did need to eat.

"I'm ready," she announced as she came out the screen door. "Was that quick enough?"

"Too quick," complained Grandmother. "Now you're stealing this handsome fellow away from me."

"Don't worry, I'll come back to visit again," Matthew assured Grandmother with a pat on her shawl-covered shoulder. He opened the car door for Meg, and she waved good-bye to Grandmother.

"She's quite a gal," said Matthew as he started the engine. "Still has that same sharp wit. I think Abner will have a tough time proving she's crazy."

"I hope so, but it's troubling just the same."

"We'll just have to keep an eye on him, maybe even take some preemptive action."

"Are there some legal steps that can be taken to keep him in line?" asked Meg hopefully. Having Abner out of her hair would certainly make life simpler.

"There might be. I'll have to talk to your grandmother about that."

They decided to have chowder at Jake's Diner. When they walked in, they spotted Cal sitting at a table, about to plunge a fork into a huge piece of coconut cream pie.

"Hi, Pop," said Matthew.

Cal looked up in surprise. "Well, you caught me, Matthew. Now, just don't tell Abby. She'll tan my hide."

"Your secret's safe with me, Pop."

Cal looked up at Meg and then back at Matthew. "Hi there, Meggie. Why don't you come sit down here and join me," he said, scooting over to make room.

Matthew looked at Meg as if to ask if she minded.

"I'd love to join you, Cal," said Meg. She slid into the booth across from him.

Matthew grinned and sat next to her.

Cal's eyebrows went up just ever so slightly, but enough to catch Meg's attention, and she quickly launched into a conversation.

"You're just the man I wanted to see, Cal. I was out at the bog today, and I think I'm going to need some help."

"What kind of help?"

"Some good advice to start with. The progress on the bog is going too slowly. I think I'll need to get a crew up there, and maybe I'll have to use some chemicals." Meg paused as the waitress took their orders, then turned back to Cal. "I don't want anything too hard on the environment, but I'm afraid it's getting to the point of picking the lesser of two evils—either compromise my stand against chemicals or lose the bog entirely."

Cal grinned. "Sounds to me like you're turning into a pretty sharp farmer. I wondered how long it would take you to figure it out. Now don't get me wrong, Meggie. Between you and me, I think the idea of steering away from chemicals is good. Just don't let that get around town, or I might be out of business. But sometimes you have to take stronger measures at the start, then let up later. There's no reason why, over a period of time, you couldn't have a completely organic cranberry bog. I've even found a couple of booklets on it for you. But all those high-and-mighty earth-friendly ideals won't do you a bit of good if you lose the bog in the meantime."

"Sounds like wise advice to me," said Matthew.

"Does wisdom run in your family?" asked Meg wryly.

Cal looked at her curiously, then continued. "The only problem, Meggie, is that this kind of plan will take some cash, and I thought you said Alexandra wasn't wanting to put money into the place."

"Right." Meg paused for a moment and thought what she was about to say was probably crazy, but she was going to do it anyway. "I want to invest some of my own funds."

"Are you sure, Meg?" asked Matthew. "You're using the word *invest*, but you have no guarantee that you'll ever see any return."

"I know. I guess *invest* is the wrong word."

"Maybe you should give this some more thought," suggested Cal.

"But how much longer can the bog wait?" asked Meg.

"Not long." Cal pressed his lips together as if deep in thought. "I think you need to get some kind of an agreement with your grandmother on this." He turned to Matthew. "Isn't there some legal thing you could draw up for them, to protect Meggie's investment if she decides to go this route?"

"Maybe." Matthew thought for a moment. "I'll see what I can come up with."

"I don't really want Grandmother to sign some legal paper," said Meg. "I just want to preserve the bog."

Cal reached across the table and patted her hand. "We know you do, Meggie. Maybe you need to have a little help, though."

Matthew's and Meg's chowder came, and they continued to discuss the various possibilities as they ate. Cal told her he'd begin to work up an estimate for what it would cost to get the bog off to a good start, and would come over to take inventory of whatever equipment she had left.

"I haven't even gone into the barn to see what's there," said Meg, almost apologetically.

"Well, it won't take me long to get it all figured out, Meggie. I know that rascal cousin of yours has probably sold off a few of the good pieces. Hopefully you've still got something to work with. I'd hate to see you have to start all over with buying harvest equipment. But then again, since you've got McFarlin berries and they come on late, we might be able to work out an arrangement with someone who does an early harvest and would be willing to rent you a beater."

They talked for another good hour, and when Matthew and Meg finally left, she felt encouraged. What had, just hours earlier, seemed like a hopeless and crazy endeavor was starting to look possible.

She thanked Matthew when he dropped her at the house. It seemed she was always thanking him these days. She wondered if she would ever be able to do something nice for him, instead of continually being on the taking end of things.

Twenty-Two

MEG ARRANGED TO PICK UP ERIN that evening before they met with Sigfried. While she waited for her sister to finish getting ready, she spent a few minutes visiting with her two older nieces in the kitchen, then slipped up to Ashley's room where the little girl was being tucked in by her daddy.

"Hi there," said Meg from the doorway.

"Aunt Meggie!" called Ashley from her bed, chubby arms out-stretched.

"Come on in, Meg," said Tom.

Meg sat down on Ashley's bed and received an exuberant hug from her youngest niece.

"I heard that you have a cold, Ashley. I hope you're feeling better."

Ashley nodded and pulled her covers up to her chin. "Mommy says if I get all better I can come help you at the bog."

"That's right. And I need all the help I can get, Ashley, so you make sure you get all well, okay?"

"Okay, Aunt Meggie."

Tom grinned at Meg. "She'll probably be better in no time now."

"I heard you working on the back porch today, Tom. How's it coming?"

"Great. But I can't believe how bad that place has gotten. The day of the memorial service was the first time I'd been out there in ages. Abner used to shoo me away every time I offered to help, but he sure hasn't done anything to make that place better."

"I know. It's a shame."

"Ready to go?" called Erin from the hallway.

"I am if you are," Meg answered.

"Sorry I took so long. I've been doing pottery all afternoon and really needed a shower."

"No problem. It's not quite seven yet."

On the way to town, Meg told Erin about the plans she was making with Cal for the bog.

"That sounds great," said Erin.

"I thought you were against my putting money into the place," said Meg in surprise. "I thought you and Tom—"

Erin interrupted her. "Well, I've changed my mind." She had a sly grin on her face. "I've decided that whatever it takes to get you to move back here for good, it's worth it."

"But just because I'm doing this with the bog is still no guarantee that I'm staying indefinitely, Erin."

"Sure, Meg, whatever you say." Erin grinned.

Meg shook her head. Well, maybe Erin was right. Meg knew she couldn't put off this decision much longer. Was she truly ready to make Crandale her permanent home? Even if it already felt like home to her heart, it still didn't make sense to her head. If she was serious about relocating up here, she should close up her apartment in order to save some money, and she'd certainly have to give notice at work. She was still hesitant about burning her last bridge at Montgomery and Tate, though.

Sigfried was waiting outside the gallery for them. Meg and Erin apologized for being a little late and then followed him up the little staircase that led to the apartment. Meg hadn't been up here since she was a girl, when it had been Grandmother's apartment. Then it had looked almost like a dollhouse, with lots of ruffles and flowers. Everything was pink, even the little refrigerator and stove. Meg realized that the house at Briar Hedge didn't look like that now. Grandmother hadn't changed any of the decor from when it had been Grandpa's house.

Sigfried turned the key and opened the door. Meg braced herself for the acrid smell of stale cigarette smoke, but to her surprise, other than a musty odor from being closed up, the air was clean.

"I thought it would smell smoky," she said, then instantly wished she could take back her words. She knew how defensive Sigfried could get about Sunny. But fortunately he didn't seem to take offense.

"Sunny really didn't smoke all that much, unless she was nervous. And she tried not to smoke in her apartment at all. She knew that it bothered other people, and she wanted to keep her home a place where she felt comfortable entertaining."

Meg looked around. The pink was definitely gone. The small apartment consisted of an open living room and kitchen that seemed bigger and taller than Meg remembered. Sunny must have had the ceiling lifted up to the rafters. Near the big window, a large sectional provided seating. It was loosely slipcovered in a milk-colored nubby cotton, and several large pillows made from pieces of old Amish quilts were artfully arranged. The old carpeting had been removed, and now the beautiful old fir floors shone with warmth and character. A few dark Oriental rugs were placed here and there, not so much to cover the floor as to add interest. Carefully hung pieces of art were lit to perfection with concealed spotlights, and the whole effect was very, very classy.

"She must have felt fairly comfortable then, Siggie. This is really nice."

He smiled. "It is, isn't it? There's a good view out over the wharf, although you can't see much at night." He walked over to an antique bureau and picked up two white boxes, each tied with a strip of red satin ribbon. One was marked with Meg's name, and the other with Erin's.

"Why don't we sit down," said Sigfried as he placed the boxes on the antique oak coffee table. "Can I get you anything? Coffee or tea?"

"I'd like some coffee," said Erin. "I can't remember what it was called, but Sunny had some awfully good decaf."

Meg and Erin sat down. Suddenly Meg became very aware that this had once been Sunny's home, and although Sunny was gone, she could almost feel her presence in this room. She looked at Erin.

"Have you been here before?" Meg asked.

Erin nodded. Apparently she was feeling the same thing as Meg. "Yes, but it feels strange to be here without her. It makes everything seem more real. More final."

"That's just what I was thinking." Meg studied the details of the lovely room. Meg's own apartment back in San Francisco was nowhere near this nice. She still had many of her things in boxes; she'd held off any special decorating for the past two years while she waited for Jerred. What a waste of time that had been.

Sigfried set three mugs on the coffee table, then returned to the bureau to retrieve a large manila envelope. He started to sit down, then straightened his shoulders, still holding the envelope in both hands.

"I could read all of this to you, but that would take all night," he said, waving the envelope in the air. "You can read it at your leisure later. I know all the important details by heart anyway." He began to pace and rub his chin, as if determining where to begin.

Meg sipped her coffee and wondered if something was troubling him. Finally he quit pacing and sat down.

"As I mentioned," he began without looking up, "Sunny has

left the gallery to both of you. She wanted to split it in such a way that if you didn't agree, there would be possible ways to work it out. Hopefully that won't be the case. As you probably know, she bought this building from her mother a number of years ago. She paid a fair price for it, and she paid cash."

He looked up now. "Sunny decided to leave the gallery, with all its equipment, computers, and whatnot, to Erin. This was because Erin has always had a strong interest in the arts, and she has been doing pretty well selling her pottery down there."

He cleared his throat and looked at Meg. She wondered why he seemed so troubled. She wasn't upset that Sunny had left the gallery to Erin. It seemed only fair. In fact, it was a relief. She smiled and opened her mouth to say so, but he held up his hand.

"And," he continued, "Sunny decided to leave the upstairs—this apartment—to Meg." He paused and looked from one to the other as if he expected problems. Meg could think of nothing to say. She was stunned.

"Now, as far as the art contents of the gallery, there are many pieces that Sunny purchased from artists or collectors, and some that are here on consignment. However, due to the rather large purchase of artifacts that Sunny made last year, before she knew of her illness, there is now a small mortgage on the building. This really shouldn't be a problem, because the gallery easily brings in enough to cover that payment as well as the rest of the expenses. But it does mean that we need to keep our doors open. To be fair, Sunny has divided the value of the art, as well as the debt of the mortgage, between the two of you. And she has had it written up that profits will be shared equally. The only reason, or rather the main reason, that she split the building like this was in case one of you wouldn't want to keep the gallery going." He looked at Meg as if she would be the one to do so.

"I don't see any reason why the gallery shouldn't continue as it always has. In fact, I would be disappointed if it didn't." Meg spoke quickly, hoping to dispel any worries.

Sigfried smiled. "Good. And the other reason, the reason that she left the apartment to you, Meg, was just in case you needed a place to live. Sunny really hoped you would be comfortable here."

Erin reached over and took Meg's hand. "Can you believe that, Meg? Wasn't that thoughtful of Sunny?"

Meg blinked back tears and nodded.

Sigfried cleared his throat. "However, there is a small problem."

They looked up in surprise.

"It's really just a tiny problem," he began apologetically. "And it has nothing to do with Sunny. It's me. I've promised my mother for the last six months that I would go back east for a visit. My father has advanced diabetes, and my mother has been begging me to come out. Well, due to Sunny's condition, I couldn't leave her, and I really hate to leave now, but I feel more strongly than ever, in light of losing Sunny, that I can't afford to delay this visit—"

"Oh, Siggie," exclaimed Meg. "You must go. Don't worry about a thing. I know Erin is busy with the girls, but I'll be more than happy to mind the shop while you're gone. Of course, you'll have to show me how things work, but that shouldn't take too long."

"Oh, Meg, how can I ever thank you?" Siggie came over and hugged her.

"You've already thanked me a million times over, Siggie. How can I ever repay you for all you have done and for being such a dear friend to my mother? Besides, I know firsthand how it feels to lose a parent when you haven't been close. I think you should go as soon as possible to visit your parents."

"I'm so relieved. I was worried that we would have to close the doors to the gallery, and I know it's important, especially as the season is just beginning, to keep things going."

"And I can help out, too," Erin offered. "I could probably even bring Ashley here in the mornings. We'll work it all out. I know Meg needs to keep giving the cranberry bog her attention. You're going to be spread pretty thin, Meg. You sure you don't want to make that decision about not returning to San Francisco now?"

"It's getting closer, Erin. But I need just a little more time."

"Sunny had already cleaned out a lot of things, since she knew her time wasn't far off," said Sigfried. "Her goal was to have it all cleared out and ready for you to move in, Meg. She was really hoping that you would want to. But, in the end, I think even she got caught by surprise, so there are still things that she didn't have time to take care of. She wanted to have it all done so you girls wouldn't have to fuss with her old things."

"I really don't mind," said Meg. "In fact, I think I'd appreciate the opportunity to sort out her things; it might help me to feel like I know her better. I've been finding out lately that she was a completely different person than the mother I grew up with."

"Is that okay with you, Erin?" asked Sigfried.

"Certainly. Actually, I appreciate your willingness, Meg. Do you think you'll have time?"

Meg frowned. "That's a good question. Of course, there's really no hurry, is there? Maybe I should consider moving in here and working in the gallery while Siggie's gone, and in the evenings I could go through her things."

"What about the bog?" asked Erin.

"I told you that Cal and I have started to work up a plan, remember? That will mean that it will take a lot less of my time and probably go ten times as fast."

Sigfried smiled. "It seems like everything is going to work out just fine. Okay, it's settled then. Tomorrow, I'll make my plane reservation, and hopefully I can leave by the middle of the week."

"Thank you, Siggie," said Erin. "Thank you for everything. You've been such a help to us through all this. I think of you as one of the family now."

Sigfried smiled sadly. "It's too bad that it took us so long to come together like this. But we will continue to be a family, right? And we'll continue to keep Sunny's Gallery alive and as wonderful as ever, right?"

"Right," said Meg and Erin in unison.

"Sunny would be very proud of both of you."

Twenty-Three

THE NEXT MORNING, MEG MET SIGFRIED at the gallery, and he spent several hours taking her over every single detail he thought she should know and then some. Meg carefully took notes and asked lots of questions. By noon, she felt confident she could handle the gallery with no problems. It might even be fun.

Then Sigfried hung the little sign that said Out to Lunch, and he and Meg headed across the street to the deli.

"I think you'll do a fine job running the shop, Meg. I know I won't be a bit worried when I'm gone."

"Good. I'm not worried, either. If you leave me your parents' number, I can always call if something comes up. But I'm sure nothing will."

"Of course." Sigfried nodded. "I called about a flight, and I can get a pretty good deal on a red-eye tomorrow night. But I wasn't sure if that would be too soon for you."

"That should be no problem, Siggie. Go ahead and book it. Like I said, the sooner you get to see your dad, the better." Meg looked down at her soup and sighed. Too bad no one had given her that kind of advice about Sunny.

"Meg, you need to forgive yourself," said Sigfried.

She looked up. "You know, I have been thinking a lot about forgiving others lately. But now I know you're right; I need to forgive myself as well. But I have a feeling that might be the toughest kind of forgiveness to carry through."

"But it might be the most important."

"Maybe so."

After lunch, Meg went out to the bog to meet with Cal. He had made lists of what it would take to make the bog profitable, as well as estimates of the costs. She tried not to gasp when she saw the total, but it was more than she had expected and much, much more than she had left in her savings. Just last year, her savings had been quite impressive. If only she hadn't impulsively purchased her car last fall—but that was when she thought that she would be married to Jerred soon, and decided it might be her last chance to get the car she'd always wanted.

She walked out to the barn with Cal to inspect the equipment. She hadn't been out here at all. The only tools she had been using had been from the shed or ones she had purchased at the Feed and Seed. When they reached the weathered old building, they found the big double doors locked tight with a brand-new stainless steel lock.

"Grandpa never locked this barn in his entire life!" Meg exclaimed hotly.

"Looks like Abner doesn't want us nosing around in here," said Cal.

"But this barn belongs to Grandmother, not Abner. What right does he have to lock it up like this?"

"Probably none, but you'd better check with your grandma. And remember, Meggie, when it comes to family, the rules can always change."

"What do you mean?"

"Your grandma may feel beholden to Abner. She may have a hard time making him do the right thing."

"Do you know something I don't, Cal?" asked Meg suspiciously. "Is there something I should be aware of?"

"Not unless your grandma tells you." He looked at her as if he wanted to say more but couldn't.

"Well, I intend to ask her about these locks, and if necessary, I will go to Abner directly and find out exactly what's going on."

"Just be careful, Meggie."

"But I thought you said Abner wasn't dangerous."

"Well, let me put it like this: there's lots of critters that aren't dangerous when left to their own devices, but you corner some of those critters and they can get downright mean."

She nodded. "I think I understand."

"You'd better talk to Matthew about this. I think he may have some good ideas for making everything neat and legal so you won't have such a hard time with Abner."

"Okay," said Meg. "In the meantime, Cal, if you could go ahead and get this plan in the works and get someone to come do the spraying and whatever else you think is necessary, I'd appreciate it. And if you give me a couple days, I'll get you a check for this amount."

"Well, hold on there, Meggie. You don't need to pay for it all at once; some of that estimate is for harvesttime. I'll write you up a proper invoice for what it will take, one month at a time. Don't you be too willing to kiss your hard-earned money good-bye."

"Thanks, Cal."

"You bet, Meggie. Now you take care."

After Cal left, Meg stayed up at the bog to pull weeds. She knew it wasn't necessary now, since there would soon be others to come and do this work, but it felt good, perhaps a bit therapeutic. After a while she heard the sound of a motorbike coming over the rise. She looked up and spotted Jason, who waved and then popped a little wheelie before cruising down the hill.

"Hey, Meg," he called. "Need any help?"

She studied him for a moment, wondering why he was so willing to help when Clive wasn't even here today. But he had a sweet, friendly smile, and she figured it wasn't fair to hold his father against him.

"Sure, if you want to," she said.

He parked his bike and launched right into a big patch of tussocks. "I never got to tell you, Meg, but I was real sorry about Sunny and all. I really liked her. She was always real good to me. She had even promised to let me work part-time in the gallery this summer."

"Thanks, Jason." Meg smiled. Here was yet another side of Sunny she hadn't been aware of. "And we may still need some good part-time help, maybe even before summer."

"Great. I used to go in and just hang out there. Sometimes Sunny would put me to work moving boxes and stuff."

"I could still use you around here some, too, Jason, although Cal Logan is setting up a crew for me to help whip this place into shape."

"Dad thinks you're nuts to keep working here. He says nothing is going to come of it."

"What do you think, Jason?"

"I'd sure like to see it stay a cranberry bog. I remember how it used to be when I was just a little kid. I loved it up here. I don't want to see a bunch of stupid condos built."

"That's good. Neither do I."

"I don't know why my dad carries on like he does sometimes...." Jason's words dwindled away at the end, as if he couldn't bear to say them.

"I don't either. But I do know what it's like to feel that way about a parent."

"Huh?" asked Jason, looking up.

"I probably shouldn't say this, especially since you have such good memories of Sunny. But under the circumstances, I don't think she'd mind if I told you something."

"Something about what?"

Meg wanted to be careful how she said this. She wanted to be honest but not disrespectful of Sunny. "Well, you see, Jason, when I was a girl, my mom—Sunny—was pretty hard to get along with. I think she'd gone through some tough times, and that made it hard for her to be a good mom. During most of my childhood she was an alcoholic, and she used to do and say things that made my life really miserable. Sort of like your dad."

"Really? Sunny was like Dad?"

"Well, not exactly the same. But she was pretty messed up a lot of the time."

"Wow. I never would have guessed that."

"Yes, and I'm not telling you this so you'll think poorly of her, because it's obvious she really straightened out her life. But what I'm saying is that I can understand how it feels to have a parent who does some hard things."

"Uh-huh," said Jason as he pulled a huge weed out and tossed it aside. "I don't know what I'd do sometimes if it weren't for my mom, but then I feel real sorry for her, too. Dad treats her pretty bad sometimes. I don't see how she can stand it. When I get fed up with Dad, I can just take off on my bike and ride through the woods or down to the beach. But my poor mom has to just sit there and take it."

"Does she have any friends?"

"Nope. She used to get out and do things, but now she stays at home most of the time, and my dad has pretty much scared off anyone who visits."

"It must be hard."

"You know, she wasn't always fat like that, either. She used to be real pretty when I was little, but I think every time my dad yells at her she gets back at him by eating. I saw a show about it on TV once."

"That's too bad, Jason."

"I'm afraid she's going to die one of these days. It's so hard for her to move around; she huffs and puffs like she can hardly breathe."

"I wonder if there's some way to get her help," said Meg as she threw an armful of weeds into the wheelbarrow.

"I sure wish there was."

Meg looked at her watch. "Oh, there was something I was going to try to do today. Do you want to help me?"

"Sure, what is it?"

"Well, it involves driving my car."

"Your Jaguar? Sure, I'd love to help." His eyes lit up.

"But first, are you willing to help me wash it and get it all cleaned out?"

"You bet."

"Okay. I need to make a couple of phone calls. Can you get started while I do that?"

"No problem. I'm on my way." He hopped on his bike and took off before her.

As Meg walked to the house, she spoke out loud to God. It surprised her how prayer was becoming more natural to her all the time.

"God, I really need some money to bring the bog back. Maybe it's foolish of me to do this, but could you help me out if I'm on the right track? You know how much I like my car, but I would gladly give it up for the bog. If it's right for me to sell it, please help me find a buyer. It's in your hands, God."

Meg made several phone calls and finally found what she was looking for. With a quick whispered "Thank you," she threw on some clean clothes and ran down to see how Jason was doing. She found Jason, in the driveway, polishing the chrome wheels. Her deep red Jaguar was spotless, inside and out.

"Great job," she said, handing him the keys. "I'm sorry you got stuck doing all the work, though. It took a little longer than I expected."

Jason didn't look as if he minded. "You're going to let me drive it? Really?"

"You bet. Just be careful, and no speeding. I already got one ticket this month. Do you think your folks will mind if you're gone for a while? You can call on my cell phone if you need to."

"Nah, they don't care. Sometimes I don't come home until really late." He carefully wiped off the soles of his shoes before climbing into the driver's seat.

"Wow. This is nice, Meg." He backed out of the driveway and started driving very carefully toward town.

"Do you realize you're only the second person I've allowed to drive this?" said Meg.

Jason shook his head. "This is cool."

"You can head onto the highway and over to Glass Cove," directed Meg.

"What are you going to do over there?"

"Trade in this car."

"No way, Meg! You're not really getting rid of this car, are you? Tell me it ain't so!"

She nodded. "Yep. I need to get some cash for the cranberry bog, and this car is not the greatest thing for farming."

"Aw, Meg. Don't you want to think this over?"

"I have. And I've made up my mind. But, hey, aren't you glad that you're getting to drive it before it's gone?"

He grinned. "You bet I am. Can I go just a little bit fast on the straight stretch of the highway, if there aren't any cars? I'll be real careful."

"Maybe just for a couple of seconds, but you'd better be very careful."

They arrived in Glass Cove earlier than she'd planned, and they decided to stop off for burgers and shakes. After that, Meg drove until she found the right car lot—Superior Import Auto Center. She drove slowly into the lot and pulled up by the showroom door.

Before she even got out, a man in a light-blue sport jacket was coming her way.

"You must be Meg Lancaster," said the man, extending a hand. He looked over the car and whistled. "This is a real beauty, Meg. And your timing couldn't be better. I had a guy in here just last weekend looking for a Jaguar in this exact model and year. I just called him, and he's on his way over. You said you were looking for something more fitting for the country life. We have a great-looking Jeep Wrangler that we just took in as a trade-in. Low miles, excellent condition. Do you want to see it?"

"Sure," she said, taking a last look at what had once been her dream car. For the first time, she realized that the color of her car was exactly the same as that of a sun-ripened cranberry.

She and Jason took the Jeep for a test drive, and it seemed to be just what she needed. When she got back, she sat down in the salesman's little office, and they began to talk about price. Certain that she would come out on the losing end of the deal, she had decided to start on the higher end of her price expectations. She understood all about depreciation and didn't expect to get anything close to what she had originally paid for her car, even if it was only six months old. But she was pleasantly surprised at the fair deal they offered her. Apparently the customer who had driven over to look at her car was extremely interested and willing to pay cash. He had even let it slip that it was the exact color he'd been looking for, and he didn't mind paying top dollar if they could close the deal tonight.

When she and Jason drove away in the little white Jeep, she was glad to have the whole thing over with.

"Are you sad, Meg?" asked Jason.

"Oh, maybe a little. But this is so much better suited to the lifestyle I have now. And everything worked out so well; I'm feeling pretty thankful."

"Does that mean you're here to stay, then? Dad keeps talking like you're just here for a visit and won't be around much longer."

Meg thought about her prayer; it seemed God had made a way for her to stay. Now she felt even more willing to stick to her decision in order to thwart Abner. "Well, don't tell your dad, but he's in for a big surprise."

Jason nodded. "Good. Someone needs to shake the old man up."

"I'd like to get to know your mom, Jason," said Meg. "Do you think it would be okay if I paid her a visit?"

"Sure, she'd like that. She really does like people, and I know she's pretty lonely."

It was dark when they pulled into Briar Hedge. Jason thanked her again when they got out of the Jeep, then hopped on his bike and headed for home.

The next day, Meg deposited her check in the bank and dropped by the Feed and Seed to pay Cal for the next month's work. Then she drove over to Erin's in her new Jeep and told her the news about deciding to stay in Crandale permanently. Erin jumped up and down in delight.

"You won't be sorry, Meg. I just know you won't."

"I don't think I will, either, Erin. But it's still sort of hard. Today I'll do all my phoning and arranging in San Francisco. And I think I'll go ahead and move into Sunny's apartment tonight so I can be ready to go to work at the gallery tomorrow morning."

"I'll come by in the morning," said Erin. "You can show me what needs to be done so I can help too."

"Great." Meg smiled. "Yes, I think this is right. I actually feel relieved. You know, I didn't fully realize until just now, but I don't think I ever wanted to go back to San Francisco. The truth is, I never felt comfortable in the fast-paced city life." She took a deep breath. "This really feels right. I may have been slow to catch on, but I think God has been leading me back here all along."

"Well, it's about time you figured that out, Sis."

Meg spent the rest of the day with the details of moving. She gave notice on her apartment, then made arrangements with a friend in San Francisco to pack up and send the rest of her things. Finally, she called Montgomery and Tate and told Mr. Montgomery that she would not be coming back. It hurt to hear the pain in his voice, but when she told him the whole story about her mother and the gallery and the cranberry bog, he began to chuckle.

"Well, considering all that, Meg, I don't know why you would ever want to come back here. But I'll tell you what—one of these days I'm going to bring the wife up there, and we'll expect you to take us out to a real nice lunch. Okay?"

"It's a deal, Mr. Montgomery. And thanks. Thanks for everything."

"Thank you, Meg. By the way, I'm awfully sorry about how things turned out with you and Jerred. But maybe it was for the best after all. It sounds as if you've landed in a good place."

"Thanks. I think so, too." Meg hesitated for a moment. "And, Mr. Montgomery, would you tell Jerred…there are no hard feelings on this end."

"I will, Meg. The best of luck to you."

Twenty-Four

MEG DIDN'T HAVE A LOT TO PACK IN HER ROOM at Briar Hedge. She had left San Francisco in such a hurry that she hadn't brought much. Maybe it was just as well, since she had been moving every couple weeks, anyway. Perhaps she would settle into Sunny's place—her place—and stay for a good long while now. The thought of living in that beautiful apartment brought mixed feelings. Part of her was thrilled, but the rest of her felt guilty and slightly uncomfortable.

She had already told Grandmother about the arrangements, and although the old woman was openly disappointed, she didn't try to discourage Meg, especially after Meg promised she would be back on a regular basis to work and check on the bog. For her last night in Grandmother's house, she ate dinner in Grandmother's room. Although Grandmother was getting up and moving around during the day, she still wore out early and took dinner in her bed. Meg figured Rosa didn't mind, since that left her free to watch *Wheel of Fortune*. Tonight, Meg offered to take care of serving dinner so that Rosa could have some time off.

"I plan on coming into town this week," said Grandmother. "I have a hair appointment at Myrtle's on Friday. I can't believe

Myrtle is still doing hair; she must be close to seventy now. No one could ever put in a pin curl like Myrtle. Maybe I'll stop by the gallery. I haven't been by there in several years. I probably can't make it up the stairs to see your place. Maybe you should think about putting in an elevator."

Meg laughed. "Now, wouldn't that be something. Did you ever see the place, Grandmother? I mean, since Sunny redid it?"

"Sure. I walked all the way up those stairs about six years ago. It just about did me in, though. Can't say I cared much for what she did to my apartment. I don't know why she didn't leave it. Those appliances were perfectly good. Top of the line in their day."

Meg smiled. "Yes, I remember them well, Grandmother. Did you do all the decorating?"

Grandmother pushed her empty plate aside and nodded. "It was my little nest. I was very happy there."

"Did you live there until Sunny bought the building?"

"Oh no, I moved back here just after your grandfather passed away. No reason to stay away anymore."

Meg didn't want to say anything to stop the flow. She knew this was uncharted territory, and hoped that Grandmother would continue. But the conversation seemed to have come to an end.

"So it was because of Grandpa that you stayed in town?" asked Meg, knowing it was unlikely she would get a direct answer.

Grandmother shook her head slowly. "No, it was because of me. I used to tell myself that it was Stewart's fault, and I think for most of my life I actually believed it." She closed her eyes and leaned back against her pillows. "Everyone else thought that I stayed in town for the sake of the business. The business did provide a good distraction at first, and it became my lifeline after a few years, but it wasn't the real reason...."

Grandmother had come to another stop, but Meg hoped it wouldn't hurt to ask another question. "So was the real reason because you and Grandpa didn't get along?"

Grandmother sighed and opened her eyes, looking up at the ceiling as if she expected to see something there. "I suppose you could say that, although we were always very civil to one another. For years I lived here, when the children were small. But when Sunny got married and moved away, I just couldn't stand it anymore. It's hard to live under the same roof as unforgiveness, Meggie."

"So had Grandpa done something you couldn't forgive?" Meg couldn't believe that her beloved grandpa could ever have done anything wrong, but then lately she had been changing the way she viewed a lot of things.

"No, dear. It wasn't your grandfather. It was me. And for all those years, those many, many years, he could not forgive me. Can you imagine what that was like?"

"It must have been like being in prison."

"That is exactly what it was like. And the only way I could escape was to live in my own apartment."

"But I can't imagine Grandpa being so mean—"

"Your grandfather was never mean, Meggie. He was always, always a gentleman. And I think if he hadn't passed away when he did, we might have even worked things out. I found a long letter he had written just a few weeks before his death. I don't know why he never sent it. It was addressed to me, and in it he said how sorry he was for not forgiving me. And he actually asked me to forgive him, if you can imagine that, after what I did to him!"

Meg desperately wanted to know what Grandmother had done that was so horrible, but she couldn't bring herself to ask. Instead she asked, "And did you forgive him, Grandmother?"

"Well, it took me a while. It should have been easier, but all those years had hardened me. I looked back on the lives of my poor children. My poor children!" Grandmother wiped her nose on the napkin. "They are the ones who suffered the most."

"How's that, Grandmother? I always imagined that their lives were just about perfect: living here at Briar Hedge with two parents, having the cranberry bog, being members of a small, close-knit community. It sounded like pure heaven to me."

"Ha! I'm sure they would have told it differently. Our house was like an ice palace in those days, and I was the ice queen. There was never fun and laughter like you would expect to find in a normal family. The children suffered the most."

"But I thought Sunny got along pretty well with Grandpa."

"That's true, she did. At least until she got married. I'm fairly certain she got married to get away from us. It was really pitiful. But she loved her daddy, and he loved her."

"And what about Bennie?"

Grandmother cleared her throat, then pressed her lips together. She sat silently for several moments before finally speaking. "Bennie and your grandpa never got along very well. I'm sure you've heard bits and pieces about it."

"Did Grandpa feel bad after Bennie didn't make it home from the war?"

"Oh, I'm sure he felt sorry for Bennie and his widow. But I don't think he ever really expected Bennie to come back to Crandale. Bennie made it quite clear when he left that he wouldn't come back. That was the one time when your grandfather and I really did come to words. Poor Sunny; she was just a teenager then and couldn't understand what was going on. Life got pretty hard for her then, and it didn't get any better when Bennie died. Poor Sunny. No wonder she ran off and married the first—" Grandmother stopped and sighed deeply.

"I'm getting worn out, Meggie. I think I need to rest now. And I'm sure you want to get settled into your new apartment before it gets too late."

Meg stood and gathered the dishes. There was so much she still wanted to know. But she knew that Grandmother was probably already regretting what she had said.

"Grandmother?" said Meg as she lifted the tray of supper things.

"Yes, dear?"

"Thank you for telling me all that. It really helps me to understand why people are the way they are when I can see some of the things that they've had to deal with."

"But there are many things that are better left unsaid, Meggie. You don't want to go digging around into too many closets; you never know what kind of skeletons you might run into."

Meg laughed nervously. "I hope you're not suggesting that we have ax murderers hidden away in our family tree?"

"No, nothing quite that dramatic. But you might turn up a horse thief or two." Grandmother smiled, but Meg could see a trace of sadness in her eyes. "Would you send in Rosa to help me get ready for bed, Meggie?"

"Sure, Grandmother. You take it easy now, and don't overdo. I'll see you later in the week, okay?"

"All right, Meggie. Say, did I tell you that handsome lawyer friend of yours called me up to make a date with me on Thursday? Hope you're not jealous." Grandmother got a mischievous twinkle in her eye.

"First of all, there isn't anything going on between Matthew and me. And second, to hear him talk, I think he's always been rather fond of you."

"Go on with you," said Grandmother, pushing her hand into the air. But Meg could have sworn she saw the old woman blush.

"Good night, Grandmother."

"Good night, Meggie. I hope you enjoy your new place. I know I always did."

It was dark when Meg carried her bags up to Sunny's apartment. Meg kept telling herself that she needed to quit thinking of it as

Sunny's, but she knew it would be difficult. And in a way, she supposed she wouldn't mind if it always felt a little bit like Sunny's.

She set down her things and unlocked the door, fumbling in the dark for the light switch. Finally, she took a deep breath and stepped inside. Her heart was pounding with apprehension, but she knew there was nothing to be uptight about. Everything looked just as it had on Monday. It felt a little cool, and she closed the door and searched until she found the thermostat, then turned it up a bit. She hadn't looked around the rest of the apartment when they'd been here with Sigfried, but now she was ready to explore.

She opened the door to the bedroom and turned on the light. This room, like the rest of the house, was very classy, with a white jacquard bedspread, tapestry pillows, and another Oriental carpet across the fir floor. The furniture was obviously antique, but like the rest of Sunny's antiques, these pieces were not frilly, but smooth-lined, classic styles. Edwardian, if Meg's memory of period pieces was still accurate. Whatever it was called, it was a style that Meg had always admired. Several times she had wanted to buy pieces similar to these, but Jerred had stopped her, insisting that they buy new furniture made to go together.

She laid her bags on the bed and started to unpack, but when she opened the closet, she realized that Sunny's things were still inside. The sight of the unfamiliar clothes startled Meg, for the rest of the house almost seemed like a nice hotel, so clean and free of everyday clutter. Meg had almost forgotten that Sunny had actually lived here. Eaten here. Slept here.

Meg stood before the closet, staring at Sunny's clothes. The space wasn't overly full; probably Sunny had already begun to thin things out. Meg could see that by simply pushing some garments aside, she would have plenty of room to hang up her own things. But for some reason, she couldn't make herself touch Sunny's clothes.

For what seemed like an eternity, she stood there with an armful of her own clothing, staring blindly into the closet. After a time, she realized that tears were flowing down her cheeks and her hands were shaking uncontrollably. That old iron clamp fastened itself onto her heart again, and she felt paralyzed, incapacitated. As the clamp tightened, she suddenly burst into action. She dropped her things on the floor and fled from the apartment, down to the sidewalk below. Telling herself she was behaving like a child, she gazed up at the apartment but couldn't make herself climb the stairs again.

She paced back and forth on the sidewalk, feeling like a fool and wondering if anyone was watching her. It was a cold, foggy, night and she was outside in jeans and a thin T-shirt, pacing like a caged tiger. There was a phone booth across the street. Maybe she should call Erin. But she didn't even have a quarter. Perhaps she could call collect. How utterly ridiculous she was being. Erin was probably helping her girls with their homework and getting Ashley to bed. Meg thought of Abby. She also thought of Matthew, but wasn't ready to take that step. But Abby had told her to call whenever she needed a friend. Meg marched over to the phone booth and called.

Matthew answered and accepted the charges. When Meg asked for Abby, he told her that Abby was teaching a painting class tonight.

"Oh," said Meg, shivering in the cold. "Well, just tell her I called then." She tried to make her voice sound light but knew it hadn't worked.

"Are you okay, Meg?"

The note of sympathy in his voice was her undoing, and she began to sob.

"Meg, what is it? Where are you? Can I help you?"

"In a—phone—booth," she choked.

"Where? What phone booth?"

"By Sunny's. But I'm okay—really—" Her words came out in short, choppy breaths.

"I'm coming right over. Wait for me."

She replaced the receiver and leaned her head against the phone, biting her lip and trying to stop the flow of tears. She did not want Matthew to see her like this. She was tempted to hide, but that would be even more childish, and Matthew would probably have the police out looking for her. She walked across the street and sat on the bench in front of the gallery, still crying. A gloomy blanket of fog was wrapped around the town tonight, creating blue circles of light around the lampposts. It soaked through her T-shirt and penetrated her bones.

"Meg," Matthew called from the open window of his car as he pulled up in front of her. He parked and leaped from his car in one swift action. "Are you okay? What is it?"

"I'm so sorry, Matthew." Her voice caught on a sob. "I'm so embarrassed. I know I'm being childish. I can't even explain it." Despite her embarrassment, she was glad to see him. If only the circumstances were different.

"It's okay. Take your time." He slipped off his jacket and wrapped it around her. She sat for a few minutes, soaking in its warmth and trying to get hold of herself.

"This seems to be becoming a habit," she said, attempting to smile, but her chin quivered so badly she knew it was a useless endeavor.

"Don't worry. I always enjoy rescuing damsels in distress."

"It's really quite silly. You see, Sunny left me her apartment to live in. And it was wonderful of her to do it. The apartment is beautiful. Fantastic. I really do love it. I was moving in tonight. And, well—" She felt the tears building up again and knew she had to talk fast. "I was going to hang my clothes in her closet. And then I saw all her things just hanging there and—that's when I lost it. I fell apart and came running down here like a baby. Here

I was, and I didn't even have my car keys, or my purse, or any money at all. Then I thought if I could talk to someone… Abby had told me to call her anytime, but I didn't really mean to drag you out here like this…."

"It's okay, Meg. I don't mind. We're friends, too, aren't we? And believe it or not, I do understand." His voice was gentle and soothing.

"Thanks." Meg noticed that he had one arm around her and was gently rubbing her shoulder. She could imagine him doing the same for Clive. But suddenly she knew she didn't want to be treated like his daughter.

"Now, before we both freeze to death, would you like me to come up there with you? Or do you want to go somewhere for a cup of coffee? You're welcome to spend the night at our house. Clive has bunk beds, and I'm sure she'd be glad to share her room with you."

Meg gave him a watery smile.

"There now," he said, giving her shoulder a final pat before removing his arm. Meg instantly felt the cold. "So what will it be?"

She looked up at the apartment. The lighted window glowed cheerfully in the foggy night. "I really should stay here. I'm just not sure if I can or not. Am I being ridiculous?"

"Not at all. Well, whatever you decide to do tonight, you'll probably need to go up there and get some of your things. Right?"

"Right. Do you mind coming up?"

"Not at all."

Matthew led the way, and she followed. It was nice and warm inside now, and again she wondered why she had reacted so strongly.

"This place is really great," said Matthew. "Very well done. Sunny obviously put a lot of time and care into decorating."

"I know. And I really didn't expect to feel like this. It's just—I don't know. Anyway, I think there's some decaf coffee in here," said Meg as she walked into the kitchen. "Siggie made us some the other night. Would you like a cup if I can figure out where everything is?"

"Sure."

Feeling Matthew's eyes on her, Meg awkwardly searched through the cupboards for the coffee and filters. After a few minutes she had a pot brewing. She sat on one of the tall bar stools across the counter from Matthew and stared at her hands for a long moment before speaking.

"Thanks for coming up, Matthew. I'm starting to feel better already. Just being in the kitchen and doing something normal helps."

"Don't feel as if you have to explain," said Matthew quietly. "I told you that I understand."

Meg poured them each a mug of steaming coffee, then turned back to Matthew. "Do you take anything in it? Although I doubt if there's any cream or anything." He shook his head as she handed him his cup to him.

"Do you want to try sitting in the living room?" he asked.

"Sure. It's not like I think the place is haunted or anything. It's just—difficult."

"I know." They moved to the sectional, and Matthew sat in the middle of one side. Meg perched on the other side. "It was like that for me the first time I came home after Gina died."

"Gina was your wife?"

He nodded. "Regina."

"Like the boat."

He nodded again. "Actually, Clive named the boat, but I thought it was very sweet."

"Clive is a very sweet girl."

"She is. She was only seven when Gina died. It was hard on her. I don't know what I would have done without Abby. She's been a lifesaver."

Meg nodded. "She seems like a very stable person to have around. That's why I called her tonight."

"Meaning that I'm not stable?" He lifted one brow.

"No, I didn't mean that." She smiled, feeling more at ease. "It's just that it felt more comfortable to call Abby. It's silly and old-fashioned, I know, but I just don't think women should call men. Silly, isn't it? No one would believe I'm the daughter of Sunny Lancaster."

"I wouldn't say that. In fact, you remind me of her in a lot of ways. Actually, much more than Erin does."

"Really? How's that?"

"Same even, controlled temperament."

"You would describe Sunny like that?"

"Sure. She may have been a free spirit, spontaneous, and somewhat eccentric, but she was also very much in control. Very strong. Very independent and confident."

Meg nodded thoughtfully, trying to take it all in. She felt it must be true. Others had told her the same thing, but the conversation felt so removed, as if they were talking about another woman. Someone else's mother.

"And I see a lot of those same traits in you. Although I think you try and repress some of them."

"Such as?"

"I think you've tried to live very carefully, perhaps too carefully. That you've been afraid to do anything too risky."

Meg didn't say anything at first. Even if he was right, it was irritating to be so neatly classified like that. "So if I'm so careful," said Meg with a trace of sarcasm in her voice, "how do you explain my coming up here? I would think that quitting my job, selling my car, and pretty much reinventing my life is fairly risky."

"So you've finally made up your mind, then?" Matthew asked mildly.

Meg nodded. "Yes, as a matter of fact. And if I hadn't gone

into hysterics tonight, I would be happily spending my first night in my wonderful apartment, ready to start my new job down in the gallery in the morning."

"I see."

Seeing the patient expression in his eyes, Meg suddenly felt contrite. "I'm sorry, Matthew. I didn't mean to sound ungrateful. The truth is, what you said about my living carefully was exactly right. Or used to be, anyway. I spent almost twenty years living in the same place, doing the same thing. I was never truly happy, but I wasn't brave enough to try anything new. If it hadn't been for an engagement that went wrong, I wouldn't be here now."

"So did you come here to run away from a relationship? Or to nurse a broken heart?" Meg noted that his tone was more intense than it had been before.

"Neither. Or maybe a little bit of both. Actually, I knew it wasn't a good relationship. But it was convenient. And at the time, it felt safe." She shook her head. "But I'm glad that I got away when I did." Meg looked at her watch. It was getting late.

"Matthew, you should probably go. I'm sure you have to get up early in the morning." She frowned. "I'm sorry. I'm not trying to push you out, after all that you've done...."

"You're not." He grinned. "But what about you, Meg? If I leave, are you going to be able to handle it tonight? You can still come bunk with Clive."

"I'd hate to disturb her, Matthew. She's probably already asleep by now, and she has school tomorrow."

Matthew set down his empty coffee mug. "Well, like I said, I know how you feel. It was really hard for me that first night."

"How did you get through it?"

"I prayed a lot. And I read my Bible."

"You know, I don't even have a Bible anymore. Isn't that awful? I'll have to get one."

Matthew reached into his jacket pocket and pulled out a small brown leather book and handed it to her.

"The New Testament," she read.

"And the Psalms."

"I've never seen such a small Bible. Maybe I'll get one like this." She started to hand it back, but he held up his hands.

"You keep it."

"Oh, could I? Just for the night, I mean? And I will get my own tomorrow."

"No, I want you to keep it for good. It's yours. Okay?"

"Really?"

He nodded.

"Thanks." She felt a warmth slowly replacing the hollow weariness inside.

"I'll mark some places for you to read. Some of the Psalms might help. And one more thing, Meg."

"What's that?"

"Can I pray with you?"

"Sure, if you want. But I have to warn you, I'm lousy at praying out loud with people. I can do okay by myself, or silently, in my heart. But when I try to speak in front of others, the words sound so silly and I forget what I'm saying—" Meg realized she was rambling and closed her mouth.

"Don't worry. God can hear silent prayers just as well."

Matthew began to pray. It wasn't a fancy prayer with flowery words, yet it sounded very real, and very powerful. He asked God to protect her and to drive away her fears, and lots of other things that she couldn't even remember with her mind, but they seemed to be rooting in her heart.

"Thanks, God," she whispered after Matthew said amen.

He looked up and smiled. "Are you going to be okay, Meg? I'd hate to put your reputation at risk, what with this being your first night in your apartment, but I was half thinking of offering to spend the night—on your couch, of course."

"That's sweet. And what about your reputation?"

"Ah, but you forget I'm a lawyer. What kind of reputation could I possibly have?"

She laughed and thanked him, then assured him that she would be fine. In fact, she thought she might sleep on the couch herself—just for tonight.

After Matthew flipped through the Bible and jotted down some passages for her, he wished her good night and left, closing the door quietly. Meg curled up on the sectional with a thick afghan and began to read the places he had marked. Finally, she felt herself drifting off to sleep. She realized that most of the lights were still on, but she didn't care. She whispered another prayer, and she didn't wake up until morning.

Twenty-Five

MEG OPENED THE SHOP AT NINE O'CLOCK the next morning
with no problem. She turned on the lights and put a stack of CDs
in the stereo, then lit a couple of large jasmine candles. Siggie had
explained that this helped cover the musty smell of the old building. After flipping over the Open sign in front, she began to brew
a pot of golden pecan coffee.

The shop remained quiet for the first hour, but Meg was
grateful for the chance to become more familiar with the pieces
on display and the layout of the shop. When a customer came in,
she wanted to appear knowledgeable. She browsed around the
perimeter of the building, taking in each artist's style and works,
as well as the unusual artifacts Sunny had collected over the years.
She paused a bit longer when she reached the photo display of her
own work, still neatly arranged on a good-sized portion of wall.
She wondered if Siggie, in his hurry to see his father, had over-
looked taking these pieces down. Perhaps she should take care of
it herself. Or maybe not. It might be interesting to see people's
responses to the photography. She gently pulled down the placard
that Sunny had made with Meg's name on it.

In a back section of the shop, divided by a long, wooden

counter, was a picture-framing area, complete with all styles and colors of frames and mat board, where Sunny and Siggie helped patrons to pick out frames and borders, then put them together. There were also several large art catalogs available for browsing, in case a customer wanted to order a special signed print or lithograph. Meg examined some of the frames and remembered that she still hadn't picked up the enlargements she'd ordered of the sailing-trip photos. She'd been very pleased with some of the shots and was anxious to see if any enlargements had turned out well enough to frame and give away.

By midmorning, Erin and Ashley arrived. Erin settled Ashley into a corner with several puzzles and a coloring book; then Meg walked Erin through the process of recording sales, making orders, and some of the other paperwork details.

"Seems fairly straightforward," said Meg as she closed the layaway notebook. "Sunny was a lot more organized than I would have ever expected."

"I suppose so," said Erin with a thoughtful expression. "Sometimes I forget, Meg, that most of your memories of her were from our childhood days."

Meg nodded. "You're lucky that you got to be here all those years, Erin."

"I guess. I never thought of it that way, though. In fact, when I think how much I complained about her, I feel so ashamed. Now I'd give anything to have her back, and she could be just as eccentric as she liked. In fact, I think I would join her."

Meg smiled. "Me, too. Then we'd become known as the Loony Lancaster Ladies. I bet Grandmother would even join us."

"Wouldn't it be great?" Erin gazed across the gallery, then back at Meg. "How was your first night in Sunny's—I mean, *your*—apartment?"

"Don't ask." Meg moaned.

"What happened?"

"Oh, not really anything. Actually, I even got a fairly good night's sleep—finally."

"Was it weird?" whispered Erin. She glanced over at Ashley, who was hunched over her coloring book.

"No, I think I was weird. I was just about to hang up my clothes in her—the bedroom. And Sunny's things were still in the closet—not a lot, probably just what she had been using recently. And, well, I freaked out."

"You're kidding! What did you do?"

Meg told her about calling Abby and how Matthew came over. She tried to gloss over the part Matthew had played. She wasn't totally sure about her feelings for Matthew, but she didn't want Erin to get curious and start questioning her yet.

"I think I'll be okay tonight," said Meg confidently. "I'm sure last night was the worst of it."

"I hope so." Erin patted her on the shoulder. "And don't be worried about calling me. Anytime—day or night. We're sisters, and we need to stick together. This hasn't been easy for me, either."

"I know. And I feel bad that I haven't been more available to you, but I figure you have Tom and the girls, and I don't want to intrude."

"Don't ever think that! We're family." Erin nodded firmly. "And, Meg, while Ashley and I are here this morning, why don't you go on upstairs and start taking Sunny's personal things out of the bedroom?"

"Erin, that would be great. You don't mind?"

"Not at all. If anything comes up, I'll just call you. I noticed some empty boxes in the storage room; you might want to use them to pack things in. We can have them picked up later."

"Okay. Thanks, Erin."

Meg spent the next two hours carefully removing and folding much of Sunny's clothing into the boxes. She left a few things on the bed that she thought she or Erin might want to keep. Meg emptied the drawers as well, laying aside some silk scarves and nice leather gloves. Finally, she pulled out the few pairs of shoes and boots that Sunny had left neatly arranged on built-in shelves, and tucked them on top of the full boxes.

At last the closet and drawers were empty. Other than some jewelry and a few framed photos, the room was stripped of Sunny's personal things. Meg looked around in dismay, wondering if she should have taken more time to examine each item and think about Sunny. But then, she didn't know if she could handle it emotionally.

Just then, Meg noticed the big cedar chest, the same one Sunny had always kept at the foot of her bed when Meg was growing up. It was the only piece of furniture that held any childhood familiarity for her. It was sitting beneath the window with a neatly folded quilt on top. Meg stared at the beat-up sides of the old chest. She knew Grandpa had made it for Sunny long ago, when Sunny was just a girl. Meg realized her work was not over yet. That chest had always been full of all kinds of memorabilia In fact, she had tried to sneak into it several times when she was a teen, but Sunny always had kept it securely locked. Meg went over and tried to lift the lid. Still locked. Suddenly Meg recalled the small brass key she'd found in the memento box from Sunny that Siggie had given her. Perhaps the chest wasn't locked to her after all. She'd have to remember to try it when she had more time.

Meg moved the full cardboard boxes out by the front door and returned to the bedroom to have one last look. The closet was completely bare now. Of course, there was quite a stack of clothes on the bed, including her own. But it was a good start. And when she came back tonight, she ought to be able to hang up her own clothes without hysterics. And hopefully she could begin to put her own mark on this room soon. Of course, she would never be able to remove all traces of Sunny, nor did she want to. But this apartment was hers now, and she thought Sunny would want her to make it her own. Meg smiled, awed at how far God had brought her, even since last night.

She made several trips to carry the boxes downstairs and place them in the storage room, making a mental note to call the Salvation Army later. She hoped her own things would arrive from San Francisco soon. But in light of Sunny's tasteful decorating, Meg thought she'd probably give away many of her own shabbier furnishings.

"Hey, you," Erin called from the front. "Are we going to take a break for lunch? Ashley's tummy is growling."

"Sure. According to Siggie, it's customary to close the shop at noon—at least during the quieter part of the year."

"Then let's go for it," said Erin. "How about the Beach House? My treat."

"Okay," said Meg, but part of her was remembering that the last time she'd been there had been with Sunny. It hurt to think that that had been the last time she'd spoken more than a few words to Sunny.

"Oh, by the way, Matthew Logan called," said Erin in a teasing, singsong voice as Meg flipped over the sign and locked the door.

"Did he leave a message?"

"Just that he would be tied up until later this afternoon, but he wanted to make sure you were okay."

"He said that? He wanted to make sure I was okay?"

"No, not exactly. But I could tell that's what he wanted to know. And I nicely told him, without going into too much detail, that you had survived the night."

Meg made a face at her sister. "Thanks, Sis."

"Don't mention it, Sis. Shall we walk? It's pretty warm today. Almost looks as if the sun's coming out."

They chatted as they walked, with Ashley holding each of their hands. It was a good feeling to be part of a family.

After they ordered the lunch special of the day, smoked salmon soup and grilled cheese sandwiches, Meg began telling Erin about the things she had salvaged from Sunny's closet.

"I really don't think I want anything, Meg," said Erin. "It was thoughtful of you to think of me. But I just wouldn't be comfortable—you know, wearing her things."

"But what about her jewelry? I don't know if there's anything valuable, but you never know."

"You go through it and see. If there's something I need to know about, you can tell me."

"Well, how about if I set aside some things for the girls?" Meg offered. She glanced at Ashley, contentedly munching on crackers.

Erin nodded. "Of course, that would be lovely of you. I wasn't even thinking."

"Okay, I'll do that. Another thing, Erin," said Meg, somewhat apologetically. It seemed to irritate Erin to talk about Sunny's things. "Have you gone through the box that Sunny left for you?"

"Yes. It was old photos and things I had made or written as a child. It was sweet of her to keep them."

"Yes, mine was the same. It was fun to see. So many things I had forgotten. But was there a key in yours?"

"A key? No, I didn't see a key."

"Well, mine had a key. And I think the key may go to Sunny's old cedar chest."

Erin nodded with downcast eyes. "I didn't realize she still had that thing. Is it in the bedroom?"

"Yes, and it's locked."

"It always was."

"Why?"

Erin looked down at her water glass, then picked up the lemon and gave it a firm squeeze. Looking back up at Meg with a steady gaze, she spoke in an even voice. "She was probably trying to protect us."

"From what?"

"Our past."

"What past?" asked Meg with a frown.

"Actually, our father's past would probably be a more accurate answer."

Meg nodded. "I see. Do we still need to be protected from it?"

"Some of us may."

Meg studied her sister's face. It was a mixture of darkness and sorrow. "Erin, I know you don't like to talk about—well, things. And I don't want to bug you about this. But I think I need to know a little more about him. Maybe it's because I know nothing."

"You might be better off knowing nothing," said Erin in a tone that sounded almost angry.

"I might. But I think I'm willing to take the risk. I think it might help me to understand Sunny better."

Erin's brow wrinkled as if she were considering this possibility for the first time. Then she slowly nodded. "You might be right about that, Meg."

"Do you want me to tell you if I find out anything?"

"I doubt there is anything you can tell me that I don't already know."

"Okay." Meg looked down at the soup that the waitress had just set before her.

"I'm sorry, Meg," said Erin in a soft voice. "I don't mean to sound cold. I just don't want to deal with this again. At least not right now."

Meg nodded. "I understand. I only wanted you to know what I was up to as I went through her things. I didn't want you to feel like I was leaving you out."

"Don't worry. You go right ahead. And unless you discover that we're heiresses to some fantastic fortune or that Mel Gibson is our long-lost brother, then don't worry about telling me. But I'm warning you: don't expect to go on some sweet, sentimental journey."

"I don't. But I think Sunny wanted me to know."

"Probably so."

After lunch, Erin took Ashley home for a nap, and Meg minded the shop. Several customers came in. One brought in some original watercolors to be framed. Another inquired about having a set of pottery made to go with her kitchen. The rest just peacefully browsed. One thing Meg had noticed was that everyone seemed to relax once they came inside Sunny's. It was as if the music, the sound of the waterfall, and the smell of the candles soothed and calmed them. It really was a pleasant place.

Just before closing time, the bell tinkled again, and Meg looked up to see Matthew step in. He was wearing a brown tweed sport coat over a soft blue denim shirt and chinos. It was a good look on him.

"Hi there, Matthew," said Meg with a smile as she stepped out from behind the counter.

"Hello, Meg. I don't see any dark shadows under your eyes, so I hope that means you got some sleep last night."

"Thanks to you and the Bible you gave me, I sure did. And I think I will again."

"Great. I'm glad to hear it." He paused, and his expression was hopeful. "I know it's last-minute, but Abby wanted me to stop by and invite you over for dinner tonight. Actually, it's Pop's birthday, and we all would love for you to join us."

"Really? I'd love to come. Can I bring anything?"

"Nope. Abby said to come around seven."

"Thanks. I'll see you then."

Matthew looked as if he was about to say something else, but apparently changed his mind. After writing out the directions to his house, he said good-bye and stepped out the door.

Meg looked at her watch. There might be enough time. Even

though it was a few minutes early, she flipped the closed sign over and dashed across the street and down a couple blocks to the photo shop.

"Hi, Joan," said Meg breathlessly. "Are those enlargements done?"

"Sure are. I hope you don't mind, but I took a peek at them when I put them in the envelope." She leaned over and said in a conspiratorial tone, "Just don't tell Gary."

Meg shook her head, wondering what Joan was getting at.

"Anyway, Meg, they look great. I think you could actually sell photos like that. You should consider doing a show or making a display at the gallery."

Meg smiled. "Thanks, Joan. As long as you say things like that, you can sneak peeks anytime."

Joan grinned sheepishly. "Well, I mean it. They are really good, Meg."

Meg jogged back to the gallery and let herself in, locking the door behind her. She went back to the framing section and spread the enlargements across the counter. They were good. The color was crisp and clear, and the shots were balanced and interesting. She hadn't cut a mat since high school art days, but she'd been looking for an excuse to start practicing.

After several botched attempts, she wound up with two fairly decent-looking framed pictures. One was a large print of Matthew, Abby, and Clive all horsing around on the *Regina,* looking beautiful with their windburned ruddy cheeks and sparkling blue eyes, with the clear blue sea and white sail in the background. The other was a smaller print of Clive at the helm, gazing out across the ocean like a Scandinavian sea princess, a pensive look on her brow. The larger print Meg wrapped up for Cal, and the smaller one of Clive she thought she'd slip unnoticed somewhere, as a small thank-you for all their kindness to her.

She dashed upstairs and took a quick shower, using Sunny's

spring rain shower gel and cucumber shampoo with just the tiniest feeling of uneasiness. She was determined that this apartment would slowly become her own. That's what Sunny had wanted. She pulled on the thick white terry bathrobe that she'd hung on the bathroom door, then went into the kitchen and made a cup of Earl Grey tea.

It was an hour until she needed to go over to the Logans', so she sat on the sectional to relax for a few minutes. She needed time to think about who Sunny had actually been: an artistic woman who had owned a business, been an important part of the community, lived in a tasteful apartment, had good friends, and pulled her life out of the ashes to create something that was truly beautiful. For the first time, Meg truly felt close to her mother, and she knew this is what Sunny had wanted, why she'd left her this place. She had wanted to leave Meg a home, the home she'd never provided while Meg was a child. Meg wiped a tear from her cheek and took another sip of tea.

"Thank you, Sunny," she said out loud. "I think I'm finally starting to get it. And thank you, God, for helping me to see things straight."

Twenty-Six

AS MEG LOOKED AT THE SELECTION OF CLOTHES spread across the bed, she wished the rest of her things had arrived. She really had nothing very festive to wear to a birthday party. Finally, she settled on the same brown dress she had worn to the exhibit in the gallery. It was a simple sheath of raw silk, ending just above the knees. When she'd first bought it she had liked how it looked on her slender figure. But now it seemed duller than dull, and the matching brown hose and suede shoes, though stylish, didn't help liven it up. The night of the exhibit, she hadn't minded looking drab. But tonight was different.

She looked across the cluttered bed until she spotted a long silk scarf that had caught her eye earlier. It was a vivid palette of rich russet, green, and gold. She picked it up and ran the smooth fabric through her fingers. She could tell by the feel that it hadn't come cheap. In fact, all of Sunny's clothes had been top of the line.

For fun, Meg tied the scarf like a belt around her waist and turned to the mirror to view the results. Not bad. She looked through the box of jewelry on Sunny's dresser and found a long gold chain with a lovely agate pendant. She put it around her neck. Smiling at her reflection, she felt like a little girl playing dress-up in her mother's clothes, something she had never done as a child. She dug a little deeper in the jewelry box and discovered a pair of gold hoop earrings that were bigger than those she normally wore, but she put them on anyway. She looked back in the mirror. Interesting.

Now all she needed was a coat. She remembered the taupe suede jacket she had saved from Sunny's things, thinking that it would look great on Erin. She pulled it from the pile and slipped her arms into the satin sleeves. It was a beautiful garment, barely worn, but the scent of Sunny's perfume still lingered on it. And for a pleasant change, she didn't mind. Finally Meg looked in the mirror to see how it all fit together, and she knew she couldn't have done any better if she had been shopping at Saks. She felt like Cinderella, with Sunny as her invisible godmother.

As Meg drove over to the Logans' she realized this was the first time she had felt good since Sunny died. She wasn't completely happy; that might still take some time. But she was beginning to feel good about Sunny, and she appreciated all that Sunny had done to make everything easier on her. She still regretted the time that had been lost, time she could have used to get to know her mother, but like Siggie had said, she needed to forgive herself for that.

Matthew met her at the door, took her coat, and quietly told her, "You look very nice, Meg."

Meg laughed lightly. "Thanks. I haven't had much opportunity to dress up lately, and I almost forgot how to do it." She carried the wrapped present for Cal, with the smaller one hidden beneath it.

"Come on in. The clan's in the kitchen," said Matthew as he gently placed his hand on her back to guide her through the large house. She knew it was simply a polite gesture on his part, but it sent unexpected, yet not unpleasant, shivers up her spine.

"Hey, Meg," called Abby. "You'd better get in here quick. These guys are gobbling up my mini clam fritters. I made a few for appetizers, because they're Pop's favorite, but they're going mighty fast."

"Hi, Meg," said Clive. "Better get some while you can."

"Happy birthday, Cal," said Meg with a big smile. She handed him the wrapped package and tucked the other one behind her back.

"Why, thanks, Meggie," said Cal. "Can I open it now, or do I have to wait?"

"Doesn't matter to me," said Meg.

"I say, let the old fellow do what he likes," Abby teased, winking at her father.

"And it's about time," he shot back, not missing a beat. He tore off the paper and stared in silence.

"What is it, Granddad?" asked Clive, leaning over his arm to see. Matthew and Abby both peered over his shoulder as well. Meg used the opportunity to slip the smaller photo of Clive onto an end table she'd spotted through the open door to the living room.

"This is just beautiful," said Cal in a choked-up voice. "Thank you so much, Meg. I know just where I'll put it."

"Yeah, that's a great shot, Meg," said Matthew. "I don't even remember your taking it."

"Can we get a copy, too?" asked Abby.

"Sure. In fact, I have another one back at the shop, a five-by-eight." She looked over the collection of pots and pans. "Can I help you, Abby?"

"Sure, Meg. You can start by putting this seafood salad on the table."

Soon the meal was ready. Besides the scrumptious-looking salad, Abby had prepared a baked salmon and fresh green beans with almonds, along with small red potatoes and a hot loaf of freshly baked French bread. Everything looked delicious. Matthew said a short blessing, ending with words of thanks to God for his dad. After the amen, Meg looked around at the family. They weren't exactly typical—widowed dad, single aunt, teenager, and grandfather—and yet they seemed so perfect together.

After dinner was over, Clive insisted on helping Abby in the kitchen. "You're the guest, Meg," said Clive. "You and the guys can go visit in the den. Go smoke a pipe or something." Clive grinned mischievously.

"Your home is really nice," said Meg as Matthew showed her to the den, where a fire was crackling.

"Thanks. Most of that is due to Abby's artistic flair."

"Yes, it reminds me a bit of Sunny's style. I like it."

"So are you getting all settled into the apartment over the gallery?" asked Cal. "Abby told me you had moved in there and that you're keeping shop while Sigfried is gone."

"Yes, and tonight I was actually starting to feel a little bit at home," said Meg, with a smile in Matthew's direction.

"That's good. Although I expect Alexandra will be missing you some."

"I know. But I plan to visit Briar Hedge a lot. Especially once Siggie gets back."

"I have a crew all lined up to start work on the bog this weekend," said Cal. "Then I've got a chemical guy scheduled to do some spraying at the end of next week. It's late, but we're using some of the milder stuff. We'll follow that up with Round-Up; it's okay to use that almost right up to harvesttime."

"Really? But doesn't it leave any residue?"

"Not according to the EPA, and they're our toughest critics. I've also ordered you some frost-detecting devices; they ought to be here by next week."

"How do they work?" asked Meg.

Cal stood up as if he were giving a favorite lecture, and Meg saw Matthew toss her a small smile, as if he'd heard this one before. "Well, Meggie, there's a specially designed thermometer that can sit in the right spots of the bog and still be easily read to let you know the exact temperature. That way you'll know whether you're in any danger of frost."

"Can't you just use a regular thermometer?"

"You can, but it's just not as reliable. You see, the way the bogs are set up is a lot like a refrigerator."

"How's that?" asked Meg.

"Well, you see," explained Cal, "there's a lot of humidity down in the peat, and it circulates with the air. The combination of moisture and air makes the temperature drop like a refrigerator, so it can actually get to be freezing down in the plants, but the air temperature might only register at thirty-six, or maybe even as high as thirty-eight, degrees."

"I can still remember Grandpa getting worried about frost coming a few times, and for some reason it seems like it was in the summer." Meg shook her head. "Is that possible around here?"

"You bet it is, Meggie. Although it's not real common. It's those earlier producers that you have to be real careful of; your late berries don't bloom until June. Still, it's when the blossoms are on that you have to watch for the frost, even if it is summer. And even if the air temperature is above freezing."

"I never knew that, Cal," said Meg. "But I'm sure glad that you're helping me out in this."

Cal smiled and hooked his thumbs into his black suspenders. "It's my pleasure, Meggie. My goal is to see that old bog get back to what it was when Stewart was alive."

"Mine, too."

"Okay, everyone," called Clive as she walked in with a cake glowing with candles. "Time to sing!" They all sang boisterously, then enjoyed generous wedges of German chocolate cake topped with French vanilla ice cream. As they ate, they talked about everything from the latest shipment of farm implements to the art exhibit scheduled to open at Glass Cove next week.

"Abby," said Meg as she sighed with pleasure, "everything has been so delicious. And you've worked so hard; now you must let me help clean up the kitchen."

"That's right, Sis," said Matthew, quickly standing and gathering all the plates. "I'll help, too. You sit here and relax a bit."

"Well, don't mind if I do," said Abby as she stuck her feet up on the ottoman with a sly grin.

When they had collected all the dishes, Meg began rinsing while Matthew loaded them into the dishwasher.

"This is a great kitchen," said Meg, grasping the first topic of conversation she could think of. "Really state-of-the-art."

"It's lost on me, but Abby has put it to a pretty good use. And Clive is becoming a fairly good cook, too."

"Lucky for you, eh?"

"I can't complain." He patted his flat stomach. "But it plays havoc with the waistline."

She laughed and rinsed the final plate, appreciating the way he always made her feel comfortable whenever there was a moment of tension between them. "Thanks for inviting me tonight," she said. "It's always so great being with your family. You guys are such fun, like what a real family should be."

"Well, like any family we certainly have our ups and downs. But with God's help, we've made it through the hard times." He neatly folded a dish towel and laid it on top of the granite countertop.

Meg glanced around the clean kitchen. "Looks like our work is done here. And I should probably be on my way, now that I'm a working girl again."

"Will you be okay tonight?"

"I think so."

He smiled. "Glad to hear it."

"Were you worried that I would call you to come and rescue me again?"

"More like hopeful," he said quietly. Then he grinned. "Like I said, I enjoy rescuing damsels in distress. And besides, it's good for my image."

Meg decided not to respond to the first part of his answer and picked up his light tone. "And would that be the evil-lawyer image?"

"Right. Lawyers are always getting a bad rap. I need all the help I can get."

"Okay, I'll keep that in mind the next time I need help."

"Good."

"Hey, where did this come from?" called Abby from the next room. "Matthew, did you see this?"

Matthew and Meg walked out to see what she was talking about. Abby had the framed picture of Clive in her hands.

"Meg, did you take this?" asked Abby as if accusing her of some horrible deed.

"Yes," said Meg hesitantly. "I wanted to leave it here, sort of as a thank-you for that great day of sailing."

"Let's see, Sis," said Matthew. Abby handed it to him, and his sandy brows knit together as he studied it.

"Meg, this is beautiful. Has Clive seen it?"

"No," Meg said. "Actually, I was hoping to slip out before it was discovered." But before she could say another word, both Cal and Clive were examining the photo.

"Thanks, Meg," said Matthew. "It's a real treasure."

"I hoped you would like it." Meg couldn't help the smile that escaped as she felt his praise warm her inside. "And now, I think I should probably get going. I've had a wonderful time. Thank you all for everything. And happy birthday, Cal."

Matthew walked Meg to the door and helped her with her coat. "You know, I think Sunny had a coat exactly like this one," he said.

"This is it," said Meg.

Matthew grinned. "Well, good for you, Meg. Sunny would like that, I think."

"I think so, too." Meg felt a strange fluttering in her stomach as Matthew's hands lingered on her shoulders, but then he drew away and wished her good night.

Meg tried not to think about Matthew on her way home, but it was almost impossible not to. Something was happening to her heart, something she wasn't ready for. She was almost certain that Matthew wasn't ready for it, either. His life seemed pretty full and complete to her. Nice and neat. He didn't need someone like her, whose life was currently rather fragmented and almost over the edge at times. Between her commitment to the cranberry bog, her responsibilities for the gallery, and her burning need to find out more about Sunny and her father, her life was too full to be upset by a romance right now. Right now, she needed to trust God and to have peace in her life. That would be more than enough. And yet, she couldn't help but sigh as she thought of the warm feeling she had when she was with Matthew. It was much more than she'd experienced with Jerred. Maybe she would be ready to explore those feelings—someday.

She walked up the steps to the apartment. All of last night's apprehension and fear seemed to be gone. She unlocked the door and stepped inside. Ah. This felt like home. She hung up the beautiful coat in her closet, and then one by one hung up the rest of the garments that were scattered over the bed. At first she put Sunny's things on one side and hers on the other, but finally she mixed them all up together. Then she stepped back and smiled. Perfect.

Meg had already decided she would sleep in the bedroom tonight. It no longer frightened her. In fact, it was becoming quite comforting. She got ready for bed, noticing the spare sets of sheets stacked neatly in the linen closet as she reached for a hand towel.

The narrow closet smelled of dried lavender. Meg removed a set of sweet-smelling sheets and carried them to the bed. She stood there for a moment, then laid the sheets at the foot of the bed and pulled back the quilt. She sat down and began running her hand across the sheet. Back and forth, back and forth, she rubbed her hand over the smooth percale. She didn't know how long she sat there, but after a while she realized she was growing cold and tired.

Sunny had slept here. Right here, in this bed. No, it was her mother who had slept here. Her very own mother. Finally, Meg curled up in her mother's bed and cried herself to sleep.

Twenty-Seven

MEG AWOKE STRANGELY REFRESHED the next morning. Almost invigorated. She opened the shop and went right to work mounting and framing some of the other photos she'd picked up yesterday. Some were from sailing, and some from the bog, and she even did a couple that she'd taken of Ashley's bunnies. When she was finished, she hung them on the wall next to the ones Sunny had saved. Meg stepped back to assess her work. She thought they looked okay, but then she had never been much of an art critic. She would wait and see how the customers reacted, and if anyone turned up their nose, she would quietly remove them all when no one was around.

Erin and Ashley came in again for the morning, and Meg used the time to do some laundry and check on the progress of the moving van coming from San Francisco. An impatient woman from the moving company told Meg that everything should be there, safe and sound, by tomorrow or the next day at the latest.

Meg brought in lunch for the three of them and arranged it nicely on the little table in her apartment. After they had finished eating, Ashley got up and started creeping around, looking in corners and around doors.

"What are you doing, Ashley?" asked Erin as she sipped her coffee.

Ashley looked up at them with a puzzled face. "Looking for Grandma."

"Oh, honey," said Erin. "Grandma is with Jesus now, remember?"

Ashley smiled and nodded her head. "Is Jesus here?"

Erin looked at Meg, and they both smiled. Poor Ashley looked even more puzzled.

"Yes, Ashley," said Meg. "Jesus is here."

"And Grandma?" asked Ashley with big eyes.

Erin explained that Grandma had gone up to heaven to be with Jesus but that Jesus could be anywhere, which meant that Jesus was here with them, too.

Erin and Ashley went home in the afternoon, and Meg puttered about the gallery, dusting and straightening just the way Siggie had told her to. In the middle of the afternoon, an older couple came in. Meg didn't recognize them, but there were a lot of people in town she hadn't met yet. Finally, the man approached her.

"My wife and I are interested in something," he said, "but we didn't see a price tag on it."

"Why don't you show me what it is," said Meg. "I'm still new at this, but I'll do the best I can." She followed him over to where his wife was standing. The gray-haired woman was staring at a neatly framed enlarged photo of Ashley wearing a big sun hat, holding a wilted bouquet of wildflowers, and sitting in a wheelbarrow at the cranberry bog. Meg had taken it the day before Sunny died.

"How much for this photo?" asked the woman without moving her eyes.

Meg bit her lip. "Um, let me go check on that," she said. She needed a moment to think. She hadn't even considered putting prices on her pictures. She had never thought anyone would want to buy them.

"You know, none of these photos have prices on them," Meg heard the man say as she walked back to the counter. "Maybe they aren't for sale, Martha."

Meg finally decided on what seemed like a fair price and quoted it to them as if she had just read it from a catalog. She was ready for them to laugh and walk out, but instead the man plucked it off the wall and carried it to the cash register.

"We'll take it," he said, pulling out his billfold. Meg tried not to gape as she counted out the bills and handed him a receipt.

The woman leaned over to Meg. "When I saw that picture, it reminded me of my childhood. It's as if the photographer captured something more than just a cute picture."

Meg smiled as she carefully wrapped the framed photo.

"Thanks," said the man.

"You're very welcome," said Meg. "Come in again."

As they left, Clive came in. "Hi, Meg. I'm here for my job interview."

"You don't really have to interview, Clive. If you want to work here after school, you're hired as of now." In the window behind Clive, Meg noticed Abner's Suburban cruise by. She winced. It seemed like whenever she saw the huge vehicle, it meant trouble.

"Great. But I can only come on days that I don't have track. Today and tomorrow they're resurfacing the track, and it's a big mess over there. So here I am."

"Good."

Meg showed Clive around and explained the basic processes for everything. As she'd expected, Clive caught on fast.

"I can work weekends, too, Meg. Either here or out on the bog—wherever you need me. Grandpa said that I could help this weekend, 'cause he's got a weeding crew coming in."

"I know. I've already arranged for Erin to watch shop for me here. I plan to go out and help, too. It'll be fun seeing the bogs pulled into shape so fast."

"Yeah, especially after seeing how long it took us to do just one bog."

Meg nodded. "Clive, do you feel comfortable watching the shop for me until closing? I have an errand to take care of."

"No problem. It doesn't look like we're exactly swamped with customers right now."

Meg laughed. "No, it doesn't usually get too busy in here. But I'll leave you my cell-phone number in case anything comes up or if you have a question."

Meg tucked a small photo that she'd framed that morning into her purse. It was a goofy shot of Jason and Clive pulling weeds at the bog. Meg hopped into her Jeep and headed out toward Briar Hedge, but she didn't stop at Grandmother's. Instead she drove past the bog and up the hill. She was thankful she wasn't driving her Jaguar anymore, because the road got bumpier the farther she went. She hadn't been out this far since she'd been a kid, but she didn't suppose it would be too difficult to find her cousin's house, since no one else lived on this road. Not that she was hoping to see Abner. If she hadn't spotted his Suburban drive past in town, she wouldn't have come out. Ever since her chat with Jason, she had been determined to pay Phoebe a visit. Hopefully she'd be gone before Abner returned.

The white double-wide mobile home looked out of place against the forested hill, sort of like a Styrofoam cup tossed into a lush garden. The yard was littered with bits and pieces of rusting machinery, a pile of old lumber, and several tires. She parked and walked up to the front door, glancing nervously over her shoulder.

"Meg?" Jason opened the door with a puzzled brow before she could ring the bell. "Whatcha doing here?"

She handed him the photo. "Hi, Jason. I thought you might like this. And I wanted to meet your mom, if it's okay. I noticed your dad was in town and thought I'd take a chance."

"Thanks, Meg. This is great," said Jason, staring at the photo. His cheeks and ears had turned a bright shade of red, but he was grinning. "Yeah, it's probably a real good time to stop by. Dad was on his way to meet his buddies. No telling when he'll be back. Let me go check with my mom, though. Okay?"

"That's fine. And if it's not a good time for her, I'll understand. I know this is spur-of-the-moment. And actually, I wanted to ask you something too, Jason."

"What's that?"

"I wondered if you were ready to start working part-time at the gallery—after school sometimes, and occasionally on weekends. I don't know how many hours there will be, since Clive is going to help out, too. But I thought you might want to work a few hours at the bog as well, unless that's a problem with your dad."

"That'd be great, Meg. I'd like working at the gallery. And I can probably help at the bog, too, but I'd have to do it at certain times, you know?"

"I know."

"I'll go see what Mom's doing."

Meg prepared herself to be sent away. She really should have phoned first, but when she'd seen Abner's rig in town, it had seemed like the perfect opportunity. But perhaps Phoebe would be embarrassed.

After a few minutes, Jason came back and said, "Come on in, Meg. Mom's in the living room."

After seeing the front yard, Meg had thought the inside of the house might be messy as well. To her surprise, it was neat as a pin, although the dark furniture and worn carpet gave the place the feel of a cheap motel. Phoebe moved toward her, smiling warmly. She wore peach polyester pants and a Hawaiian shirt in bright tropical colors.

"Hello, Meg," said Phoebe. "I'm so glad you stopped by. I wanted to meet you at your mother's funeral—well, it wasn't exactly a funeral.... Anyway, I wanted to meet you and tell you how sorry I am. Sunny was such a dear woman. I miss her a great deal, more than I can say. Now, come on in and sit down. I hardly ever get visitors out here, although your mother used to come once in a while. That would just make my day." Phoebe sank down on the sagging brown couch and seemed to need a moment to catch her breath.

"I didn't mean to barge in on you, Phoebe, without calling. I didn't even think."

Phoebe waved her hand. "Your timing couldn't have been better. Abner's out with the boys and probably won't be back until late. Jason, can you get us some coffee? I just put a pot on. Would you like some coffee, Meg? And I just baked a pound cake. Bring in some of that, too, won't you, Jason?"

"Sure, Mom," he called back.

"Jason is a great kid," said Meg. "I've appreciated his help at the bog. And I hope you don't mind, but I offered him some part-time work at the gallery."

"That would be nice. He needs to get out more. How is it going with the gallery? Will it continue to stay in business like before?"

"Sure. Nothing's changed with the business."

"Good. Sunny would like that."

"I didn't realize that you and Sunny were friends," said Meg as Jason set down mugs of coffee and generous slices of pound cake.

"Oh, it wasn't as if we were real close. I know Sunny had dozens of friends. But she was a friend to me, and I don't have many." Phoebe pressed her lips together and stared down at the coffee table. "Well, now, you had better try some of my pound cake, Meg."

Meg took a plate and tried not to think of how many calories

268

were in this huge slice. After the first bite, she no longer cared.

"This is absolutely delicious, Phoebe!"

Phoebe ducked her head shyly. "Thanks, Meg. If there's one thing I do take a bit of pride in, it's my baking."

"Grandmother has mentioned that you've sent baked goods over, and she loves them."

Phoebe smiled again.

"Mom's the best cook ever," said Jason proudly. "There's nothing she can't bake, and better than anybody else."

"Oh, go on, you," said Phoebe, obviously enjoying every minute of it.

"My grandpa—well, Abner's too, although I know he never met him—was quite a good cook. In fact, I recently found all his old cranberry recipes. You might be interested in some of them."

"Oh, I sure would, Meg. I just love trying new things."

"I'll get copies made and bring them out to you."

"That would be wonderful. But, Meg?"

"Yes?"

"Next time, you might want to call first. You see, with Abner around, well—"

"I understand. Sure, Phoebe, I'll be glad to call first. And I hate to run, but I need to get back to help Clive close the shop."

"Clive's working today?" asked Jason, his eyes bright.

"Yes, this is her first day. She's also coming out this weekend to help on the bog." Meg glanced at Phoebe, unsure of how Abner's wife felt about the cranberry bog. She imagined Phoebe sided with her husband, because they'd probably make quite a bit of money if the land was sold for development. So she was surprised by what Phoebe said next.

"Meg, I know you won't repeat this, but I don't mind saying I'm real glad you're doing what you are. I don't understand why Abner has given up on the cranberries. Everything was going so well the first few years we were here, and then he seemed to get lazier and started drinking more, and now I just don't know what to do about him half the time."

"I understand. Maybe if he sees them being brought back, that will encourage him to look at things differently."

"I don't know, Meg. But I sure hope so."

"Thanks for the cake, Phoebe. It really was delicious."

"Jason," Phoebe said. "You wrap up the rest of that loaf for Meg." She turned to Meg. "You take it home with you. Maybe you can slice it up for your customers in the gallery. Sunny used to do that sometimes."

"That's a great idea," said Meg. "Thanks again for everything."

As Meg set the foil-covered loaf on the car seat beside her, she wondered if Phoebe would like to bake things on a regular basis for the gallery. It would give her some extra money, and it might be smart marketing to have some good snacks at the gallery.

Just as Meg expected, Clive had had no problems managing the gallery. Meg thanked her and locked up, while Clive departed to the Feed and Seed to catch a ride home with her grandpa. Then Meg dashed upstairs and called Grandmother, inviting herself over for dinner.

"I'll tell Rosa to put another plate on," said Grandmother.

"I'll be there in ten minutes," said Meg.

And she was. Rosa served dinner in Grandmother's room, since she had been up a lot already today. Meg told her about the gallery, how she was settling into the apartment, and that she had actually sold a photo. When Grandmother had finished her last bite, Meg poured her another cup of tea.

"How was your visit with Matthew?" asked Meg as she sipped her tea.

Grandmother stiffened slightly. "It was fine."

"I asked Matthew to discuss putting something together for us in regard to the bog."

"Yes, he told me about it. I don't quite understand why we

need anything drawn up. After all, we're family."

"Well," Meg began, searching for the right words, "I plan to invest a bit of my own money—actually, quite a bit—and I don't want Abner to sell the bog out from under us."

"He can't sell what isn't his," said Grandmother indignantly.

"Yes, I know, but I was a little worried. It will be pretty costly to restore the bog and—"

"But, Meggie, you know I don't have much money to spare," said Grandmother, her eyes wide. "I never—"

"No, Grandmother," Meg interrupted gently, "you don't understand. I don't want you to put a single penny into this."

"But then, how will you manage?"

"I decided it was something I wanted to do."

"But how can you afford it?"

"Don't worry, I'm not bankrupting myself. Besides, I want to do this for Grandpa, for the family. The cranberry bog is part of our heritage. And everyone—well, everyone but Abner—seems to want to see it preserved."

Grandmother set down her teacup and looked at Meg with concerned eyes. "I never meant for you to get this involved, Meggie. Putting money into this place..." She shook her head. "It was one thing when it was just you kids working on it. It seemed to amuse you—"

"It's more than amusement, Grandmother. And I thought you wanted to see it brought back. You told me that I could—"

"But what about Abner?"

"What about Abner?" Meg tried to keep the irritation out of her voice. After all, Abner was as much Grandmother's grandchild as Meg was.

"Well, I just don't know what he's going to say about all this. Bringing in crews, spending all that money—"

"My money, Grandmother. And remember, it is your land."

"I know, I know. I just don't want to upset Abner."

271

"But what about all the upsetting that Abner is doing?"

"I know; he's not an easy one. But he has his problems, Meggie. You have to understand."

"Well, I understand that he doesn't give a hoot about the bog and that he would sell this whole place in a second if he could."

Grandmother looked down into her lap. She started rubbing her hands together and then began to tremble.

"Oh, I'm sorry, Grandmother," said Meg, feeling guilty. "I thought I was doing something good. But if it's not right, or if it upsets you, I'll call Cal and tell him you've—tell him *we've* changed our minds."

"No, no. I don't want you to do that, Meggie. Not exactly." Grandmother paused and shook her head. "If only there was some way to make everyone happy. If only—if only..." Grandmother's eyes got a faraway look, and her lips continued to move as if she were speaking, but Meg couldn't hear or understand the words. It frightened her, and she went out to ask for Rosa's help.

"It's okay, Meg," said Rosa as she turned off the TV. "She gets like that sometimes. But don't you worry, I'll take care of her now."

Meg drove home and wondered if she should tell Cal to put a stop to their plan. In all fairness, she would still need to pay him something for his efforts. But on the other hand, Grandmother had said to go ahead. Even if there was the tiniest chance that Grandmother might change her mind again, would it hurt anything to at least get things going to save the bog? Besides, if they stopped now, it would be too late—forever.

Before she went to bed, Meg read some more in the Bible that Matthew had given her. Last night, she had started reading the Gospel that he was named after, and in it, she found a verse where Jesus told people not to worry about things but to trust their heavenly Father. She asked God to help her with that one.

Worrying was such a natural thing for her to do. It would be hard to let go of. But she would try.

Twenty-Eight

CAL AND THE CREW STARTED TO WORK on the bog on Friday. On Saturday, Meg went out to help while Erin kept shop. To Meg's surprise and pleasure, Matthew dropped off Clive. But he didn't leave. Jason joined them, too, and just before noon, Tom and the girls showed up. By late afternoon, Meg looked around and was amazed at how much had been accomplished in two short days. For the first time since she'd started, she believed that the bog might produce something besides weeds when it came time to harvest.

"I'm real pleased," said Cal at the end of the day. "I think by Tuesday we'll be ready to start spraying." He looked at the clipboard in his hand. "See here, Meggie, I've been keeping track of what kind of weeds are most prevalent in each area so we'll know exactly what to spray."

"And I thought you were just doodling, Pop," Matthew teased.

"We're not going to be able to save the four bogs on the east end, Meggie. They're just too far gone; it's not worth it. They can be replanted next fall."

Meg nodded. She had expected as much. "I guess we should be glad there's only those four."

"That's right. It's downright amazing what good shape these plants are in, considering what they've been through. I never expected to see this many uprights."

Meg knew, from what Grandpa had taught her long ago, that uprights were one of the most important parts of the plants. The upright was where the berries would grow, and the more uprights on the plant, the better. She knew there weren't nearly as many as there would be in a normal bog, but she was glad they had any.

"I can't believe I almost gave up, Cal."

"A lot of people would have, Meggie. The truth is, it's nothing short of a miracle that things are looking this good."

"Well, I think someone's looking after Meg," said Matthew, putting his hand on her shoulder. She knew it was just a friendly gesture, like something a big brother might do, but just the same it made her breath catch in her throat.

"But, as good as things are looking, we're nowhere near done," said Cal. "We've still got the herbicides, and you'll still be needing lots of hand weeding because believe me, Meggie, these weeds may look like they're under control now, but they'll keep coming back. Then we've got to get some fertilizer on here, and there's always the frost—"

"Okay, Pop," said Matthew. "Let's not rain on her parade yet. I'm starving. How about we all head over to Mario's for pizza? My treat."

"No, it should be my treat," Meg protested.

Matthew's sandy eyebrows drew together in a mock frown. "Are you sure you want to argue with a lawyer, Meg?"

"Maybe not." Meg smiled. "But do you think they'll let us in like this?" She held out her stained hands and looked down at her dirty shirt and jeans.

Matthew gave a little tug on her French braid. "Sure. Mario's a good buddy of mine."

They invaded Mario's and were treated to excellent service and even better pizza. They stayed late, eating and talking until they were the only ones left in the restaurant.

Meg thanked everyone as they left. It was incredible how helpful and friendly people were here. It reminded her of stories she'd heard about the good old days, with barn raisings and quilting bees. She realized that if she hadn't been in such need, she probably never would have made all these friends.

Back at her apartment Meg took a long, hot bath and then felt ready to collapse into bed. She was getting ready to do just that when she spotted the cedar chest. Each night she had been telling herself that she would get to it the following day, and when the next day arrived, she was just too busy. It was only ten o'clock now, and she used to stay up much later than this in the city, but that was before all this fresh air and exercise. Maybe she could stay up a little later, just this one night. Somehow, she felt it was time to look into Sunny's past.

She went over and carefully removed the old quilt from the top, then fit the key in the lock. It turned easily, and opened with a soft click. She lifted the lid and was met by the strong smell of cedar. Sunny had opened it for her once when she was little, and had shown her some old baby clothes inside. Meg couldn't remember what else had been in it, but she remembered the smell.

The chest wasn't as full as Meg had expected it to be. She wondered if Sunny had already gone through and removed things that she didn't want to leave behind, or if the things she'd taken out were in the boxes she'd already put together for Meg and Erin. Meg fingered through a stack of diplomas and awards that Sunny had received over the years. Sunny had devoted so much time and energy to her education during those early years, going to college year-round, taking night classes, and being on committees to win points with the administrators. And this was all that was left to show for it. No, Meg corrected herself. There was more. A lot more.

Meg dug deeper, rifling through piles of old photos, programs, and newspaper clippings about art exhibits Sunny had directed at the university. She was getting close to the bottom and was about ready to go to bed when two things caught her eye. One was a stack of old letters, and the other was what looked like a journal, but the journal didn't look old at all. The two were tied together with a red ribbon. Meg untied the ribbon and opened up the journal first, since it was on top. To her surprise, the very first entry was written to her. Sunny must have put this together, hoping that Meg would find it. She sat down on the floor and began to read.

Dear Megan,

I hope that somehow this finds its way into your hands because it might help explain many of the things that I've never had a chance to say to you. First of all, I must say that I am very sorry. I'm sorry for all that I put you through as a child, and I'm sorry that you felt the need to remove yourself so completely from my life, for what appears to be forever. I don't ever expect to see you again, Megan, and if you're reading this, it must mean that I am gone. Please understand I don't hold that against you. No, it is my fault, Megan.

I realize now that I was a complete failure as a mother. You told me that many times as a teenager, and you were right. I did let you down. I let Erin down, and I let myself down. And I am very, very sorry. I've considered trying to find you, but I want to respect your privacy. I know that should you ever want to, you'll know where to find us. I pray that someday you will.

The reason I'm writing this is because I've just discovered that I have only a few months to live, and I'm afraid I might die without having a chance to make things right with you. Or to at least try. I hope that you will be able to forgive me, because I know how terrible it feels to not be able to forgive someone in your family. I saw my father do it to my mother, and I saw myself do it to your father.

*Although everyone suffers, it is the children who pay the greatest price,
and for that I'm truly sorry. I've already talked about this with Erin,
and fortunately for her and her children, she believes in a Christian
forgiveness. She has managed to break away from this vicious cycle.
Megan, I hope that if you have children, you are not living in bitterness toward me—because if you are, watch out. It will spill over and
poison your children, the way it did to me and the way it did to you.*

Meg could no longer read. Her eyes were filled with tears. She
closed the journal and thought about Sunny's words. For the first
time, Meg was thankful she had no children, because what Sunny
said was painfully true. Unforgiveness had been poisoning Meg
over the years, and it eventually spilled out onto anyone who got
close to her.

She took a deep breath and thanked God that he was starting
to teach her about forgiveness, even if she had a long way to go.
Then she continued to read in the journal. Sunny wrote more
about how the unforgiveness and bitterness in her life had begun
with her own parents, but Meg still couldn't figure out exactly
what had happened. Like what she'd heard from Grandmother,
Sunny also implied that Grandmother had done something
wrong and that Grandpa had held it against her for a long time.
Meg wondered what it could have been, but it seemed that Sunny
was purposely not disclosing this information in the journal.

After several more entries with apologies and reflections, Meg
found an entry that began to talk about her father. Her grip tightened on the small book, and she read the words with fierce inten-
sity, almost as if they would vanish off the page before she could
take them all in.

*When I met your father, he seemed like a good man, although
Daddy told me differently. But I was only eighteen, and I thought I
knew it all. And besides, I was more than ready to get away from*

home. Bennie had been dead several years by then, but the cold war between Mother and Daddy seemed to go on and on, growing worse with each passing year.

Finally, I just couldn't stand it anymore. John provided me with a welcome escape from all that. What I didn't realize was that I had just jumped from the frying pan into the fire. For several years, I blamed myself. I told myself if I were only a better wife, or if I cooked better or cleaned better, or if I were prettier or funnier. Perhaps the problem was that I had gotten pregnant with Erin so soon after we were married. But the truth is—and I don't blame you if you can't believe this, Megan—I kept the house spotless, and I cooked better than I ever had, before or since. And I wasn't bad-looking, if I do say so myself. Just look at the photos if you don't believe me, Megan. I have saved some. I know, you probably thought I blacked out your father's face on all of them. But I didn't. I saved a small box for you. Erin said she doesn't want any, and I don't blame her. I can't stand to look at them myself. They are for you, and they are in the cedar chest. Go ahead and look at them. Then do whatever you like with them.

Meg looked through the few remaining items in the chest and picked up an old Christmas candy box. She opened it and looked at pictures of what appeared to be a nice, ordinary family. The house behind them was neat and clean. The parents were both very attractive. Her father had thick, dark hair and eyes just like Erin's. And Sunny was blonde and beautiful; she looked almost like a movie star. The dark-haired baby, whom she knew was Erin, was pretty and wearing frilly little clothes. There were shots in front of Christmas trees. Shots outside in the yard. Shots in the nursery. Everything looked very nice and normal, just like a fifties television family might look. What could have gone so horribly wrong? Meg picked up the journal again and flipped to the next page.

*So now, if you've looked at the pictures, you're probably thinking:
"Gee, Sunny, things couldn't have been that bad. You lived in a cute
house, he looks like a nice guy; why did you go and blow it?" For years
I told myself the same thing. Besides, he only beat me once, sometimes
twice, a month. Usually he tried to avoid my face, although I did
have to use a lot of makeup more times than I care to remember in
order to cover up bruises and the occasional black eye. But I stayed
home a lot in those days. And fortunately for him, we lived away from
my family, and I had no friends. His family lived someplace on the
East Coast, which is why he had moved out west. You see, he hated his
father. I suspect it was because his father had taught him, by example,
everything he knew.*

Meg shut her eyes tight and took a quick breath. Her heart
was racing now. It was almost too painful to read, yet she couldn't
stop. Not yet.

*The confusing part was that he would always apologize profusely
afterwards. He would bring me flowers and gifts, and promise never,
never to do it again. At first I believed him. I felt sorry for him. I
knew when I married him that he was a creative person, with that
artist's temperament. You probably never knew that your father was
an artist, Megan. Actually, he was quite good. He worked for one of
the top graphic-design firms in Seattle back then.*

*But by the time Erin turned four, I knew beyond a shadow of a
doubt that I despised him. I even wondered if I had the nerve to kill
him. I actually considered arsenic in his morning coffee. Or perhaps I
could drop the electric radio into his bath. Finally, I decided it would
be better to just run away. You see, it was one thing when he hurt me,
but another thing when he hurt my child. When he started venting
his anger on Erin, I knew we were through. I couldn't even believe he
did it at first. He had always treated Erin like his little princess, and
she looked so much like him. I hate to admit it, but sometimes I was*

actually jealous of the attention he gave her.

When he began to lash out at her too, I knew it was time to leave. But he made sure I had no money, no car, nothing. I was his prisoner, and Erin was his hostage. If I ever mentioned leaving, he would beat me and threaten to do something dreadful to Erin. I won't bother to horrify you with the details of how I became pregnant with you, Megan. Just know I was never sorry that I had you. I may not have been much of a mother, and you may not have known this, but I always loved you. I still do.

Meg closed the journal. She couldn't take any more. Why did she have to read this right now? Just when she was starting to get over losing Sunny and getting used to her new life. Why had Sunny even left these things here? Erin had been right when she had said that some stones were better left unturned. Too bad Sunny hadn't burned all of this. Ignorance in this case would have been blissful.

Meg crawled into bed, more lost and alone than she had felt in ages. All the pain of her family seemed to be wrapped into one huge bundle, and now it lay upon her chest like an enormous boulder about to crush the life out of her. She reached over to turn off the light and saw Matthew's Bible on the bedside table. It seemed to take every ounce of strength for her to pick it up. When she did, the pages flopped open, and she stared blankly at the print. She felt bone weary, and very tired of reading. Finally her eyes focused on one spot in the middle of the right page.

"Come to me, all you who are weary and burdened and I will give you rest." She stared at the words, which seemed to leap from the page, reading them over and over. She thought she could hear Jesus himself speaking to her. She closed her eyes and leaned back into the pillow, repeating the comforting words in her mind again and again until she finally fell asleep.

Twenty-Nine

THE NEXT MORNING, MEG IGNORED the cedar chest with its gaping lid, and the contents spilling across the bedroom floor. She would deal with it later. First she was going to church.

The words of the service felt dull and flat to her today, and she slipped out before the benediction, then drove down toward the beach. She parked the Jeep and got out. It was a beautiful day, with a blue sky and almost no wind, perfect for a pleasant stroll along the shore. She began to walk, not really sure what her purpose was, but she knew she needed time to sort things out. Before long, she noticed that sand was filling her shoes, and she realized belatedly that her silk dress and leather pumps weren't exactly beachwear. She slipped off her shoes and carried them, continuing along.

After a while she sat down on a piece of smooth driftwood and looked out over the sea, watching the waves curling in, one after the other, over and over again. Finally, she realized why she had come.

"Sunny," she whispered, "I don't know if you can hear me or not. Maybe it doesn't matter. But I want to tell you again how sorry I am. I never knew you had it so tough, Sunny. I held so much against you. I just didn't know. I never realized that my father was such—such—" She burst into sobs and buried her head in her hands. If only Meg had known. Why hadn't Sunny told her about all this? Was it to protect her? Poor, poor Sunny.

"Thanks, Sunny," Meg continued. "I know you did the best you could. And I appreciate it." She whispered a prayer of thanks to God for bringing her to this place, as painful as it was. It helped her to finally understand why Sunny was the way she was. Once again, Meg felt the icy edge of bitterness pressing in upon her heart, but this time it was directed toward her father. How could her very own flesh-and-blood father have been such a cruel and unfeeling person? He was really the one to blame for the mess that had been made of their lives.

"Oh, Lord," she prayed. "Now you're going to have to help me forgive him, too, because I don't think I can on my own." She stared out toward the ocean. Would she ever be done forgiving people, or did it just go on and on forever? Like the waves that kept rolling in.

"Hey, Meg," called a voice from up the beach. She turned and looked, and saw Matthew walking toward her. She wiped the last traces of tears from her cheeks and waved.

"Thought I'd find you down here," he said as he came closer. "Can I join you?"

"Sure, pull up a piece of log." She smiled and patted her hand on the driftwood.

"I saw you sneaking out of church," he said. "And I wondered if you were okay."

If he hadn't sounded so kind and sympathetic, she might not have started crying again. But with a sense of déjà vu, Meg's tears started afresh. At least she wasn't sobbing like last time.

He pulled out a handkerchief and handed it to her.

"Valiant knight to the rescue again?" she said as she wiped her cheeks and tried to stop the tears.

He grinned a lopsided grin. "Sure."

"Thanks. You always manage to catch me at my emotional worst," said Meg. "I might start to get a complex."

"It's okay. I know you're going through some tough things right now. It hasn't been that long since you lost your mother. I know it's not easy."

"But the thing is, I'm really okay with Sunny now. I think I'm finally beginning to understand her. I'm just sorry I didn't get acquainted sooner."

Matthew smiled. "So what's the bad news?"

Meg looked out over the ocean, wondering how much to tell. Or whether to tell anything. It was so awful to think her father had been such a loser. Matthew probably wouldn't understand, since his father was such a great guy. And yet she needed a friend to talk to.

"The bad news is, I've just found out some extremely unpleasant things about my father."

Matthew nodded with a creased brow.

She shook her head. "And now I know I have to forgive him, but I don't want to."

"I know. That's not going to be easy."

"What do you mean, you know?"

Matthew looked at her with clear blue eyes. "Sunny told me a lot about it. It wasn't easy for her, either."

"But did she forgive him?"

He nodded. "Eventually."

"Then I can, too," said Meg firmly.

"God had to help Sunny. I think it was the biggest obstacle to her coming to faith."

"But God got her through it. He'll have to help me too."

Matthew grinned. "That's the spirit. Now, the other reason I was looking for you was because we are taking the *Regina* out and we need another crew member."

"I'd love to come."

"Great. Clive invited Jason yesterday. In fact, she was wondering if you'd mind picking him up."

"No problem," said Meg. She wondered what she'd say if she ran into Abner.

"Jason said he'd be waiting at your grandmother's house."

"That's good," said Meg, relieved.

Meg went home and changed, then picked up Jason before driving down to the dock. It was another perfect day for sailing, and Meg even managed to help Abby in the galley without getting seasick. Later, Clive allowed Meg to take the helm while she gave Jason a few sailing tips. Breathing the fresh sea air and riding the waves seemed to sweep Meg's concerns about her father far away. She wished they could go on forever like this, but finally it was time to turn back. When they pulled into the slip, the sun was turning pink and sinking low in the sky.

Meg took Jason back to Grandmother's and returned home. After a shower, she sat down on the bed and looked at the cedar chest, still open, still waiting. She had to finish Sunny's journal and lay these things to rest once and for all.

To Meg's relief, there were no more unpleasant surprises. The remainder of the journal was quite encouraging and uplifting. Sunny shared what Matthew and Abby were teaching her about how God forgave the world through Jesus Christ, and how for the first time it made sense to her. She even wrote that she realized she needed to forgive John.

I know that John will never know that I forgave him, and perhaps that's not that important right now. But I understand that if I don't forgive him, it will be impossible for me to accept God's forgiveness for my life. That might not make sense to you, Meg. But let me explain it with a picture that I believe God gave me.

Imagine, if you will, that you have a beautiful puzzle that is all put together, but is missing one piece. You're holding a puzzle piece in your hand, but it doesn't fit. No matter how you try, it just won't work. It's because you need to give that piece to someone else; it's the missing part of their puzzle. And only when you let go of that piece can God hand you the missing piece to your puzzle. I know that's sort of silly, Meg. But you know how I always liked doing jigsaw puzzles.

Meg closed her eyes and considered her mother's words. It did make sense. Meg prayed again that God would help her forgive her father, and this time she imagined God taking her piece of forgiveness to her father, wherever he was, and then placing his own piece of forgiveness in her hands. So simple, yet it gave her heart a tremendous feeling of peace.

She sighed and looked back at the journal. Flipping the next page, she sadly realized that she had come to the final entry, apparently written on the same day that Meg had returned to Crandale after nearly twenty years.

Dear Megan,

When I saw you today, I couldn't believe it. My own dear Meggie standing right before me! When I hugged you, I never wanted to let go. But I didn't want to scare you away, either. It was such an answer to prayer to see you again. Unfortunately, I put my foot right in my mouth—as usual! If only I had more time, perhaps God could show me how to manage my tongue better. But I don't. I'm afraid that you might disappear as quickly as you came, and I so want to do and say everything just right, but I know that I can't. So I'll write it all down, and that way perhaps I won't spoil it.

You are beautiful, Meg. See there, I called you Meg. You are not only beautiful on the outside, but I see a deep inner beauty in you as well. Sure, I know that you're not at peace yet; I can see that in your eyes. But I see a deep sense of caring and rightness in you. I know that you are going to be okay, Meg. I can feel it. And I believe that God has some special plans for you and that you were supposed to come back home. I hope you will stay. You belong here. I believe that with my whole heart.

For that reason, I want to leave my apartment to you. I worked hard to make this a place I felt comfortable in, and I hope you will, too. I always felt bad that I never gave you the home you needed as a child, and I hope this will help make up for it. I want you to have a place to come home to, Meg. But more than this apartment, I want you to have God. Because, you see, I have found that he is my place to come home to. And I know it won't be long until I'm there. I love you, Meg.

Love,
Your mother, Sunny

Meg hugged the journal to her chest, and the tears in her eyes were not from sadness tonight. She knew the time would come to read the journal again, but for now she returned it to its place in the trunk, along with the photos and other bits of memorabilia. Perhaps she would add her own things to it someday. Maybe she would have children one day who would go through it like she had, and they, too, would be blessed.

Life went smoothly for the next few weeks. The moving van arrived from San Francisco several days late, and as she unpacked, Meg was pleased at how nicely her strange collection of household goods melded with Sunny's things. Those that didn't, she had never cared much for anyway, and she donated them to charity.

Sigfried came back and took over the major responsibilities for the gallery, and with the coming of summer, it became increasingly busy. The warmer weather seemed to draw the shoppers to Crandale like homing pigeons, and many spent their money at the gallery. Sigfried sold a number of Meg's photos and begged her to bring in more. Now Meg went nearly everywhere with her camera, and she was pleased to notice that her photos were getting better all the time.

Matthew took Meg and Erin and Tom and the girls for a short sail on Mother's Day, and they tossed flowers into the water in remembrance of Sunny.

Life seemed just about perfect when June came along, and the cranberry plants began to bloom profusely, as if they, too, were enjoying their second chance at life. Meg loved walking around the bogs, inhaling the fresh, sweet fragrance of the fragile white blossoms. And although she knew Cal's fertilizer formulas had a lot to do with the results, it felt more like a miracle to see them blooming like this.

"Looks like we could have ourselves a freeze tonight, Meg," said Cal one early June day as Meg purchased a new set of work gloves and some water hoses at the Feed and Seed.

"Really? Where did you hear that?" asked Meg. "The air is a little cool today, but it's nice and sunny."

"Hank Whitmore was just in. He still raises McFarlin berries, too, and he was more'n a little worried. You know, most everybody else's blossoms are over by this time, so they're not too worked up. But you need to keep a watch on things tonight, Meggie. Remember to check all those thermometers, because freeze is a strange thing. It can hit one bog and miss another one altogether. Is your sump pond and irrigation system all in order? You know that's the only way to beat the freeze."

"Yes, it seems to be just fine. I haven't had to use it yet, but I gave the whole thing a trial run a couple of weeks ago after we replaced those sprinkler heads. Thanks for the tip, Cal. I'll stay on top of it. I'd hate to lose them now, after all this work."

"Not to mention the expense," Cal added.

"Any luck finding a buyer for the berries yet, Cal?"

He frowned and shook his head. "It's awful hard getting in so late. You know most folks get set up a year or more in advance. The lucky ones have ongoing commitments from the big buyers. Your granddad used to be one of those lucky ones."

"I know. But surely there's someone who will want the berries. We couldn't have come this far for nothing."

Cal rubbed his chin. "Maybe this is going to be one of those blind faith things where you just gotta trust God."

Meg picked up her bag and tried to smile. "I usually do have to learn things the hard way, Cal."

"Some folks say the school of hard knocks produces the best results."

"Or at least the lumpiest heads. Thanks, Cal."

Meg drove straight over to Briar Hedge and up to the bog. Naturally, there was no sign of frost this early in the afternoon. In fact, it was hard to believe it could even be possible; the sky was clear, and the air was warm from the sun. Meg strolled around the bogs, drinking in the sweet fragrance. The tender blossoms blanketed the bogs like fluffy white quilts. Cal had been pleasantly surprised at the number of blossoms. If all went well, it would be a pretty good harvest.

Meg was about to grab the pruning shears to cut back some overzealous blackberries when a strange sound made her stop. She cocked her head to one side and listened for a long moment. It was a gushing sound, like the sound of water running. She walked up toward the big sump pond that was used for irrigation and that would provide the needed water for harvest. If there was a frost tonight, Meg would need its water to cover the plants in order to keep them from freezing. The pond was fed by a stream shared by a number of cranberry growers, the same precious stream she had worked so hard to preserve water rights for.

When Meg reached the sump pond, the water level was way down. Water was pouring freely over an opened gate and down the stream that led to the next holding pond, which happened to be someone else's farm. She dashed over and tried to force the wooden gate back into place, but it was open wide, and the sheer force of the water made it impossible to budge. Finally she jumped into the pond and used her body to slow the fast-running water as she tried to shove the gate back into place.

After what seemed like years in the frigid water, Meg finally got the gate closed and climbed out of the pond, soaked and freezing cold. Exhausted, she slumped to the ground. As she sat in the dirt trying to catch her breath, she realized that the water level had been reduced to about a third of what it had been. She stared hard at the gate. It had not come open on its own. Someone had sabotaged it, and she had a pretty good idea who that someone might be.

Despite her bedraggled appearance, she wanted to settle this now. Meg walked over to her Jeep, telling herself she would remain calm and make no accusations. She would simply ask Abner if he had any idea who might have done such a thing. Or maybe she would ask him if he had seen anyone prowling around the property.

She drove quickly down the hill, trying to control her anger as she watched the muddy water dripping from her clothes and soaking into the upholstery of her Jeep.

"Hi, Meg," called Phoebe, waving happily as Meg hopped out and walked toward the house. Phoebe was sweeping the front porch. "I was just thinking of an idea—my goodness, Meg, you look like a drowned rat. What in tarnation have you been doing?"

"Trying to save my water," said Meg in a tight voice. "Is Abner home?"

"No, he left this morning. Don't know when he'll be back. Are you all right, Meg?"

Meg flopped down on the porch steps in a wet heap. "No, I'm not all right. I'm really mad. Someone opened the water gate at the sump pond, and I've lost nearly all my water. And Cal said there's a chance of frost tonight, which means I'll need that water to keep my plants from freezing."

Phoebe's forehead creased with concern. "Oh, dear, Meg. What can we do to help? Do you suppose we could run hoses from the house and fill up the pond again?"

Meg almost smiled. "Thanks, Phoebe, but that would probably take several days and about a mile's worth of hoses, and I doubt Abner would appreciate it."

"No, you're probably right about that. You don't think—"

"I know who did it," said Jason solemnly as he pushed open the screen door and stepped onto the porch. "I saw Dad park up there this morning and walk over to the pond. I didn't know what he was doing, or I sure would have gone up and closed it for you, Meg."

"I'm so sorry, Meg," gasped Phoebe. "And I'm so ashamed. I just don't know what to say."

"It isn't your fault, Phoebe," said Meg woodenly. "I just don't know what to do about it. I tried to look the other way when I learned he had sold off the farming equipment, but this is much worse." She paused. "Do you think it would do any good if Grandmother were to speak to him?"

"I don't think she would stand up to him, Meg," said Phoebe sadly. "Hardly anyone stands up to him. Except for you." Phoebe looked at Meg from the corner of her eye. "And you know what that's like...."

"I'll stand up to him," said Jason with fire in his eyes.

"No, Jason," said Meg calmly. "I don't want this to come between you and your dad. This is my problem."

"Well, it just ain't fair!" said Jason. He stomped off the porch, and a moment later they heard the roar of his motorbike.

"He'll be okay," said Phoebe in answer to Meg's worried face. "He just needs to blow off some steam."

"I can relate to that," said Meg. She turned to Phoebe and tried to smile. "You know, I'd probably feel a whole lot better if

292

you had something warm and wonderful and sweet just out of the oven, Phoebe."

"Well, you've come to the right place, Meg. Come on in."

"I can't, Phoebe. Look at me. I'm all wet and muddy."

"Nonsense. We don't have that ugly brown carpet for nothing. Abner comes in dirty all the time. In fact, you can sit in his chair, and I hope you get it all muddy and wet, too." Phoebe grinned with a spark of mischief in her eye.

Meg went inside and got a small measure of satisfaction from messing up Abner's chair. As usual, Phoebe's baking was exceptional. Today she had made oatmeal cookies with cranberries, from one of Grandpa's recipes that Meg had given her.

"Since you're here, Meg, I want you to hear my idea. Of course, I wouldn't do it without your permission."

"Sure. What is it?"

"I'd like to put all your grandpa's recipes onto our computer. Abner bought the crazy thing for the business, but he never learned to use it. I've taken some correspondence courses, and I'm no whiz at it, but at least I can use the word processor. Anyway, I'd like to try to organize the recipes into a cookbook. Maybe I could insert some bits and pieces of local history about the bogs, and even some old photos. I've been trying out the recipes with cranberries I have in my freezer. And they are good. And what better place to sell a cranberry cookbook than Crandale?"

"Phoebe, I think that's a super idea. Of course you can have my permission."

"Can we be partners in it, Meg?"

"Sure, if you want to. But it seems like you'll be doing most of the work, Phoebe."

"But they are your recipes, Meg. And I'd love to have any help you could give me."

"Well, it sounds like a good partnership, Phoebe." Meg stood and shook her hand.

"Thanks, Meg," said Phoebe. "And I'm real sorry about the water problem. If there's anything I can do…"

"No, Phoebe. And please don't mention this to Abner. I don't want you to get caught in the middle. But I do plan to talk to Grandmother. She needs to know what's going on."

"You're right, Meg."

"And please tell Jason not to worry. Everything will be okay."

Thirty

AFTER LEAVING PHOEBE'S, Meg stopped by to talk to Grandmother, but Rosa said she was napping. Meg decided to go back into town to gather supplies for spending the night up at the bog. She had never spent the night there before, and she felt excited, like she was going on an adventure, but she was still concerned about the water level. Would there be enough water pressure to run the irrigation system if she needed to ward off the freeze? She stopped by the Feed and Seed to discuss the problem with Cal.

"Boy, Meggie, I don't know," said Cal with a frown. "If it's just a one-night freeze, you may be okay. But if it hits a second or third night, you could be in for some trouble. Let me call around and see what I can do. It's a dirty shame, Meg."

Meg hadn't told Cal that she suspected Abner, but she felt pretty sure that Cal would have his own ideas anyway. She put the gear she'd purchased into the Jeep and headed back to Briar Hedge. She carried everything up to the cabin and flung open the door to air the place out. Erin's girls had played house in it quite a bit lately, and it was pretty neat from their little sweeping and dusting binges. There was even a wilted bouquet of flowers sitting in a tin can on the wobbly metal card table. Meg smiled as she tossed the drooping flowers out the door, grateful for her nieces' domestic efforts.

She set up her new kerosene lantern, sleeping bag, and other camping supplies. She had never been much of a camper, but she remembered Grandpa used to have all sorts of useful items on hand to get him through cold nights when he was watching for a freeze. She glanced around the small room with satisfaction. Now all she needed was enough firewood to keep the tiny woodstove going so she didn't freeze. She knew there was a stack of old wood next to Grandmother's back porch, so she drove back down the hill, hoping Grandmother had woken up from her nap by now.

Meg poked her head in the kitchen door and greeted Rosa. "I'm spending the night at the bog tonight," she explained. "Do you mind if I take some firewood?"

"I wish you would take that whole pile," said Rosa. "Your grandmother doesn't want me to make fires in the fireplace anymore; she says it gives her bronchitis. Right now the only thing that pile is good for is for rats to hide in. Why are you staying at the bog, Meggie?"

Meg began to pick up some pieces of wood. "There could be a freeze tonight, and I need to be there to turn on the irrigation. Hopefully by next year we'll be able to afford a good thermostat system that will turn on automatically."

"Here," said Rosa, grabbing several chunks of wood. "Let me help you." By the time they finished loading the wood into the back of the Jeep, Meg thought she had enough to last for several nights.

"Thanks, Rosa," said Meg, brushing wood chips off her jeans. "Is Grandmother up now?"

"She's up, but I don't think she's feeling too great, Meg. She's been moving real slow lately. And she's been acting kind of strange, too. You know, Abner was here several days ago, and I think it might have upset her."

"Do you suppose it would be okay if I talked with her?" asked Meg. She was suddenly uncertain about the wisdom of mentioning Abner's most recent activities.

"Oh, sure. She's always so glad to see you, Meg. Do you want to stay for dinner tonight? I've got some nice red snapper I'm going to fry up."

"Sounds good, Rosa. Thanks."

Meg washed her hands and tiptoed into Grandmother's room. The old woman was sitting up with her eyes wide open, but she had a blank stare on her face.

"Hi, Grandmother," said Meg. But Grandmother didn't even look at her. Meg sat down and waited a long moment. "How are you doing today?" she asked finally.

Grandmother slowly shook her head. "Not well, Meggie," she said in a raspy voice. "Not well at all."

"What's the matter?" asked Meg. "Has the doctor been by to see you?"

"It's my heart, Meggie. Ready to quit on me. Could be any day now."

Meg leaned over and looked into Grandmother's pale eyes. Was she serious? Was something really wrong? Only a week ago, Grandmother had been as lively as ever. "Is there anything I can do for you, Grandmother?" Meg asked with growing concern.

"No," said Grandmother slowly. "Nothing anyone can do. I'm just too old. And I'm getting feebleminded, too. I couldn't even remember the names of Erin's girls today. Pretty soon, I won't even know my own name."

"Don't say that, Grandmother."

"It's true, Meg. My mind is wandering something terrible. I woke up from my nap and started to call Sunny on the phone." Grandmother broke into sobs. "But I can't. My baby is gone. Both my babies are gone. I need to go to them. My time's a-coming."

Meg didn't know what to say. She had never seen

Grandmother like this before. She reached out and took the old woman's hand and held it in her own, wishing for the right words to say to make everything better, but none would come. Finally she looked up to see Grandmother leaning back against the pillow, eyes closed and apparently sleeping. Meg gently released her hand and went to join Rosa in the kitchen.

"Rosa, you're right. Something does seem to be wrong with Grandmother. I think you should call her doctor in the morning. Maybe he should check her medication or something."

Rosa flipped the fillets in the big cast-iron frying pan. "Okay, Meggie, I'll give him a call. But you know, she is getting old. It may just be life taking its course."

"I suppose. But she had been doing so well, and this seems to have come on so suddenly."

Meg ate by herself in the kitchen while Rosa watched *Wheel of Fortune*. Grandmother was still asleep. Finally, Meg rinsed off her plate and said good-bye to Rosa before heading up to the cabin. She started a fire to ward off the chill that she knew was coming. It was still light out and would be for a couple of hours, so she decided to start cutting back the blackberry vines that were trying to creep into the east bogs. After she'd made a good start on the vines, it became too dark to see, so she put her tools away and watched as the clear sky began to fill with bright stars. It was definitely getting colder, but when she checked the temperature gauges, they showed that it was still well above fifty. She knew it wouldn't get really low until the early morning hours, and she figured it would be smart to get in a few hours of sleep before that. The cabin was toasty, and soon she had the kerosene lantern glowing warmly. She set her alarm clock for 2:00 A.M., then lay down and read until she fell asleep.

She awoke with a start, but it wasn't the alarm clock that disturbed her. The lantern had burned out, and in the darkness she could hear the roar of an engine and then the crash of breaking glass. She lay frozen in bed, too frightened to move or breathe, listening to the night with a pounding heart as another piece of glass shattered, then another. Finally, the engine roared up again, followed by the sound of tires spinning through loose gravel. And then all was silent.

Meg silently crept out of her sleeping bag and peered out the window to see red taillights disappearing over the rise that led to Abner's place. Of course, it must have been Abner. The breaking glass was probably just him throwing out his old beer bottles. She took a deep breath and willed her heart to return to its normal beat.

She looked at the clock. It wasn't two o'clock yet, but she decided to check the temperature gauges as long as she was awake. She grabbed her flashlight like a weapon and went outside. She was not about to let Abner keep her from watching over her berries. She walked to each bog, using her flashlight to check the gauges. The coldest one was just below forty degrees, and she knew that was getting close to the danger zone. Cal had said that if it reached below the midthirties, it was time to start the sprinklers running. But she knew she didn't want to start too soon because of her limited water supply. It was possible that this freeze could last more than one night. She looked up into the starlit night and whispered a prayer.

"God, you know what I need better than I do. But I really don't want to lose these blossoms to a freeze, and I'm worried about having enough water. Please help me to know what's the best thing to do, and to do it. Thanks."

To her mind, it seemed like a silly little prayer, but it felt right to her heart. She went back to the cabin and waited, reading from the little New Testament that Matthew had given her, and tried not to think about Abner's behavior. He was just a harmless drunk, she tried to convince herself. Besides, God was watching out for her.

At two-thirty, she went out to check again. This time she started with the bog that had been the coldest. Thirty-three degrees. It was time to turn on the irrigation. She dashed back to the pump house and turned on the pump that would start the sprinklers. One by one they came on. At least there was enough water pressure for now. She would worry about tomorrow later.

She sat down on a stump and watched as the water sprayed out with its rhythmic *chinka-chinka* sound. The droplets of water were illuminated by a nearly full moon. She wished she could capture its beauty on film. Perhaps with a tripod and a manual shutter. For now, she would just enjoy the spectacle with her own eyes. She knew that if the temperature continued to drop, the plants would begin to be coated with a thin covering of ice. It seemed a strange remedy to prevent freeze damage, but she knew it was the standard way. It was exactly what Grandpa used to do, although she had never been allowed to stay up long enough to see it herself. But Grandpa had described to her how the ice-coating process actually produced and then trapped heat in the plants, protecting them from the colder temperatures of the freezing air.

Soon she was forced to return to the cabin to get warm. After half an hour she went out to see how the plants were doing. To her amazement, it had happened. The plants were now coated with a layer of sparkling ice. It looked just like the middle of winter, yet it was June. She sat for a long time, watching in amazement, until the cold got to her and she was forced back into the cabin. She checked the plants off and on throughout the rest of the predawn hours. She wasn't sure what she was looking for, but like a mother fretting over a sick child, she watched over the bog and longed for the morning sunlight.

Finally the sun began to come up, but she knew it would be some time before the temperature warmed up, so she went inside and boiled some water on her propane stove for a cup of instant cocoa. When she came back out she noticed that the ice had softened and was starting to melt from the plants. Before long, she turned off the sprinklers. She still wasn't sure how the plants could have survived the freeze, but as the air grew warmer, she noticed that they appeared to be just fine, with their white blossoms intact. She had done it! She breathed a thank-you prayer and fell into her sleeping bag, exhausted.

Meg didn't wake up until after ten o'clock. By then the sun was high in the sky, and the bog looked as if last night had never even happened. Like a proud mother, she returned to town, took a shower, then went over to the Feed and Seed to tell Cal about her success.

"Good for you, Meggie," said Cal. "I knew you could do it."

"Do what?" called a familiar voice from the front door. Meg turned to see Matthew coming in. He was wearing a nice gray suit and looked out of place next to the farm tools.

"Meggie saved the bog from freezing last night," Cal said proudly.

"That's great," said Matthew.

Meg smiled. "I just hope it doesn't freeze again tonight. I don't know if I'll have enough water. You know, I didn't even check the level of the pond this morning," said Meg. "I guess I'd better run back up and see, not that there's anything I can do about it."

"Yep," said Cal with a curious twinkle in his eye. "You'd better go check."

"Can I give you a lift?" asked Matthew.

Meg looked at him with raised brows. "You sure? You look like you're ready to go sue someone."

"Thanks a lot," said Matthew. Then he grinned sheepishly. "Actually, I just did. And I think it went rather well. But it wound up much quicker than I'd expected, and now I have some free time. I sure could use some fresh air and sunshine."

"That'd be great," said Meg. "And I could probably use some company. Last night, I started to feel a bit like a hermit living in my little old shack."

Cal chuckled. "See you two later."

Matthew had already removed his tie by the time they reached his vehicle. He opened the door for Meg, then tossed his jacket in back and undid the top button of his shirt.

"Ah, much better," he said as he climbed into the driver's seat. "Sometimes, I think I should have been a farmer, too."

Meg laughed. "You make it sound like farming is easy."

"No, that's not what I meant. I just get tired of the suit-and-tie routine sometimes, and all the rules and formality of the corporate world."

"Yeah, I understand," said Meg. "Actually, it wasn't so long ago that I was one of those people, performing every day for the corporate world."

"Do you ever miss it, Meg?"

She thought seriously about it for a moment. "Maybe sometimes. Just a little. I think I really am a people person, or at least I used to be. I suppose it could get lonely being a farmer. But then there's the gallery. And friends. And—" Meg broke off and turned to look out the window.

"And?" Matthew glanced at her from the corner of his eye.

"And…I guess I wouldn't trade my life for just about anything right now."

Matthew grinned.

They reached the bog just then and climbed out. Meg breathed in the aroma of the fragrant blooms. Their scent was even stronger than yesterday. "Doesn't it smell just luscious?"

Matthew took in a deep breath and sighed. "I had almost forgotten that smell, Meg. But there isn't anything else like it on earth. Someone should bottle that and sell it as perfume."

"Eau de cranberry." Meg laughed. "I'd be their best customer!"

"What's this?" asked Matthew as he stooped down to examine some broken glass.

"Oh, I almost forgot about that." Meg frowned. "I don't know for sure, but I think it was Abner on a drunken rampage. Last night I got a scary wake-up call about one o'clock in the morning." Meg bent over and began to carefully pick up the broken shards of glass.

"Doesn't this worry you a little?" asked Matthew. He looked into her eyes with concern.

"Of course. I was completely terrified last night—at least for a few minutes. After that I got pretty consumed in fighting off the freeze. But I just don't know what to do about him. The fact is, yesterday I was ready to have him tarred and feathered for letting most of the water out of the sump pond."

"So he's the one who did that?"

"Well, I don't know for certain. But that would be my guess, and Jason said he saw him messing around up here. I had planned to talk to Grandmother about it, but she was acting sort of odd last night, so I didn't want to bring it up. I didn't want to upset her."

Matthew shook his head. "It just seems to get messier and messier. I wish you had something legal written up. Your grandmother seemed interested the first time I mentioned it to her, but when I drafted a document, she backed off completely. I told her to take some time to think about it. But she's never gotten back to me on it. I hate to hound her."

"She needs to make up her own mind," said Meg. "Hopefully, I'll catch her in a better state of mind, and maybe I can explain what's going on with Abner. I'm sure everything will be okay."

"I hope so. But I think you should be careful when you're up here alone at night."

"I'm only up here when there's danger of a freeze."

"Which could be again tonight."

Meg nodded solemnly. "I have my cell phone with me, so I'm not completely isolated. And really, I don't think Abner even knew I was up here last night. My lantern had gone out by then.

Besides, I'm sure he was pretty wasted."

Matthew held up a piece of a gin bottle. "Judging by these, you're probably right. But I don't see how that makes the situation any better."

Meg tried to push thoughts of Abner from her mind as they dumped the broken glass in a trash pile. Then they went up to check on the pond.

"I can't believe it!" Meg exclaimed when she saw the water level of the pond. She began to walk faster. "I thought it would be nearly empty now, but look, it's almost half full. How can that be?"

Matthew joined her. "Looks as if water is coming in to fill it up again."

Meg shook her head. "But how?"

"Maybe Pop let the other farmers know about your misfortune."

"You think so? Do you think they would actually care enough to help me out?"

"Sure, Meg. These are good folks around here. Farmers usually stick together. Besides, almost everyone in these parts thought the world of your granddad. And I'm sure they respect what you're doing here."

Meg felt tears building in her eyes, and she swallowed hard as she shook her head in disbelief. "That's about the nicest thing I can imagine, Matthew. They must be a little worried about having enough water to protect their own plants from freezing. To think that they would actually share with me…"

Matthew put his arm around her shoulders and gave her a gentle squeeze. "You've come home to quite a place, haven't you, Meg?"

She sighed. "Yes. Quite a place."

"Hey, I have a crazy idea, Meg."

"What's that?" She turned to face him. His blue eyes were sparkling with excitement.

"How about a dog?" he said.

"Huh?"

"If you had a dog up here, he could be like a burglar alarm. You know, to ward off unwelcome intruders or drunken relatives. A watchdog."

Meg thought about it for a moment. "But where would I get a dog like that? One that's trained and everything."

"The animal shelter is always doing TV spots about pets you can adopt. I've often thought about it myself. Usually the dogs are full grown, and some are even trained. In fact, I saw this beautiful dog just today on the morning show. Some kind of a shepherd mix."

Matthew's enthusiasm was contagious as he described the dog. Meg could already picture it.

"What do you think, Meg? I'd be happy to drive you over and check them out. But I don't want to talk you into something you don't want. This is a perfect place to keep a dog, though. Lots of room to run—"

"All right, all right!" Meg laughed. "Let's go check out this dog." Suddenly the idea of a good dog to keep her company did sound comforting. She wasn't sure how many nights she'd need to spend up here, but having a dog with her might be nice.

They found the dog Matthew was talking about, a loving two-year-old named Toby. Toby proved to be more than just a watchdog. Part German shepherd, part black Lab, and 100 percent loyal, Toby quickly became Meg's best buddy, and she took him almost everywhere she went. With Matthew's help, she put up a run with a sturdy doghouse right next to the sump pond, but before long she was letting Toby spend an occasional night in her apartment. He was very well mannered and good company, and although Meg had never had a dog before, she couldn't imagine being without one now.

The sump pond remained full, and she managed to keep the

cranberry plants from freezing. Soon the blossoms dropped off, and little buds began to grow. Summer fell into a comfortable routine for Meg between working in the gallery and out on the bog. Her free time was divided between Erin and her family, and Matthew and his. There were sailing trips and gallery showings, and the days seemed to speed by.

Often Meg found herself worrying that her wonderful life was only a vacation, a brief interlude, and that one day she would be forced to return to the busy city and the old working grind. So much of her previous life had been spent as a workaholic that she often felt guilty for having fun.

But as summer drew to an end, she became more and more comfortable in her new life, and she finally allowed herself to relax and settle in. She was at home, and it felt right.

Thirty-One

ONE DAY IN LATE SEPTEMBER, Meg walked up the hill toward the Beach House to meet Erin and Ashley for lunch. Erin's girls were all in school now; even Ashley had started going half-days to kindergarten this fall. The air was cool, and a brisk breeze was blowing in from the sea. Normally, Meg loved this time of year because it meant harvesttime was around the corner. But with no buyer for her berries lined up, autumn made her nervous. She had heard that some cranberry growers were already harvesting, but they had earlier varieties of berries, and she knew her McFarlin berries still had two to three weeks to go.

She found her sister and niece in the parking lot, and Ashley ran up and threw her arms around Meg.

"Hi, Aunt Meggie!"

"Hi, Ash. How's school?" asked Meg.

Ashley pressed her lips together and furrowed her brow. "I don't like it."

"Why not?" asked Meg as they entered the restaurant. She glanced at Erin for clues, but Erin just grinned.

"There's this boy," said Ashley, rolling her eyes.

"Ah," said Meg. "A boy?"

"Yes," said Ashley with exasperation. "His name is Jonathan Murphy, and he just won't leave me alone!"

Meg nodded. "I see. Sometimes that's what boys do when they like you."

"I know," said Ashley patiently. "But the teacher made him move to another table."

"So what's the problem?" asked Meg.

"Because, Aunt Meggie," said Ashley, as if it should be perfectly obvious, "he doesn't get to sit by me anymore!"

Meg nodded, trying not to laugh. "I see."

"Meg, how are your berries doing?" asked Erin.

"They're looking really good. They should be ready to harvest by mid-October."

"Great! So you have a buyer lined up?"

Meg frowned. "Cal still hasn't got anything nailed down. I'm trying not to worry about it, though. I keep telling myself that God is in control."

"Sounds like good advice," said Erin. The waitress took their orders and filled their coffee cups.

"But it's hard not to worry," Meg continued. "I've put so much into those berries, Erin. I know it must sound ridiculous, but I think this is the closest thing to a pregnancy that I've ever gone through. Now my due date is so close, and I don't really know what's going to happen."

Erin laughed. "I think you're right; it is a lot like a pregnancy. I never thought of it that way before. Should we give you a baby shower or something?"

Now Meg laughed. "No. Just promise to come help me deliver my baby. Or perhaps I should say babies."

"We wouldn't miss it for anything, Meg. I can't wait. Have you had any run-ins with Abner lately?"

Meg sighed. "As a matter of fact, I was just out in the barn yesterday, cleaning and sorting what's left of Grandpa's old harvesting equipment—the things that Abner couldn't sell off. He stopped in to say hello."

"Oh dear. Did he make a scene?"

Meg glanced at Ashley, who seemed preoccupied with coloring the children's menu, and continued in a quiet voice. "He asked me what I thought I was doing, and I told him. Then he told me in no uncertain terms that I had totally overstepped my boundaries and that he had engaged a lawyer to put me in my place. Of course, he didn't say it that nicely or coherently. In fact, by the smell of his breath, I'd bet that he doesn't even remember exactly what he said."

"Are you telling Grandmother any of this, Meg?"

"Erin, you know how she's been lately. She seems to go back and forth. Either she's sharp and witty, or dull and depressed. But whenever I bring up the subject of Abner, she always resorts to the latter. It seems useless to try to talk to her. But I figure Grandmother has authorized me to work on the bog, so what can Abner possibly do to change that?"

"Probably nothing, other than make your life miserable."

"Well, he only makes it miserable once in a while. And I'm a big girl; I can take it. Besides, for the sake of Phoebe and Jason, I'd really like to work things out with Abner. Phoebe's almost done with the cranberry cookbook, and it's actually looking pretty good. If only I could befriend Abner somehow. I'm just not sure how to go about it."

"I don't know, Meg. Tom said talk in the construction circle is that Abner's acting like Briar Hedge is going to be sold for sure. He says development will begin by next spring."

Meg shook her head. "Maybe I need to get Matthew to come over and talk to Grandmother again."

"Couldn't hurt, Meg." The waitress set down their food, and their conversation moved more comfortably to the new exhibit that Sigfried was putting together for the gallery next month.

"It's going to be a pictorial history of cranberry growing on the Oregon coast," explained Erin. "At first, Siggie wanted to surprise us with it, but then he decided he needed your help. He wants you to go out and photograph some current pictures of how they harvest nowadays. I told him I was sure you'd be willing."

"I'd love to," said Meg. "In fact, this week I'm going out to the Henningers' to look at their beater and elevator. I need to see how it's run. Cal set it up for me to rent some equipment from them for my harvest."

"Perfect. And now that you know what Siggie is up to, you should see the old photos he's lined up for the exhibit. They're really great, Meg. Some are from Sunny's collection from Briar Hedge when it was just starting out."

"You know what would be great for the exhibit?" said Meg. "We could get Phoebe to make some of her cranberry recipes. Maybe we could even get the cookbook printed before the exhibit and sell it at the gallery."

"Isn't she having it printed and bound locally?"

"Yeah, but I promised her some black-and-white photos to put in it, and that I'd help her with the layout. We'll have to see if we can get going on it. That would be a great way for her to start selling them."

"Sure would. Siggie wants to run the exhibit for at least a month."

"Well, this sounds like fun," said Meg. "Maybe it will help keep my mind off other problems."

"Don't forget to talk to Matthew about seeing Grandmother, Meg. I understand wanting to befriend Abner, but you need to be smart about it."

"Don't worry, Erin. I'll talk to him tonight. We're going down to Gold Beach to see a play."

Erin's brows went up. "You sure have been spending a lot of time with him. Are you still going to tell me that it's nothing serious, Meg?"

Meg took a sip of coffee. "Listen, Erin, if it ever gets serious, as you say, you'll be the first one to know, okay?"

"I just don't get it, Meg. Every time I see you two together it seems so perfect. I watch him look at you, and I could swear he's in love. Doesn't he ever say anything? Don't you?"

Meg sighed. "I think maybe he still hasn't completely gotten over losing Gina. And besides that, he's so well set up with Abby to take care of the house, and Clive only has two more years of high school. I just don't know...."

Erin shook her head. "Neither do I. And I suppose it's none of my business. I just don't want to see my little sister get hurt."

Meg smiled. "Don't worry about me. I have my eyes wide open. And I enjoy every minute that I spend with Matthew. Even if we only remain friends, he's one of the best friends I've ever had."

Erin rolled her eyes. "And I'm sure you don't want anything more than that."

"I can wait," said Meg. "If it's meant to be, it'll be."

Erin laughed. "Well, you sure have come a long way in the last six months, Meg. I'm impressed."

"Don't be. I've got a long way to go."

Erin glanced over at Ashley's drooping eyelids. "I think this little schoolgirl is ready for a nap."

They parted in the parking lot, and Meg walked down the hill, suddenly reminded of the time she had stormed down the same hill after that last unpleasant lunch with Sunny. So much had changed since then. Now thinking of Sunny filled Meg with a pleasant warmth, mixed with only a trace of lingering sadness.

Meg stopped in at the Feed and Seed to see if Cal had gotten lucky with any prospective berry buyers. But she knew what the answer was as soon as she saw his face.

"Sorry, Meggie," said Cal. "I haven't heard anything. But don't lose hope. I've seen deals made at the eleventh hour before."

"It's okay. I figure this is part of my life lesson in the school of faith, right?"

Cal smiled. "You bet, Meggie. Nothing gets wasted."

Meg drove out to the bog to check on Toby. As always, he was eager to see her, and she took him down to the beach for a run. Toby loved the water and wasn't afraid to go right out into the surf. After about an hour, she whistled for him, and they headed back.

There were several unfamiliar, expensive cars parked up by the bog when she returned. As Meg drew closer she noticed several men in business suits over near the pond, talking to Abner. She knew they must be the developers or the investors, or both. Abner was pointing in the direction of the ocean; she could just hear his voice telling them what a great view could be seen from there. What nerve! Anger boiled up inside her, taking her by surprise.

What right did Abner have to act as if he were sole owner of Grandmother's land, as if he could sell it right out from under them? Or was something going on here that Meg didn't know about? Was it possible that Grandmother had struck up some sort of agreement with Abner? Perhaps that explained why she had become so depressed in the last few months. Not eager to face Abner or the businessmen, Meg cut down toward Abner's house, hoping to catch Phoebe for a moment or two. She could tell Phoebe the good news about the cranberry exhibit, as well as glean any helpful information about Abner's latest business dealings, if Phoebe knew anything. Most of the time, Meg suspected that Abner kept both Phoebe and Jason in the dark about his plans.

"Hi, Meg," called Phoebe through the screen door. She opened it and waved. "Come on in. I want you to try this new candy recipe."

"Stay here, Toby," Meg commanded as she went up the porch steps. "Hi, Phoebe. I've got some good news." Meg walked in and sat down on a stool by the kitchen counter. She watched as Phoebe cut a piece of candy. Meg was pretty sure that Phoebe was losing weight. It seemed that her interest in the cookbook, as well as baking goods to sell to the gallery, had given her a good distraction.

"Here," said Phoebe proudly. She handed Meg a square of dark red candy with nuts. "I decided to try the recipe a little different this time. See if you like it."

Meg bit off a corner. "Mmm. Phoebe, this is terrific. Much better than Grandpa's version. In fact, that's exactly what I want to tell you." Meg launched into her ideas for the exhibit.

"Sounds like a wonderful plan," said Phoebe. "The cookbook is all on the computer now. If you have time to help me with the layout, it should be ready to be printed." Then Phoebe's face clouded over. "The only problem is, I've been saving my baking money to cover the printing costs, but I still don't have enough—"

"Hey, I thought we were partners, Phoebe. It seems only fair that I should pay for part of the printing, especially since you've put in so much work on the book."

"But you were going to do the layout and the photos. And you provided all the recipes...."

"I know, but if you hadn't worked on refining them, they wouldn't be worth much. Besides, I'd planned to help pay for the printing," said Meg.

Phoebe's face lit up. "Meg, sometimes I think you are an angel sent by God just to rescue me and Jason."

"Oh, Phoebe," said Meg, embarrassed. "Maybe it's the other way around. I mean, here you are putting together a wonderful book of my grandpa's recipes, and right now, Jason is working at the gallery. You two are an important part of my life."

"Thanks, Meg. Here, have another piece."

Meg ate another piece and then decided to bring up the unpleasant subject of Abner's business dealings. "I saw Abner showing some guys around the bog, Phoebe. They look like developers or something."

"No!" gasped Phoebe. "He wouldn't."

Meg nodded. "I think he is, Phoebe. Do you know anything about it? Has he ever talked to you about legally getting something set up with Grandmother?"

"No, he's never said a word. He's been like a clam when it comes to that nasty business, ever since he figured out you and I are friends. At first, he forbade me to have anything to do with you, but Jason stood up to him. It was awful at the time, but something Jason said must have sunk in because Abner's never brought it up since."

"I didn't think you'd know anything about it, Phoebe. Actually, I'm glad that you don't. But I sure wish I could get to the bottom of it. Do you think it would do any good for me to try and talk to Abner about it, face-to-face?"

"Honestly, Meg, when it comes to this subject, there just seems to be no reasoning with him. Believe me, I know just how contrary he can be. But he does, or at least he used to, have another side to him. You see, Meg, his mother was a real unhappy woman. I mean, she was bitter something awful. I'm not sure why, but I know she held a lot of things against your grandfather. And in some ways, I think she poisoned Abner. When we moved up here, he had a good-sized chip on his shoulder about his grandpa, even with the old man dead and all. But he seemed to get along okay with Grandmother, at least to start with."

Phoebe frowned. "Then I think Abner started getting too big for his britches. He started taking over everything from your grandmother, and it was real odd, but she just let him. I'd always heard that she was a strong woman, and a businesswoman to boot, but somehow she let Abner walk all over her. And before long, Abner took to drinking more than ever; then he started letting the bog go to ruin. I swear, Meg, I've never been able to get to the bottom of it. At first I blamed it on the alcohol, but now I'm not sure which came first."

Meg nodded slowly. "I wish I understood why. I'd really like to be able to work this out with Abner and Grandmother together. Grandmother has said she wants me to preserve the bog, but she gets all soft when Abner steps in, almost as if she's afraid of him. I just don't get it."

"Me neither, Meg. I'm sorry that Abner keeps bringing you so much grief. But surely he can't make any deals without your grandmother's signature. As far as I know, everything is still in her name. I don't think he'd resort to anything illegal." Phoebe paused and looked down at her hands. "But nowadays I'm not so sure about that, Meg. Sometimes he scares me a lot."

Just then they heard the sound of tires grinding in the gravel, and Toby began to bark wildly. Meg and Phoebe ran out to see what was going on. Meg had never heard Toby sound so ferocious. Abner was standing frozen in the driveway, his face paler than usual, and Toby was holding him off, growling loudly. When Abner saw Meg on the porch, he let loose with a string of curses unlike anything that Meg had ever heard. But Toby stood his ground.

"Toby!" called Meg with a shaking voice. "Stop it, right now! Come." Toby turned and looked at her, then back at Abner as if he wasn't sure whether to obey or not. Finally he walked over to Meg and sat beside her.

"Get that blasted mongrel dog off my property right now!" yelled Abner. "If I ever see him down here again, I'll be getting my gun."

"Come on, Toby," said Meg. She headed toward the bog, too shaken to respond to Abner's nasty threat. "It's okay, Toby," she said soothingly as soon as they were out of earshot. "You thought you were protecting me, didn't you, fella?" She patted him on the head, and he looked up with trusting brown eyes.

She opened the gate of the dog run, and Toby went right in. As she filled his food and water dishes, she wondered why Toby had had such a strong reaction to Abner. She had heard that animals could sense things about people; maybe Toby knew something about Abner. She knelt down and stroked his smooth, dark head. "You're a good boy, Toby. A real good boy." She double-checked to make sure the gate was latched securely, then told Toby good night. "I'd bring you home with me, but I'm going to be out late tonight. I'll see you in the morning, though."

The play wasn't too bad for a small-town, small-budget production, and Meg reminded herself that this was not San Francisco. Besides, the best part was seeing it with Matthew. They went out for a late dinner afterwards, and she told him all about seeing Abner and the businessmen up at the bog.

"I know I said I wanted you to wait until Grandmother makes up her mind," said Meg. "But now I'm wondering if you shouldn't sit down with both of us and see if we can come to some understanding."

"Under the circumstances, it would seem wise. If Abner is actually showing the property to investors, it's time your grandmother is in the know. Unless she already is. Do you think there's a chance that she and Abner have already made some sort of agreement?"

"I suppose it's possible," said Meg. Just the thought of Grandmother going behind her back made Meg feel sick to her stomach. It reminded her of the way she used to feel as a child about Grandmother, only many times worse. "I just can't imagine that she would do that, though, not after I've put so much work into the bog."

"Maybe she didn't mean for you to get so involved. Maybe she thought that you were just playing at being a cranberry grower or that you wouldn't have the tenacity to stick with it. After all, she knows how much goes into making a cranberry bog run."

"Maybe. But she seemed to be so encouraging. At least, early on. But then she became more and more removed and moody. A lot of times I get the feeling she's covering something up. Like she gets this close to telling me something—" Meg held her thumb and forefinger close together— "and then she shuts off or goes into one of her 'I'm dying' speeches. I just don't get it."

"We need to get all the cards on the table, Meg. Someone is holding out on you. It may be that Abner is trying to force your grandmother's hand, or it may be that your grandmother has already made some agreement with him."

"You know, it would only stand to reason—" Suddenly, it was as if a light clicked on in her head.

"What's that?"

"Of course! Oh, how could I have been such a fool?" Meg shut her eyes, trying to shut out what had just hit her.

Matthew reached across the table and placed his hand on her arm. "Meg, tell me. What is it?"

Meg felt sick. "I never really thought about it before. You see, Abner's father hadn't gotten along with Grandpa, and there was quite an argument before he went off to the war. I know Grandmother was devastated when he died, although I'm not sure why he and Grandpa never got along. But the point is, Grandmother must have felt she needed to make something up to Abner for what happened with Bennie. After all, he did move up here to help with the bog, and he is the only grandson. It only stands to reason that he considers the property his. And perhaps Grandmother has told him as much. But why wouldn't she have told me?"

"Meg, you're only speculating. You don't know anything for certain—"

"But think about it, Matthew. It makes sense. Abner *should* get

317

Briar Hedge. I just never looked at it like that, because when I came all I could see was how he had neglected and abused the bog. But it's quite likely that Grandmother intends for Abner to have Briar Hedge. If that's the case, I have been a fool."

"Meg, you're getting worked up about what might be nothing. For you to speculate like this is silly; it'll only worry you for no reason."

"But what if I'm right?"

"Then you'll have to trust God for the next step. Just the same as if you were wrong. Right?"

Meg smiled a tiny smile. "Thanks, Matthew. You're right. I'm sorry; I don't know why I got so carried away. But it is upsetting, and it's probably my own fault for not getting things nailed down sooner. Everyone warned me. You and Cal, Erin and Tom. Even Sunny warned me."

"Since tomorrow is Saturday and I don't have anything else planned, how about if I meet you at Briar Hedge; then we can ask your grandmother the hard questions together."

"That would be good. Thanks, Matthew. I just hope she'll cooperate."

"I'm sure she will. She's a smart woman, and I know she doesn't want to see you get hurt, Meg."

Meg smiled. His words reminded her of what Erin had said today at lunch. His hand was still on her arm. She looked down, and he gave her fingers a warm squeeze before taking his hand away.

"Everything is going to be okay, Meg. You'll see."

"Thanks, Matthew. I hope you're right."

Thirty-Two

THE NEXT MORNING, Meg wanted to get down to Briar Hedge early enough to take Toby out on the beach for a little exercise. She wasn't looking forward to the ten o'clock meeting with Matthew and Grandmother, and she hoped a short walk would calm her nerves a bit. Still it needed to be done. She parked the Jeep and started toward the dog run, but she didn't see Toby or hear him barking his friendly greeting.

As she got closer, she saw that the gate was open. How could that be? She had securely closed it last night. In fact, she had double-checked it, and it didn't open that easily. She whistled for Toby and waited. But he didn't come. She looked around the bog and even down toward the beach, but she didn't see him anywhere. Suddenly, she imagined Toby wandering down toward Abner's house, and Abner's threat from yesterday echoed in her ears. No, he wouldn't do such a thing. Would he? She ran to the Jeep and called Matthew on her cell phone.

"Matthew," she said breathlessly. "I'm not going to be able to meet you at ten."

"What's wrong, Meg?"

"It's Toby. He's out of his pen. I can't find him."

"Well, that's no big deal. He'll show up."

"No, Matthew. You don't understand!" Meg's words choked as she tried to hold back tears. "I know that it's Abner—"

"What do you mean, Meg? Calm down and talk to me." Matthew's words were slow and calming.

Meg took a breath. "You see, yesterday when I was at Phoebe's, Abner came home, and Toby was barking and growling at him. And Abner was furious. He said if he ever caught Toby in his yard, he would shoot him."

"But why would Toby go to Abner's?"

"I don't know. All I know is that I fastened the gate to his pen before I left, and now it's open. Somehow, I just know that Abner is behind it."

"Did you look around the pen at all?"

"No."

"Meg, just sit tight. I'm on my way. I'll be there in ten minutes. Promise me you won't do anything until I get there, okay?"

"Okay." Meg hung up the phone and sat down in the Jeep. She leaned her head against the steering wheel and prayed. For a moment, she thought it seemed silly to pray for a dog, but she believed that God cared about everything. She was certain that he cared about Toby.

In less than ten minutes, Matthew was there, and Clive was with him. Meg felt a little foolish, making them both come out here. Perhaps she had overreacted. There was probably some reasonable explanation for Toby's absence.

"Thanks for coming, Matthew. Hi, Clive," she said, forcing a smile.

"Meg, Dad told me about Toby. Let's go look right now," said Clive.

"First let's investigate the dog pen," said Matthew. "Let's see if it looks like there's been any foul play."

"All right, Sherlock," said Meg, hoping to sound lighter than she felt.

Matthew smiled. "I always wanted to be a detective when I was a kid."

They walked up to the pen. "Now let's not touch anything, just in case," warned Matthew. They all stopped by the open gate and stared. There in the dirt was a small, dark puddle. Matthew knelt down and dipped a finger in it. When he held it up, it was red. Clive gasped, and Meg covered her face with her hands.

"Clive, go get my cell phone," said Matthew. He wiped off his fingers and put his arms around Meg. "We don't know if he's dead yet, Meg. We need to look for him. Do you want to wait here?"

"No, I want to look for him," said Meg stiffly.

"Here, Dad," said Clive, breathless from running to the car and back. Matthew quickly called the police and explained the situation.

"We're going to start looking for the dog. We'll probably end up at Abner Lancaster's house since we have reason to think he may have something to do with this."

They looked around the pen and inside the doghouse but could find nothing more that was out of the ordinary.

"I'm going down to Abner's," said Matthew. "But you two should stay here."

"I think Clive should stay here," said Meg. "But I'm going to Abner's with you."

Clive began to complain, but Matthew remained firm. "Clive, I want you to sit in Meg's Jeep with the cell phone. You keep an eye out for the police. Meg and I will drive down there, so if we find Toby, we can put him in the car."

Clive agreed, and Meg and Matthew drove slowly down the road, looking out the windows as they went. Finally, just within sight of Abner's house, Meg spotted what looked like some dark fur near a tangle of blackberry vines. She let out a cry, pointing toward the spot. Matthew stopped the car and leaped out, with Meg right behind him. Matthew reached the dog first, then quickly turned, catching Meg in his arms. She tried to push past him, but he held her tightly.

"It's too late, Meg," said Matthew. "I'm sorry."

"Why? Why?" cried Meg. "Why would he do that to an innocent dog? It's so senseless. Why?" Matthew held her until she stopped crying. Then Meg wiped her eyes and began to walk toward the house. She didn't know what she would say or do, but she was not going to let Abner get away with this. She felt Matthew's presence by her side, but she didn't speak. She wanted to take care of Abner herself. She knocked loudly on the door, and when Phoebe answered pleasantly, Meg didn't even say hello.

"Where is he?" Meg demanded.

"Who? What's wrong, Meg?" asked Phoebe, her eyes filling with fear.

"Abner," said Meg. "Where is he?"

"I don't know, Meg. He left late last night. I haven't seen him. I thought I heard him drive in, but if he did, he never came inside the house. What's wrong, Meg?" cried Phoebe. Then Jason popped his head out.

"I heard him come home, Meg," said Jason. "I think he's out in the garage."

Meg headed for the garage.

"Wait, Meg!" yelled Matthew, but it was too late, she was already opening the door. She peered into the dark garage and spotted him sitting in an old lawn chair with a blank expression on his face. She stepped forward, ready to light into him, but suddenly she stopped. In his hands was a revolver.

Matthew touched Meg's shoulder, and she looked back at him, catching the look of alarm in his clear blue eyes. "Come on, Meg," he whispered. "Get out of here. Let me handle this."

"Why?" came a raspy voice from the other direction.

Meg turned to see Abner's eyes fixed on them. Suddenly, Meg realized that not only had she endangered herself, she had also endangered Matthew.

"No, you go," she whispered over her shoulder to Matthew. But he didn't leave. Instead, he stepped beside her.

"No reason to leave," said Abner. "Stick around; see the show."

"What's going on?" said Jason from behind them. Meg turned to see both Jason and Phoebe standing in the doorway.

"Good," said Abner. "The more the merrier."

"What are you doing, Abner?" asked Matthew in a quiet voice.

"Doing?" said Abner. "What am I doing? That's a good question." He lifted the revolver and waved it slightly. As he moved his arms, Meg could see dark red bloodstains on his shirt. She knew it was from Toby, but her anger had evaporated, leaving in its place fear, not only for herself and Matthew, but for Phoebe and Jason as well.

"Abner," Meg began, trying to imitate Matthew's calm tone. "I know what you did. But it's not too late for us to work this out in a reasonable manner."

Abner laughed a sad, haunted laugh. "No, you're wrong, cousin. It is too late." He held up the gun, turned the muzzle toward himself, and placed it firmly against his temple.

Meg heard Phoebe gasp behind her.

"Dad!" choked Jason.

"Abner," said Meg, with a sob in her voice. She prayed for the right words. "Please, don't do this, Abner. Think about what you're doing. You have a fine son to finish raising. You have a wife who loves you. Why would you want to do this?"

Abner didn't move the gun. "Why?" he echoed. He said nothing more for a long moment. The silence in the garage was almost suffocating, and Meg was afraid even to breathe. "I'll tell you why. Last night, I went out and shot a dog. Then I carried him down here and listened to his last whimpering breaths. What kind of a person have I become?"

Meg felt tears streaming down her cheeks, partly for Toby, but mostly for Abner.

"But you want to know why?" said Abner. "That's only part of it. Because I'm a lousy father who beats his son, maybe not with my fist, but with my tongue. Because I'm a lousy husband who has turned his wife into—" He closed his eyes and his fingers tightened on the trigger as he continued to speak in a monotone. "And because I've even swindled my own grandmother. Yep, that's right. For a long time I told myself she owed it to me. Then I started to believe it. I took just about everything she had, and it still wasn't enough. I was even willing to declare her insane to get her property. Now I'd rather end it all here than go to prison."

"No one is sending you to prison, Abner," said Matthew calmly. "Nothing has been done that can't be worked out. You need help, Abner. Everyone knows you have a drinking problem. Don't take a coward's way out, Abner. You can fight this. You can get your life back under control, but you need help. And there are people who are willing to help you. There are people right in this room who are willing to help you."

"That's right," said Phoebe.

"I'll help you, Dad," said Jason.

"Abner, I'll do anything I can to help you," said Meg. Abner still held the gun against his temple. Meg continued to pray with every breath. "I had hoped that you and I could work together on the bog, Abner. I wanted to be friends, but you never let me."

"I can help you find legal help, Abner," said Matthew. "You don't need to throw everything away just because you've made a few mistakes." Matthew slowly took a couple of steps forward. "Abner, let us help you."

"No, stay back, Matthew!" yelled Abner, waving the gun wildly.

"Please, Dad," cried Jason. "Please, don't do this. Let us help you."

Abner's hand began to shake. "I've turned into a monster," he sobbed. "I deserve to die. I'm good for nothing. I've failed at everything. I'm a drunk and a coward. My life is worthless. All I wanted to do was make some money. I've never had anything. But I got too greedy. I wouldn't let anything stand in my way."

"God doesn't think you're worthless, Abner," said Meg. "God can take any mess and make it better. If you let him."

Abner's arm suddenly went limp, and the gun slipped from his grasp. In one quick movement, Matthew had the weapon safely in his hands.

"It's going to be okay, buddy," said Matthew. Phoebe and Jason came over and wrapped their arms around Abner as he sat and sobbed like a baby. Matthew and Meg stepped outside to give them some privacy. A patrol car was making its way slowly down the hill. Meg couldn't remember afterward how she got to Matthew's car, but once she was in the passenger's seat, she sat there in shock, unable to believe what had just taken place. Matthew talked to the police for a few minutes, then took them into the garage. After a while they came out with Abner, placed him in the patrol car, and drove away.

Finally, Meg went to check on Phoebe and Jason. No words would come to her, so she just hugged them both for a long time. Jason, acting very grown-up, helped his mother get ready to go to the police station.

Matthew was waiting outside for Meg. Before he opened the car door for her, he gathered her into his arms and held her, gently stroking her hair.

They drove back to the bog in silence. Clive was still sitting in Meg's Jeep, but she hopped out as soon as she saw them coming.

"How about if I take you down to your grandmother's while Clive and I take care of Toby?" said Matthew.

"No," said Meg. "I want to help."

They buried Toby under the fir stand behind the bog, and Meg thanked Matthew and Clive, assuring them that she would be fine but that she needed some time to herself. After they left, she sat down on the stump and looked out over the bog. Suddenly, nothing seemed to make sense. She stared at the ripening red berries growing from plants that had survived years of neglect but now might not even be harvested if no buyer came forward. She thought of her cousin, Abner, whose obsession for getting rich had nearly destroyed his life and the lives of those around him. She thought of Grandmother and the possibility that she had lied to Meg. She thought of the way she'd tossed aside her career and spent her life's savings on what might very likely be a futile mission. She thought of the time spent with Matthew over the last six months and the possibility that it might only be a friendship. Not that friendships weren't valuable. She looked upon the freshly dug grave of the first dog she had ever owned, and suddenly her life felt almost as out of focus as it had when she first returned to Crandale last spring.

The only thing she could really cling to was that she still believed God had her life in his hands. She didn't know how, couldn't understand why, but somehow she knew it was true.

Thirty-Three

HOLDING TO THAT ONE THREAD OF HOPE, Meg worked her way through the next few weeks, and slowly her life came back into focus. For the most part.

She didn't press any charges against Abner for shooting Toby, under the condition that he be placed in a substance-abuse facility. And according to Phoebe, Abner was making good progress there.

Siggie had gotten almost everything ready for the exhibit, and Meg managed to get some decent photos of cranberry harvesting. She and Phoebe put together the layout for the cookbook. It was due from the printers on the day that the exhibit was scheduled to open. Phoebe had made some minor alterations to her kitchen and had actually managed to get a license for commercial food preparation. She was now working night and day, producing all kinds of cranberry products to sell at the gallery.

Still Meg felt shaken, and unsure about her future. She had put off meeting with Matthew and Grandmother after the episode with Abner, partly out of guilt, and partly out of fear. It was almost as if she didn't want to find out that Grandmother had indeed promised Briar Hedge to Abner. Matthew had gently nagged her to talk to her grandmother, but with so many other things pressing, it was easy to delay.

Nearly every grower in the area had harvested their berries by now, but Cal still had no news of a buyer. She knew that in another week it would be too late for her berries. She drove up to the bog and sat looking at her berries, now fully ripe and ready to be harvested, but unlikely to ever leave the bog. She wondered if this could be, in a small way, similar to how a mother might feel knowing that her child would be stillborn.

She leaned down and picked a few of the dark red berries and studied them in her hand. Her berries. Then again, they weren't really hers. Originally, they had been Grandpa's, and legally they were probably Grandmother's. Maybe one day they would be Abner's to plow under if he liked. Of course, ultimately, they were God's.

She remembered some verses in the Gospel of Matthew that had comforted her after Sunny's death. Since then she had read them over and over again, until she knew them by heart. The passage always felt so personal, as if God were speaking directly to her. "But seek first his kingdom and his righteousness, and all these things will be given to you as well."

She sighed as if a heavy weight had just been lifted from her chest, then tossed the berries high into the air, watching their dark color against the clear blue sky.

"There you go, God!" she shouted. "They're your berries. Do with them as you please." She turned and walked away, feeling lighter than she had in days.

By the time she reached Grandmother's house, she was smiling. Maybe she should stop to visit Grandmother. Just to visit. It had been a while since she had stopped for a visit with no other agenda. No tales to tell on Abner, no deals to make.

"Good morning, Grandmother," she said as she went into the bedroom. "It's a beautiful day out there today."

"Hello, Meggie," said Grandmother with a faint smile. The

old woman looked tired and fragile. And for a change, Meg thought that maybe Grandmother was right about her health. Maybe she was, in fact, dying.

"How are you feeling, Grandmother?" asked Meg with concern.

"Oh, not too bad. Just weary."

"Can I get you anything? Would you like a cup of tea?"

"Now, that would be nice. Do you have time to join me, Meggie?"

"Sure do. I'll be right back."

Meg found hot water on the stove and quickly fixed a pot of Earl Grey.

"There you go," said Meg. "Just the way you like it."

Grandmother took a sip. "Perfect."

"I remember when I was little, you taught me how to make tea in a teapot," said Meg. "Before that, I thought tea only came in bags."

Grandmother chuckled. "You were such a funny little girl, Meggie. You always had such strong opinions. But you have certainly grown into a fine young woman."

Meg smiled. "Thanks. I especially like the young part. Lately, I've been feeling rather old."

"Oh, pish-posh, Meggie. You're just a young thing. And I should know. Now, tell me, how are the cranberries doing? Should be harvesttime about now."

Meg sighed. "They look absolutely beautiful, Grandmother. But I'm afraid they may not get harvested."

"Why not?"

"Cal hasn't found a buyer." Meg paused. "Maybe it's just as well."

"What do you mean, it's just as well?"

Suddenly Meg's eyes filled with tears. "I shouldn't be so upset, Grandmother," said Meg. "Especially after I just gave them to

God. They're really not mine, you know."

Grandmother's face was puzzled. "I have no idea what you're talking about, Meggie."

"I'm sorry, Grandmother. I mean the cranberries. I think I care too much about them, so I just gave them all to God. Besides, they were never really mine. I know the land belongs to you, and I wanted to preserve the bog. You let me do it. Now you and Abner will probably sell the property anyway, and it will all be plowed under and built into condos."

Grandmother set down her teacup. She looked stunned.

"I'm sorry, Grandmother. I didn't mean to upset you. It's just that I realized I've gotten way too attached to the bog, and I need to let it go. That's why I'm saying that it's probably for the best that they don't get harvested."

Grandmother shook her head. "You think it would be for the best to waste perfectly good cranberries, after all your hard work?"

"Well, I don't know what to think," said Meg. "It's very frustrating. I'm trying not to make myself crazy over the whole thing. I've put everything I have into that bog, and I don't even know why."

"Meg, go look in the bottom drawer of my bureau. There's a brown box. Bring it to me."

Meg followed Grandmother's instructions, placing an old hatbox in Grandmother's lap. Grandmother opened it. Inside was a pile of old papers. Some looked official, and others were letters.

"Remember when I told you about the letter that your grandfather wrote to me before he died? Well, there's a part in it that I didn't tell you about. It's not that I wanted to keep it from you, Meggie, but I wasn't sure when the right time to tell you would be. I think the time has come."

Meg waited as Grandmother's shaky fingers opened the letter.

"I don't suppose I need to read the whole thing to you. You can read it yourself later. You might remember that this letter was to tell me about how your grandfather had finally come to a place where he could forgive me, Meggie. I know what I did was a horrible thing, and I wouldn't have blamed him if he never forgave me. Not that any good would come from that." She paused to catch her breath, and Meg tried again to imagine what sort of horrible thing her grandmother would be capable of.

"I suppose for this to make any sense, I'll have to fill you in on all the details," said Grandmother. "It's been my secret all these years, at first because of my pride, but then to protect the family. You see, Bennie wasn't your grandfather's son. And therefore, Abner is not his grandson."

Meg tried not to act as shocked as she felt. She knew this was hard on Grandmother, and she didn't want to make it any harder by probing. If Grandmother wanted to give any more information, Meg would wait.

"As you might imagine, that was the source of many problems. For a long time, I didn't tell your grandfather that Bennie wasn't his own, but I think he knew all along. He always seemed to be too hard on Bennie. When Bennie became a teenager, he got wild and hard to manage. And one night, he and your grandfather got into quite a fight. I won't go into all the details, but Bennie had done something very wrong, and your grandfather wanted him to put it right. But Bennie refused, and ran off and joined the army when he was only seventeen. Your mother was just a girl then. Anyway, I was so angry at your grandfather that I exploded, and I let the secret out. From then on, your grandfather rarely spoke to me, and your poor mother grew up in a house full of hostility and bitterness."

"You told me a bit about that before. That must have been hard on all of you."

"In the letter, your grandfather said that he hadn't made a will, but it was his dying wish that Briar Hedge be passed on to you but that I was to live out my last days in this house. But he also said that if by some chance you didn't want it, he would leave the decision to me."

Meg was stunned. Grandpa had wanted to leave the bog to her. And Grandmother had known for all these years. If only Meg had known, would her life have been different? Maybe. Maybe not. Maybe it didn't matter now.

"You have to understand, Meggie. You never came back after all those years, and the whole time Abner was here, working at first, but slacking off later. I began to think that I would leave it all to him. Not that I wanted to cut you out, but when you never came back…"

"It's okay, Grandmother. I understand."

"To be fair, I've left Erin a nice little nest egg, taken from my business. I figured the rest would go to Abner. I never expected to see you again."

"So, I guess I upset the applecart."

"No, no. Not at all, Meggie. When you came back, I couldn't have been happier. It seemed perfectly right that you should be the one to rescue the bog. Your grandfather would have been so proud. But I just didn't know what to do about Abner. Don't think that I haven't known there were problems. Believe me, I did. Rosa tried to tell me. Abner, in his own way, revealed that all was not well. I just didn't know what to do. And I realized, the more you became attached to the bog, that I would have to honor your grandfather, because there was no denying that you had cranberry juice running through your veins."

Meg smiled. "I want to be fair to Abner, especially since he's trying to turn his life around. I'm really not in it for the money. But it would be nice to break even."

"That's good of you, Meggie. It has worried me a great deal, especially when I think of poor Phoebe and Jason. I don't know what they would do."

"Matthew Logan could probably help us work out something

that would make everyone happy, Grandmother."

"Yes, tell your friend Matthew I want to see him. The three of us shall sit down and work it all out. Oh, Meggie, I feel so much better having this out in the open. I think it was killing me holding it all inside like that."

Meg took the cup out of Grandmother's hands. "You must need a rest, Grandmother. I'll talk to Matthew, and we'll set up a time to meet with you."

"Good, good." Grandmother closed her eyes. "And when I wake up, I'll give a call to one of your grandfather's old friends. I think he might know what to do with those berries."

Meg leaned over and kissed her grandmother's cheek. A little smile fluttered across Grandmother's lips. "Thanks, Grandmother," whispered Meg as she gathered the tea things. "Thanks for telling me all this. I know it wasn't easy, but I really appreciate it."

As Meg tiptoed from the room, she could hear Rosa in the laundry room, singing as she worked. Meg quickly rinsed out the cups and pot, and slipped out the back door.

She sat down on the front porch steps and slowly replayed all that Grandmother had just told her. It was amazing—utterly amazing. Suddenly it was all beginning to make sense, how entangled all their lives had been for three generations. Even after Meg had completely removed herself from her family, the threads that tied them together had reached out to her and eventually pulled her back. Back home.

"Thank you, God," she said quietly. "Thanks for bringing me back. Not just back home to Crandale, but back home to you. You knew all along exactly what I needed. I'm so thankful that you never gave up on me, and so glad to be home. I'll never, never leave again!"

Epilogue

IT WAS A PERFECT FALL DAY. Crisp nip in the air, clear blue sky, just a slight breeze blowing in off the sea. Perfect conditions for a cranberry harvest.

Cal had already predicted that this year's harvest would be more than twice as big as last year's. And last year's hadn't been bad, all things considered. Grandmother, true to her word, had called up Greyson Landers, an old buddy of Grandpa. Greyson's family owned a big cranberry-processing company on the East Coast, and in no time Meg was set up with an account. Her berries were harvested right at their peak.

"Let her rip, Jason!" yelled Meg from below. Everyone cheered as the first bog began to flood. As the water level slowly rose, everyone bustled about setting up equipment. Tom was arranging the big wooden booms that would float on the water, and Matthew was gassing up the new beater that Meg had purchased just last month. Meg watched with pleasure as the dark red cranberries floated up to the surface of the water.

"Do you want me to start up the beater yet?" called Matthew. He was hunched over, studying the water level of the flooded bog. He looked right at home in his rubber hip waders held by thick suspenders over an old gray sweatshirt. "Come here, Meg," he called. "I need your professional opinion."

"I don't think the water level's high enough," said Meg as she squatted beside him and peered at the submerged plants and floating berries.

"Maybe not," said Matthew with a grin. "But look at this." He plunged a closed fist into the water and pulled it out again. Then he opened his hand and held it up in front of her. Meg's eyes grew wide as she stared at the glistening ring lying in the palm of his dripping hand.

"What is it?" she gasped, staring at the diamond surrounded by dark red rubies, just the color of ripe cranberries.

He took her hand in his. "Something I picked for you." He looked into her eyes. "Will you have me, Meg? You already know how much I love you. Will you marry me?"

"Yes!" she cried as she threw her arms around him. After a long embrace, he slipped the ring onto her finger.

"Hey, you two!" yelled Cal. "Better check that water level. We need to get that beater running, Matthew."

Matthew winked at Meg. "I'm getting right on it, Pop!"

"Well, this was one sure way for you to get back into the cranberry business," Meg teased as Matthew wheeled the beater into the flooded bog.

"Sure, and with lots of fringe benefits," called Matthew. "Shall I start her up then, boss?"

"Go for it!" Meg grinned, studying the ring on her hand. She felt like shouting for joy.

The machine started up, and before long, more and more cranberries became loosened from the submerged plants and floated to the surface.

"Aunt Meggie!" cried Ashley as she ran back and forth along the edge. "Here they come! Just like jewels floating on the sea!"

Meg laughed and gave her little niece a hug. The other two

girls were ready with their plastic rakes. They would gather the shining cranberries onto the elevator that Abner was running. Abner still had his ups and downs, but he had changed greatly in the past year. He was trying his best to be a good father and husband and cousin, and that's all any of them could ask.

Meg, Erin, and Abby began slipping the floating booms into place on the bog. The booms would corral the berries into one area so they could be loaded onto the elevator. Meg had paused for a moment to adjust the suspenders on her hip waders when Erin cried out. Meg looked up, startled. Erin was pointing to her hand.

"What's that on your finger?"

Abby stopped and looked toward Meg as well. Meg blushed and quickly explained.

"Well, it's about time," said Abby as she gave Meg a hug. "Welcome to the family, Sis!"

Erin hugged her, too. Then Clive looked up from where she and Jason were getting the big truck ready and gave Meg a big thumbs-up.

"I helped pick it out, Meg," called Clive. "Doesn't it remind you of cranberries?"

Meg grinned. "That's exactly what I thought!"

There wasn't much time to chat. Everyone had a job to do. Even Siggie had come out to help. He was overseeing the shaker that cleaned the stems and debris off the berries. Meanwhile, Phoebe and Rosa were working in the kitchen, getting a big lunch ready for the crew.

The only one missing this year was Grandmother. She had slipped away peacefully in her sleep just after last year's harvest. And, whether or not it was biblically correct, Meg liked to imagine that Grandpa and Sunny and Grandmother were all looking down from heaven and delighting in the harvest.

Meg glanced over at Matthew and smiled. Maybe someday her

own children would participate in this tradition. And hopefully the story of God's goodness and how he brought Meg back home to restore the bog would be passed down from generation to generation.

Dear Reader,

When I started this book, my goal was to create three generations of strong women and show how their lives impacted one another as they all sought their place in the world. But, as is often the case, my story began to take on a life of its own; and before long I realized that the main theme was really about forgiveness. Since I know better than to argue with my stories, I let this one transport me down its bumpy road of hurts, heartaches, bitterness, and ultimately forgiveness. And now that it's all said and done, I can see how it takes us to the place where we need to live—a place called grace.

Like Meg, many of us try to unravel the mysteries of our past generations in hope of shedding a little light on life's current conflicts. And often, understanding *will* follow, and we will say, "Aha, so that's why Aunt Claire is so introverted." And without a doubt, this type of knowledge is a helpful tool to foster empathy and deeper levels of understanding.

But occasionally we forget to take the next step. And that's when we become stuck in the process of trying to understand the reasons behind everything, and consequently tend to overlook the power of grace. It's easy to forget that forgiveness is often the most important key to healing a broken relationship; or that love can cover a multitude of sins.

I hope Meg's story will challenge you, as it has me, to try to live in a constant state of forgiveness—both in receiving and giving. Because I'm certain that God desires for us to forgive others as naturally as we breathe in and out. Perhaps that's why He gives us so many opportunities to practice. Not to mention how He forgives us over and over, again and again.

Melody Carlson

Write to Melody Carlson
c/o Questar Publishers, Inc.
P.O. Box 1720
Sister, Oregon 97759

PALISADES...PURE ROMANCE

⌒ PALISADES ⌒

Reunion, Karen Ball
Refuge, Lisa Tawn Bergren
Torchlight, Lisa Tawn Bergren
Treasure, Lisa Tawn Bergren
Chosen, Lisa Tawn Bergren
Firestorm, Lisa Tawn Bergren
Surrender, Lynn Bulock (August, 1997)
Wise Man's House, Melody Carlson
Arabian Winds, Linda Chaikin
Lions of the Desert, Linda Chaikin
Cherish, Constance Colson
Chase the Dream, Constance Colson
Angel Valley, Peggy Darty
Sundance, Peggy Darty
Moonglow, Peggy Darty
Promises, Peggy Darty (September, 1997)
Love Song, Sharon Gillenwater
Antiques, Sharon Gillenwater
Song of the Highlands, Sharon Gillenwater
Texas Tender, Sharon Gillenwater
Secrets, Robin Jones Gunn
Whispers, Robin Jones Gunn
Echoes, Robin Jones Gunn
Sunsets, Robin Jones Gunn
Clouds, Robin Jones Gunn (July, 1997)
Coming Home, Barbara Jean Hicks
Snow Swan, Barbara Jean Hicks
Irish Eyes, Annie Jones
Father by Faith, Annie Jones (September, 1997)

Glory, Marilyn Kok
Sierra, Shari MacDonald
Forget-Me-Not, Shari MacDonald
Diamonds, Shari MacDonald
Stardust, Shari MacDonald
Westward, Amanda MacLean
Stonehaven, Amanda MacLean
Everlasting, Amanda MacLean
Promise Me the Dawn, Amanda MacLean
Kingdom Come, Amanda MacLean
Betrayed, Lorena McCourtney
Escape, Lorena McCourtney
Dear Silver, Lorena McCourtney
Enough!, Gayle Roper (August, 1997)
Voyage, Elaine Schulte

⌐ ANTHOLOGIES ⌐
A Christmas Joy, Darty, Gillenwater, MacLean
Mistletoe, Ball, Hicks, McCourtney
A Mother's Love, Bergren, Colson, MacLean
Silver Bells, Bergren, Chaikin, MacDonald (October, 1997)

THE PALISADES LINE

Look for these new releases at your local bookstore. If the title you seek is not in stock, the store may order you a copy using the ISBN listed.

Surrender, Lynn Bulock (August, 1997)
ISBN 1-57673-104-9
As a single mom, Cassie Neel works hard to give her children the best she can. This year, young Sarah and Zach want to show their appreciation for what she does by giving her a date with handsome police officer Lee Winter as a birthday present! Surprised and flattered, Cassie accepts. But little does she know where that one date will lead....

Wise Man's House, Melody Carlson
ISBN 1-57673-070-0
Kestra McKenzie, a young widow trying to make a new life for herself, thinks she has found the solidity she longs for when she purchases her childhood dream house—a stone mansion on the Oregon Coast. Just as renovations begin, a mysterious stranger moves into her caretaker's cottage—and into her heart.

Moonglow, Peggy Darty
ISBN 1-57673-112-X
During the Summer Olympics set in Atlanta, Tracy Kosell comes back to her hometown of Moonglow, Georgia, to investigate the disappearance of a wealthy socialite. She meets up with former schoolmate Jay Calloway, who's one of the detectives assigned to the case. As their attraction grows and the mercury rises, they unwrap a case that isn't as simple as it seemed.

Promises, Peggy Darty (September, 1997)
ISBN 1-57673-149-9
Elizabeth Calloway, a Christian psychologist, finds herself in over her head when a client tells her about a dangerous twin sister. Elizabeth turns to her detective husband, Michael, asking him to find the woman. Unexpected events plunge the couple into danger, where they rediscover the joy of falling in love.

***Texas Tender,* Sharon Gillenwater**
ISBN 1-57673-111-1
When Shelby Nolan inherits a watermelon farm, she moves from Houston to a small west Texas town. Spotting two elderly men digging holes in her field each night, she turns to neighbor Deputy Sheriff Logan Slade to figure out what's going on. Together they uncover a long-buried robbery and discover the fulfillment of their own dreams.

***Clouds,* Robin Jones Gunn**
ISBN 1-57673-113-8
On a trip to Germany, flight attendant Shelly Graham unexpectedly runs into her old boyfriend, Jonathan Renfield. Since she still cares for him, it's hard for Shelly to hide her hurt when she learns he's engaged. It isn't until she goes to meet friends in Glenbrooke, Oregon, that they meet again—and this time, they're both ready to be honest.

***Sunsets,* Robin Jones Gunn**
ISBN 1-57673-103-0
Alissa Benson loves her job as a travel agent. But when the agency has computer problems, they call in expert Brad Phillips. Alissa can't wait for Brad to fix the computers and leave—he's too blunt for her comfort. So she's more than a little upset when she moves into a duplex and finds out he's her neighbor!

***Snow Swan,* Barbara Jean Hicks**
ISBN 1-57673-107-3
Life hasn't been easy for Toni Ferrier. As an unwed mother and a recovering alcoholic, she doesn't feel worthy of anyone's love. Then she meets Clark McConaughey, who helps her launch her business aboard the sternwheeler Snow Swan. Sparks fly between them, but if Clark finds out the truth about Toni's past, will he still love her?

***Irish Eyes,* Annie Jones**
ISBN 1-57673-108-1
When Julia Reed finds a young boy, who claims to be a leprechaun, camped out under a billboard, she gets drawn into a century-old crime involving a real pot of gold. Interpol agent Cameron O'Dea is trying to solve the crime. In the process, he takes over the homeless shelter that Julia runs, camps out in her neighbor's RV, and generally turns her life upside down!

Father by Faith, Annie Jones (September, 1997)
ISBN 1-57673-117-0

Nina Jackson may not know much about ranching, but she knows business. So when she buys a dude ranch and hires recuperating cowboy Clint Cooper as her foreman, she figures she's set. But her son, Alex, doesn't think so. He's been praying for a father, and the moment he sees Clint, he tells everyone that God has answered his prayers and sent him a daddy!

Stardust, Shari MacDonald
ISBN 1-57673-109-X

As a teenager, Gillian Spencer fell in love with astronomy...and with Max Bishop. But after he leaves her heartbroken, she learns to keep her feelings guarded. Now that she's a graduate student studying astronomy, she thinks she has left the past far behind. So when she gets an exciting assignment, she's shocked to learn she's been paired with the now-famous Dr. Maxwell Bishop.

Kingdom Come, Amanda MacLean
ISBN 1-57673-120-0

In 1902, feisty Ivy Rose Clayborne, M.D., returns to her hometown of Kingdom Come to fight the coal mining company that is ravaging the land. She meets an unexpected ally, a man who claims to be a drifter but in reality is Harrison MacKenzie, grandson of the coal mining baron. Together they face the aftermath of betrayal, the fight for justice...and the price of love.

Dear Silver, Lorena McCourtney
ISBN 1-57673-110-3

When Silver Sinclair receives a polite but cold letter from Chris Bentley ending their relationship, she's shocked, since she's never met the man! She confronts Chris about his insensitive attitude toward this other Silver Sinclair, and finds herself becoming friends with a man who's unlike anyone she's ever met.

Enough! Gayle Roper (August, 1997)
ISBN 1-57673-185-5

When Molly Gregory gets fed up with her three teenaged children, she announces that she's going on strike. She and her husband Pete stand back and watch as chaos results in their household, in a hilarious experiment that teaches their children how to honor their parents.

A Mother's Love, Bergren, Colson, MacLean
ISBN 1-57673-106-5

By Lisa Tawn Bergren: A widower and his young daughter go to Southern California for vacation, and return with much more than they expected.

By Constance Colson: Cassie Jenson wants her old sweetheart to stay in her memories. But Bruce Foster has other plans.

By Amanda MacLean: A couple is expecting their first baby, and each plans a surprise for the other that doesn't quite turn out as it should.

Silver Bells, Bergren, Chaikin, MacDonald (October, 1997)
ISBN 1-57673-119-7
By Lisa Tawn Bergren: Noel Stevens has to work up the ranks in her new job, but being assigned to Santa's workshop is too much. Until she gets to know Santa....

By Linda Chaikin: Christmas at the family lodge doesn't sound too exciting until Jennifer meets a handsome young cadet.

By Shari MacDonald: Madison Pierce feels lonely at the thought of her best friend's wedding...until she meets the best man.

PASSAGES
Romance, mystery, comedy....Real life.

Homeward, Melody Carlson
ISBN 1-57673-029-8
When Meg Lancaster learns that her grandmother is dying, she returns to the small town on the Oregon coast where she spent vacations as a child. After being away for twenty years, the town hasn't changed...but her family has. Meg struggles with her memories of the past and what is now reality, until tragedy strikes the family and she must learn to face the future.

Arabian Winds, Linda Chaikin
ISBN 1-57673-3-105-7
World War I is breaking upon the deserts of Arabia in 1914. Young nurse Allison Wescott is on holiday with an archaeological club, but a murder interrupts her plans, and a mysterious officer keeps turning up wherever she goes!

Lions of the Desert, Linda Chaikin (October, 1997)
ISBN 1-57673-114-6
In 1915, Allison Wescott arrives in Cairo to serve the British military and once again encounters the mysterious Bret Holden. And to mix things up even further, the chaplain she is thinking of marrying comes to Cairo as well.
Watch for the final book in the trilogy, coming in spring 1998!

***Chase the Dream*, Constance Colson**
ISBN 0-88070-928-6
After years apart, four friends are reunited through the competitive world of professional rodeo, where they seek fame, fortune, faith...and love.

***Song of the Highlands*, Sharon Gillenwater**
ISBN 1-57673-946-4
Kiernan returns from the Napoleonic wars to find out he's inherited a title. At his run-down estate, he meets the beautiful Mariah, and finds himself swept up in the romance and deception of a London Season.
Watch for more books in Sharon Gillenwater's Scottish series!

***Promise Me the Dawn*, Amanda MacLean**
ISBN 0-88070-955-3
Molly Quinn and Zach MacAlister come from very different backgrounds, but both seek to overcome the past. Enduring hardship and prosperity, the promise of a meeting at dawn brings them through it all.

***Redeeming Love*, Francine Rivers**
ISBN 1-57673-186-3
The only men Angel has ever known have betrayed her. When she meets Michael Hosea in the gold country of California, she has no reason to believe he's any different. But Michael *is* different. And through him Angel learns what love really means—the kind of love that can wipe away the shame of her past.